OXFORD MEDICAL PUBLICATIONS

Therapeutic Factors in Group Psychotherapy

Therapeutic Factors in Group Psychotherapy

SIDNEY BLOCH

Consultant Psychiatrist and Clinical Lecturer
Warneford Hospital and University of Oxford

and

ERIC CROUCH

Consultant Psychiatrist, St John's Hospital
Aylesbury, Bucks

OXFORD NEW YORK TOKYO
OXFORD UNIVERSITY PRESS
1985

Oxford University Press, Walton Street, Oxford OX2 6DP
Oxford New York Toronto
Delhi Bombay Calcutta Madras Karachi
Kuala Lumpur Singapore Hong Kong Tokyo
Nairobi Dar es Salaam Cape Town
Melbourne Auckland
and associated companies in
Beirut Berlin Ibadan Nicosia

Oxford is a trade mark of Oxford University Press

British Library Cataloguing in Publication Data
Bloch, Sidney, 1941–
Therapeutic factors in group psychotherapy.—
(Oxford medical publications)
1. Group psychotherapy
I. Title II. Crouch, Eric
616.89'152 RC488

ISBN 0-19-261365-0

Library of Congress Cataloging in Publication Data

Bloch, Sidney.
Therapeutic factors in group psychotherapy.
(Oxford medical publications)
Bibliography: p.
Includes index.
1. Group psychotherapy. I. Crouch, Eric.
II. Title. III. Series. [DNLM: 1. Psychotherapy, Group. WM 430 B651t]
RC488.B56 1985 616.89'152 85-7277
ISBN 0-19-261365-0

Filmset by Latimer Trend & Company Ltd, Plymouth, Devon
Printed in Great Britain
at the University Press, Oxford
by David Stanford
Printer to the University

Preface

Although group psychotherapy is a long-established and popular mode of treatment in psychiatry, the fundamental question of how it works remains ill-understood. For example, is it the patient's sense of belonging to a cohesive group that is important? Is it his interaction with other group members? Is it his acquisition of self-understanding? Or is it his disclosure of highly personal information? Any attempt to obtain a clear answer to these sorts of questions by perusing the group therapy literature is often more confusing than illuminating. The exercise is made more complicated by the broad range of theories that seek to explain the therapeutic process. The experimental research that has been done is also confusing: it is scattered, not always relevant to the clinician, and uneven in quality.

Our main aim in writing this book is to offer what we hope is a coherent account of the knowledge that has accumulated on how group therapy works, and specifically on those elements of the group process likely to be responsible for its beneficial effects. In tackling these 'therapeutic factors' we have assembled from the group therapy literature the clinical lore, the theoretical advances, and the empirical research that have a close bearing on the subject and merit our attention. Because of the vagueness that typifies the subject, we set out immediately in the first chapter the important matters of definition and classification. We also briefly consider there the methods used to study therapeutic factors.

In the following seven chapters we examine the ten therapeutic factors that comprise our own classification, although we certainly do not confine ourselves rigidly to it. As we shall see in Chapter 1, any particular selection must be arbitrary to some extent. While knowledge of the subject is rudimentary, there will remain uncertainty about its precise boundaries and taxonomy. In Chapter 9 we consider the work done on therapeutic factors as a group rather than as independent entities. Emphasis is given to theoretical models in which the relative role of a constellation of factors is elaborated and linked to relevant systematic research. In Chapter 10 we summarize the progress made on the subject as a whole and comment briefly on the implications of available knowledge for the clinician. Such implications are also contained, where appropriate, throughout the book.

We have also included an appendix covering virtually all the systematic research studies under review. Its purpose is twofold; to spare the reader getting bogged down in the text with excessive detail of methodology and results; and to provide, at a glance, these same details for anyone with a deeper interest in the research that has been done.

We need to make several general points before proceeding to the first chapter. Our major focus is on therapy groups, but research on non-therapy groups is dealt with where pertinent, and extrapolations to the clinical context considered. Even in the clinical context, however, we have not covered every conceivable form of group treatment. Had we done so the book would have become unmanageably long. Thus, for example, we have not dealt with the application of cognitive therapy to groups, since this form of treatment is primarily individually based and its therapeutic elements are not directly associated with group processes.

The review is mainly of work done since the mid-1950s, especially as regards systematic research. Precious little experimental work was done prior to this period. But where it has been useful to trace the evolution of a certain line of thought, we have not felt bound by rigid time boundaries.

Originally, we embarked on our review of systematic research with the aim of including only those studies that met specified criteria. For the record they were: sufficient sample size; specified patient characteristics; clear descriptions of the therapy used; measures of process and outcome that validly and reliably reflect the phenomena studied; appropriate statistical analysis of results; and use of control groups, where applicable. We soon recognized the impracticality of employing these criteria. Many studies we looked at failed to fulfil them and yet were worth reporting on, even if only to learn from their limitations. So, the quality of the work reviewed necessarily varies.

The process of group therapy is not as tidy as the theorizing about it. Indeed, in the multi-coloured fabric that so typifies group treatment, therapeutic factors are often intertwined, both in their operation and effects. We take the liberty of putting this consideration aside in the pursuit of clarifying the intrinsic features of the various therapeutic factors. Each factor is therefore tackled as if it were an entirely discrete entity and we recognize that this approach is, to a degree, contrived.

Although our principal purpose throughout is to review contributions to the subject of therapeutic factors and not to offer a textbook of group therapy, we should express our conviction that the practice of group therapy is in need of a pause from both the immediacy of the group room where clinical judgements must be made as perceptively as circumstances will allow, and the stream of published empirical findings often inconsistent and sometimes contradictory. During this pause, the therapist may take the opportunity to reflect on the group processes he is customarily engaged with in terms of their relevance, validity, and efficacy. The present volume is in a sense the product of our own pause to reflect.

Finally, it is our pleasure to thank most cordially the many people who have helped us in one way or another with the preparation of this book. We are indebted to Irvin Yalom for stimulating our interest in the subject in the first place. It will be obvious from our many references to him in the text how central a role he has played in the study of therapeutic factors. One of us (SB) worked with Dr Yalom for two-and-a-half years in the Department of Psychiatry at Stanford University and would like to thank the Commonwealth Fund of New York for providing him with a Harkness Fellowship which made this possible. Janet Reibstein was exceedingly industrious in ferreting out relevant references and also co-authored some earlier contributions that we made to the literature. Several colleagues read the manuscript and offered constructive criticism: Liz Burrows, Irene Freeden, David McNab, and Geoff Pullen. We are also grateful to many other colleagues in the Oxford Psychotherapy Department with whom we discussed our ideas.

Judith Tuck and Andrea Jarrett, the librarians of the Warneford and Littlemore Hospitals, and the staff of the Mental Health Authority Library of the State of Victoria were most helpful in tracking down material. Pauline Madden, Carolyn Clarke, Diana

Eldon, and Doris Plater typed the manuscript in most co-operative and helpful fashion. The staff of Oxford University Press have been most encouraging at all times.

Our own research studies were done with the support of the Oxford Regional Health Authority to which we are deeply indebted.

Finally, we thank our families for their constant support and patience.

Oxford and S. B.
Aylesbury E. C.
April 1985

Contents

1 Definition, classification, and methods of study

In the course of research we conducted in the late 1970s on ingredients of group psychotherapy with apparent therapeutic effect, we were struck by how much more attention had been paid to elaborating different theoretical models than to the identification of discrete elements of the group process which seemed to account for clinical change. Throughout the eighty-odd year history of clinically orientated group treatment, there has been a consistent interest on the part of clinicians in theorizing about their activities but at the expense of discerning and studying the elements that constitute the therapeutic process. Moreover, work that has been done on these elements has been intermittent and non-cumulative.

We believe that this state of affairs has hindered the development of group therapy. We have witnessed the formation of several schools, each grounded in its own theory and claiming advantages over its rivals. Exponents of these schools have largely ignored the possibility that underlying their theoretical differences there might exist a set of basic therapeutic components held in common. They have been disinclined to seek understanding of this, surely finite, set. And this despite the convincing work of such a figure as Jerome Frank, who has highlighted the salience of a basic set of non-specific factors in psychotherapy generally.[1]

Mulling over these points, we concluded that the matter might be ameliorated through a comprehensive review of the literature concerning therapeutic elements in group therapy. Its chief goal would be to establish what body of knowledge (and of what quality) had accrued in this area. The result was our evaluation of nearly a hundred papers and the publication in 1981 of *Therapeutic factors in group psychotherapy—a review*.[2] Because of limitations of space, the original draft had to be substantially reduced in length and a detailed, tabulated appendix of empirical research dating from 1955 to 1979 was omitted. Furthermore, in preparing the review we had perforce been selective. These limitations led us to think that a more comprehensive scrutiny of the literature was warranted; this volume is the product of that more extensive review.

In this introduction we consider the evolution of the concept of therapeutic factors, noting in particular the role of pioneering clinicians, the contribution of theorists to the subject, and the part played by the systematic research investigator. We also outline the customary methods of study used by them in their work. But before proceeding we must define our terms.

The concept of a therapeutic factor

The concept of a therapeutic factor rests on the premiss that the process of group therapy embodies a finite number of elements distinguishable from one another by virtue of their highly specific effects on the group member. The epithet 'therapeutic' is intentionally omitted thus far since the specific effects may be to the member's detriment as much as to his benefit.[3] The crucial point is the notion of discrete, identifiable elements bearing an impact on the patient.

Obviously, if these elements work in his favour (that is they facilitate clinical improvement of some kind, whether it be the amelioration of symptoms, desired changes in particular patterns of behaviour, or personal growth) they can be categorized as exerting a therapeutic effect. Conversely, if these elements work to the patient's disadvantage (that is they produce a deterioration of his symptoms or pave the way for new, undesired patterns of behaviour) they can be categorized as exerting an anti-therapeutic effect. A third possibility exists. An element inherently therapeutic may be misused—whether through the ineptitude of the therapist or because the group member's motivations, in some way linked to his disturbed psychological state, disrupt the harnessing of the element's potential—so that the result is anti-therapeutic.

Illustrations of these three possible effects may help in arriving at a definition of what is a therapeutic factor. Consider firstly the example of an element exerting a desired effect. It is most probable that a patient will derive benefit from a sense of being valued by his fellow group members. The experience of feeling cared for, supported, and understood by his peers brings in its turn a sense of belonging and comfort with a distinct potential for the bolstering of self-esteem. Few would quibble with the therapeutic potential of the element we have just identified and which we could conveniently label 'acceptance'. Of course, not every group member may reap the benefits of acceptance. For example, the need for such an experience may be entirely superfluous, inasmuch as the sense of being valued is not lacking in a patient's life; in other words, in this particular sphere, he is problem-free. On the other hand, a patient may be so grossly disabled—with an intractable lack of self-regard—that acceptance fails to penetrate his psyche, its potentially positive effect consistently bouncing off him. Thus, despite the possible operation of acceptance in the group, this member is unable to exploit it.

Turning to an element producing an anti-therapeutic effect, a useful example is that of dependency on the therapist. Members of a group inevitably pass through a phase of feeling reliant on the leader, perceiving him as the omniscient expert who has created the group and who will promote its welfare and interests. As the group evolves, so members come to realize that their appraisal of his role was distorted by their own needs at a time of vulnerability and that they must necessarily become more self-sufficient. For reasons residing in the therapist (for example, his need to be loved or to feel powerful) or in the patient (for instance, a long standing trait of dependency) the element, which we may conveniently term 'fostering of dependence', may come to have a decidedly deleterious effect so that a patient is robbed of any possibility of autonomy. (This is not to negate the purposeful use of dependency—especially on the group itself rather than on the therapist—in certain clinical situations, such as when a patient is in the throes of an acute crisis and requires a lifeline until he can harness his own resources.)

Finally, we illustrate the misuse of an inherently therapeutic element so that it comes to have the opposite effect: anti-therapeutic. Common observation, buttressed by theoretical and empirical work, suggests that the act of self-disclosure by a patient—revealing to fellow members personal information which he has hitherto concealed out of a concern that to divulge it would prove embarrassing, painful, or anxiety-provoking—is a beneficial experience. Thus, we can assume that this element is intrinsically therapeutic. But its application may go awry. Consider the following case:

A voluble young man revealed a torrent of private details about himself in the first few sessions of a new group. This pronounced level of self-disclosure remained unmatched by his peers and unchecked by the therapist. Before long he became identified as deviant in respect of a prevailing norm in the group, a norm which pointed to a gradual entry into personal exchanges. The group, intimidated by the pace of the deviant member's self-disclosures, steered a self-protective course around him. His subsequent sense of isolation was the prelude to bitter disillusionment which culminated in his premature dropping out.

In the aforementioned examples, we have cited the therapeutic impact of two elements, acceptance and self-disclosure, but in each case alluded to a 'probable' effect. In other words we have intentionally remained tentative in commenting upon their role in generating clinical change. As subsequent chapters will demonstrate, elements of the group process commonly regarded by clinicians as being therapeutic have not been adequately investigated to confirm or refute clinical consensus. Thus, the term 'therapeutic factor' is a misnomer. If we were to be more honest and accurate, we should apply the epithet 'putative' in order to clarify that, in the present state of knowledge, a number of elements of the group process are likely to yield positive effects on patients in group therapy. To avoid the cumbersome use of 'putative' on every occasion, we shall take it as read that reference to therapeutic factors does not assert a claim for their proven status as therapeutic but instead reflects a traditional, consistent view held by observant clinicians of their probable benefits.

What is a therapeutic factor?

With this important qualification in mind, we are now in a position to define a therapeutic factor as: *An element of group therapy that contributes to improvement in a patient's condition and is a function of the actions of the group therapist, the other group members, and the patient himself.* The use of the term 'element' is obviously vague but so are any of its potential substitutes—mechanism, dynamic, operation, event, component, and the like. The reason for this vagueness is straightforward; the means whereby various therapeutic factors exert their influence differs considerably. We can note this readily by returning to our earlier examples of acceptance and self-disclosure. Acceptance is a feeling arising in a patient as a result of specific forces within the group, both explicit and implicit. These forces, constituents of a particular climate, include support, caring, validation, and friendliness, and rely to a considerable degree on the therapist's inculcation of certain norms from the outset and the adherence to them by group members.

Self-disclosure, by contrast, is very much an individually orientated factor, although the reception by an audience of the personal revelations is mandatory (otherwise it could be done equally well in the bath!). The discloser gains from a specific activity, initiated and executed by himself. Even if nudged by his peers or the therapist to share private details about himself, the decision to carry this out is ultimately his alone. Thus, in the case of acceptance, the all-important process is the cultivation of a certain milieu with the therapist playing a prominent role to promote it, whereas in self-disclosure, the key process entails the protagonist and his decision to act in a particular fashion.

What it is not

On occasion, defining a concept is illuminated by ascertaining what it is not. In this context, a therapeutic factor can be distinguished from two other facets of group therapy closely allied to it: *conditions for change* and *techniques*. The former, although they do not exert therapeutic effects, are aspects of the groups structure and procedure without which therapeutic factors could not operate. We commented earlier on the need for an audience to facilitate the act of self-disclosure. Obvious here, is the basic requirement for at least one other person to hear out the protagonist. The participation of several co-members in a group enhances the process by providing more listeners and, moreover, includes peers to whom the discloser may find it more important to reveal personal matters than to a professional expert. Therefore, the sheer presence of group members constitutes a condition for change. The basic act of verbal participation is another obvious condition for change. Without the exchange of words, naturally accompanied by non-verbal communication, most therapeutic factors cannot operate. This is not to negate the important role of silence in the experience of a group; it too is a mode of communication, but a continually silent group will become a dull, vacuous place. A third example is a shared sense of motivation. A group marked by absenteeism, unpunctuality, and dropouts is invariably dispiriting and demoralizing, and the ground in which seeds of therapeutic import may germinate is too arid and impoverished.

Just as conditions for change are a requisite for the operation of therapeutic factors, so the latter are necessary for the application of techniques.[3] Therapeutic factors and techniques are commonly not differentiated from each other. The blurring is a major limitation in some schools of group therapy, which rely excessively on, and become bewitched by, technical expertise and innovation. A commonly heard catch-phrase in this context is: 'Have you heard about the latest strategy to . . . stimulate a group . . . promote intimacy . . . encourage assertiveness . . . etc.?' Ignored in this thinking is the fact that techniques are merely devices available to the therapist to promote the operation of therapeutic factors. Like conditions for change, techniques do not intrinsically exert therapeutic effects, except possibly indirectly as a spin-off. To illustrate the difference between therapeutic factors and techniques, consider the strategy of 'doubling' pioneered by Moreno[4] and used extensively in psychodrama. A group member identifies with the protagonist who is, for example, emotionally blocked—wanting to ventilate intense grief arising from the recent loss of a relative but also anxious lest such expression should be accompanied by loss of control. The judicious deployment of a 'double' to empathize with the bereaved person may pave the way for the therapeutic factor of catharsis to operate, that is, a release of intense feelings leading to a sense of relief. Clearly, the technique of doubling is a means to an end. Its therapeutic effect, if any (the perception by the protagonist of the 'double's' empathic act may be one of gratitude or relief at being understood), is totally subsidiary to its primary function—the facilitation here of catharsis.

Although we have distinguished between conditions for change, therapeutic factors and techniques, we should add that all three are interdependent and commonly overlap. Certainly, none can operate optimally without the other two, and the efficacy of group therapy is undoubtedly limited by neglect of this mutual dependence.

In the hope that the three terms are conceptually clear, we now sketch briefly the evolution of the concept of therapeutic factors. Since we shall be examining various aspects of this development in later chapters (see Chapters 2–9), our treatment of it here is limited and schematic.

Development of the concept of therapeutic factors

If we date the beginning of professional group therapy in the first decade of this century, when the physician Joseph Pratt[5] described his 'class method' of treating patients with tuberculosis, we note that the attention given to group-based psychological treatments from that point through to the Second World War was exceedingly slender. Dreikurs and Corsini[6] cite the publication in the USA of only 11 papers between 1900 and 1919, a mere 20 in the following decade, and a slightly more respectable number of 90 in the 1930s. Within this small corpus of work (and the picture was similar elsewhere), the notion of therapeutic factors did not emerge as an identifiable concept although it was recognized implicitly by a minority of therapists reporting on their clinical experience.

As a physician, Pratt was primarily occupied with the physical treatment of his tubercular patients, but recognized that a group approach had specific advantages. Holding the notion that encouragement and support were crucial forces in the patients' recovery, he pinpointed at least one mechanism in his 'class method' that later became established as the therapeutic factor of 'instillation of hope' (see Chapter 8). On the arrival of a new patient, one of the 'star' members was usually asked to convey how he had personally benefited from Pratt's treatment. As he reports: '. . . this [was] done with the enthusiasm that exerts a powerful influence on the newcomer.' A previously demoralized patient is then described, who, upon witnessing the substantial progress of fellow members, moved from his position of complete discouragement to one of hope '. . . that he, too, might recover.'

It was several years before Pratt's model was tried out with psychiatric patients. Although the two notable exponents involved—Edward Lazell[7] and Cody Marsh[8]—provided accounts of their efforts, they made no reference to the therapeutic mechanisms operating in their groups. Both seemed more engaged with the subject of technique, remaining relatively naïve about group processes. Marsh, for example, carefully specified the constituents of his programme—lectures, note-taking, grades, class exercises, homework, progress cards, etc.—but ignored the question of what were the factors exerting a therapeutic effect on his patients.

The advent in the 1930s of psychoanalytic theory on the group therapy scene did not, at least initially, mark any change in the neglect of the concept of therapeutic factors. Then, the all-embracing question was how to apply psychoanalytic concepts to the group process. Trigant Burrow,[9] for instance, while pioneering the practice of psychoanalysis with groups of patients from the early 1920s, was preoccupied with this issue of transfer. But he did identify some advantages of the group method and, in so doing, alluded to therapeutic factors, including vicarious learning—the opportunity for a patient to identify features of his own neurosis in his peers—and universality—the patient taking note that he is not alone with his problems and that they are not unique.

Louis Wender[10] was an exception among the pre-war analysts experimenting with the group mode, in so far as he specified the 'dynamics', in essence the therapeutic factors, operating in his groups. He identified four factors. The first, intellectualization, i.e. a patient's understanding of his own emotional reactions, facilitates greater self-awareness. The second concerns the effects exerted by one member on another. In Wender's view it contains elements of transference which can be exploited more widely than in classical psychoanalysis by serving as the forerunner of improved socialization. The third factor, clumsily entitled 'catharsis-in-the-family', is also linked to transference. Therapist and patients represent parental and sibling figures respectively; this constellation enables group members to resolve long-standing parent–child conflicts chiefly through their perception of patterns of transference within the group. Interaction, the final factor, is a process which facilitates the development in the patient of a changed perspective on his behaviour. For example, he can compare his own problems with those of his co-members, thus realizing their universal manifestations and obtaining a sense of hope that they are soluble. In pinpointing such factors as family re-enactment, universality, and hope, Wender was highlighting the forces unique to a therapy group.

The application of psychoanalytic concepts to group therapy blossomed during and immediately after the Second World War. In the USA, Samuel Slavson[11] and Alexander Wolf[12] were especially prominent, while S. H. Foulkes[13] and Wilfred Bion[14] were influential in Britain. Not all of them were as explicit as Wender about the therapeutic forces operating in their groups. Slavson, as we will see in Chapter 9, did identify them most clearly but maintained that his five elements—transference, catharsis (chiefly free association), insight, reality testing, and sublimation—were similar in virtually every respect, whether featuring in individual or group treatment. Although he commented on minor differences, and, like Wender, cited universality as a uniquely group-orientated factor, Slavson's allegiance to the classical psychoanalytic position may have prevented him from recognizing group-specific therapeutic factors.

Foulkes[13] was the foremost exponent of the group analytic approach in Britain. Though he had been impressed by the ideas of Trigant Burrow (see above) as early as the mid-1920s, it was only during the Second World War that he turned to the practice of group therapy based on psychoanalytic principles. Unlike Slavson, Foulkes was as impressed by the intrinsic therapeutic power of the group process as by the incorporation into it of analytic thinking, and it was therefore no surprise when he began to tease out group-specific therapeutic factors. Among these can be identified: acceptance (the member feels understood and an equal with his co-members); universality (the member senses that fellow patients have 'similar morbid ideas, anxieties, or impulses'); vicarious learning (another patient's therapy may be helpful to the observing member through the process of identification); guidance (the exchange of explanations and information); and the 'activation of the collective unconscious' (the group process facilitates the pooling of free associations). In addition, Foulkes also distinguished between two categories of therapeutic factor—analytic and supportive. The former encapsulates typical Freudian notions, particularly the exploration of transference within the group (responsible for fundamental change), whereas the latter covers such elements as encouragement, support, and reassurance. A blend of the two sets of factors is a requisite for optimal group function.

The immediate post-war years saw further elaboration of the psychoanalytically orientated approach to group therapy (the quartet mentioned was joined, for example, by Henry Ezriel[15]). But only minimal attention was devoted to the specific therapeutic factors involved.

The beginnings of a systematic taxonomy—Corsini and Rosenberg

The authoritative review by Corsini and Rosenberg[16] of the 'dynamics that lead to successful therapy', published in 1955, marks a distinct watershed in the evolution of the concept of therapeutic factors. Posing the critical question of 'what within the group therapeutic situation is of the essence?', they attempted to answer this by searching the literature for material on therapeutic mechanisms. Up to that point, the literature was principally composed of contributions by clinicians—as we have seen, they were by and large from the psychoanalytic fold—who reported on their experience of leading groups, and to some extent focused on theoretical issues. Accounts of systematic research, certainly in the clinical field, were virtually non-existent.

The review by Corsini and Rosenberg marked a critical step as the first attempt in almost half a century of group therapy to produce a unifying classification of the therapeutic elements at the core of the group process and shared by therapists whatever their orientation. Setting out with the premiss that all writers on the topic of therapeutic factors warranted attention since they were expressing opinions stemming from their own clinical observations, Corsini and Rosenberg conducted a form of 'factor analysis'. The exercise involved four steps: a search of the literature for references to therapeutic elements (of the 300 articles examined, 67 were ultimately referred to); statements reflecting therapeutic elements were extracted (220 were found); identical statements were combined (this resulted in 166 different statements); and finally, according to a series of hypotheses suggested by their examination, these 166 statements were categorized as far as possible.

The result was a classification comprising nine factors (plus a tenth, miscellaneous category). They are:

(1) acceptance—a sense of belonging, being emotionally supported, and accepted by the group;
(2) altruism—a sense of being important in the lives of other patients by virtue of being helpful to them;
(3) universalization—the realization by the patient that he is not unique and that others share similar problems;
(4) intellectualization—the process of learning or acquiring knowledge (insight is the product but not a mechanism in itself);
(5) reality testing—the evaluation by the patient of such issues as personally held concepts, hostility, frustration, family conflicts, and personal defences through events which occur in the group;
(6) transference—strong attachments to either the therapist or to co-members take place;
(7) interaction—the opportunity for relating within the group,

which brings beneficial results;

(8) spectator therapy—the patient gains from observation of co-members, in part through the process of imitation;

(9) ventilation—the release of feelings and expression of ideas previously repressed.

The miscellaneous category covers a range of mechanisms, including suggestibility, sublimation, sharing common experiences, and the opportunity for spontaneity.

The nine factors were further assigned to three broader categories:

(1) intellectual—consisting of universalization, intellectualization, and spectator therapy;

(2) emotional—comprising acceptance, altruism, and transference;

(3) actional—consisting of reality testing, interaction, and ventilation.

In discussing their classification, Corsini and Rosenberg were clearly aware that their taxonomic effort might have yielded different results in the hands of therapists using other assumptions, but nevertheless felt that their schema constituted a rational beginning in the search for a set of discrete factors. They also expressed the hope that their work might spawn improved communication between therapists (they presumably were thinking about the limited dialogue between different schools of therapy) as well as provide a framework for research into therapeutic factors. In the chapters that follow, we shall examine whether their hopes have been fulfilled. For the moment, we need to comment on the review itself, and its aftermath.

Their classification captured the essence of group therapy as seen through the eyes of some of its prominent practitioners. The factors they delineated make clinical sense for the most part even though the statements listed under each of them are not always entirely consistent. Consider 'ventilation'. In its definition, the authors combine the release of feelings and the expression of ideas, and list under its rubric a variegated array of items, including ventilation of guilt, anger, anxiety, and tension (all examples of emotional release) and verbalization of fantasy and unconscious material. As we shall comment later, the factor of ventilation fails to distinguish between the effects exerted by the release of intense feelings, and by the disclosure of highly personal material.

Similarly, intellectualization, while defined broadly as the process of acquiring knowledge, encompasses a diverse range of items, including the analysis of dreams and resistance, the understanding of defences used by co-members, and awareness of interpersonal relations. A minority of factors, particularly transference and interaction, are nebulous and not adequately defined. To state, for example, that transference implies the existence of strong emotional attachments to the therapist, individual co-members, or to the group as a whole, reveals little of therapeutic import. Are these attachments intrinsically therapeutic? Is the understanding of the nature of an established transference in the group the necessary feature of the therapeutic factor? We face similar problems with regard to interaction. Corsini and Rosenberg actually conceded the difficulty they encountered in defining it, and the result, that interaction seems 'to have beneficial results', conveys nothing about its therapeutic basis.

Despite these limitations the classification was, as Fawcett Hill[17] puts it, 'the first and all important step in bringing some taxonomic order into the group therapeutic scene'. In our own observation, it not only served as a forerunner of other attempts at identifying and classifying therapeutic factors, but it also ushered in a phase of systematic, investigatory research into the subject.

What about subsequent efforts at taxonomy since Corsini and Rosenberg? Hill[18] was first to follow in their footsteps when he sought the views of therapists on 'what do patients get out of group therapy'. Nine factors emerged from the responses. Five were similar to categories in the Corsini and Rosenberg classification (in parentheses): catharsis (ventilation); feelings of belonging (acceptance); spectator therapy (ditto); insight (intellectualization); and peer agency (a double-barrelled factor comprising universalization and reality testing). Four additional factors were specified—ego development, sensitivity to one's own emotions, improvement of defences, and socialization. The first three are not therapeutic factors but rather the product of their operation. Socialization is too vague a concept upon which to comment adequately. Recalling our definition of a therapeutic factor as an element of group therapy contributing to improvement, we note that Hill's respondents were confusing process and outcome; not surprising in view of the question they were asked. A more appropriate question would have been: 'By what mechanism do patients benefit from group therapy?' This is not to glide over the real difficulty of how to separate process and outcome. Take again the factor of insight. This could be conceived as an outcome variable as much as a process one. After all, we commonly talk about acquisition of insight (or greater self-awareness or self-knowledge) as a goal of treatment. Careful distinctions are required here. Corsini and Rosenberg illustrate this well in referring to their factor of intellectualization as a process of learning or acquiring knowledge, but stipulate at the same time that insight is the result, i.e. the outcome, of such a process.

Another classificatory attempt followed in 1963 when Berzon[19] and her colleagues used the 'consumer' rather than the provider of therapy as the respondent. Using an indirect method of enquiry (see Chapter 2, reference (5)), the investigators asked group members to select from the events occurring in each session the one they regarded as having 'contributed most to [them] personally'. An inspection of the responses led to the identification of nine categories (nine seems to be a magical number in this area of work!). Again, as with Hill, there was substantial overlap with the Corsini and Rosenberg categories. The following factors were more or less similar (Corsini and Rosenberg categories in parentheses): ventilating emotions (ventilation); feeling warmth and closeness generally in the group (acceptance); feeling responded to by others (acceptance); increased awareness of personal emotional dynamics (intellectualization); recognizing similarity to others (universalization); witnessing honesty, courage, openness, or expression of emotionality in others (spectator therapy); and feeling positive regard, acceptance, or sympathy for others (altruism). The remaining two factors in the Berzon classification—seeing the self through others (usually through feedback) and expressing the self congruently, articulately, or assertively in the group—seem to represent the factor Corsini and Rosenberg struggled to define, i.e. interaction.

Yalom and the interpersonal factors

Thus far, the adage *plus cą change, plus c'est la même chose* applies to developments in the field of therapeutic factors. But the publication in 1970 of Yalom's *The theory and practice of group psycho-therapy*[20] constituted a new milestone. For the first time, a text devoted considerable attention to the concept of therapeutic factors, combining clinical observation, theoretical formulation, and systematic research. All three sources were used in an attempt to arrive at a classification and understanding of the therapeutic factor concept. The result is an extension of the work of Corsini and Rosenberg, chiefly in the sphere of interaction.

The weight given to the interpersonal sphere is not surprising considering Yalom's neo-Freudian approach, particularly his espousal of the interpersonal theory of psychiatry formulated by Harry Stack Sullivan. Following Sullivan's central thesis that the personality is to a considerable extent the product of a person's relationships with significant other people, Yalom incorporated into his classification two interrelated factors concerned with interaction: interpersonal learning-input (mainly via feedback; see Chapter 2) and interpersonal learning-output (a process whereby the patient attempts to develop more desirable modes of relating to others; see Chapter 3). Although aspects of this pair of factors are embedded in the Corsini and Rosenberg classification, the result there is unsatisfactory and confusing. The explicit specification by Yalom of the interactional dimension is a distinct advance. Three other factors (there are a dozen in all) are added: instillation of hope—on noting progress made by his peers, the patient feels optimistic about his chances of improvement; guidance—receiving advice or suggestions from therapist or co-members; and an existential factor—the patient recognizing that he must inevitably face life alone and take responsibility for the way he lives.

Yalom's remaining seven factors are familiar, even if named differently and given somewhat different emphases (self-understanding, altruism, group cohesiveness, universality, catharsis, identification, and family re-enactment).

Our own efforts to classify

We now turn to our own efforts at classification.[21] In conducting a study that required the careful delineation of therapeutic factors we examined the available schemata, namely those by Corsini and Rosenberg, Hill, Berson *et al.*, and Yalom. That by Yalom as we suggested earlier, was an improvement on its predecessors, but close examination reveals the presence of certain limitations. Firstly, we could not justify the inclusion of an existential component. This did not fulfil the criterion of our definition of a therapeutic factor as an element of the group process that exerts a beneficial effect. Instead, the existential factor calls for the patient to think in a particular way, along lines laid down by a specific body of theory; its constituents are, in our view, more accurately conceptualized as goals of treatment. Secondly, in this context we also opted to delete transference, or its parallel—family re-enactment, since this presupposed that the patient was required to identify and understand a specific cause to his problems, namely, unresolved family conflict. As with the existential factor, this invoked a special theoretical formulation.

We need to return for a moment to Corsini and Rosenberg to appreciate the point of a unifying classification—it is to locate the common ground between different theoretical schools of group treatment. Thus, one cogent criterion for inclusion is that the prospective factor is not bound up exclusively with a particular theory. We have tried to deal with this issue by including an all-embracing cognitive factor—self-understanding—whose basis is that the patient learns something important about himself. This could be in one or more specific areas according to the nature of the patient's problems and his related goals in therapy. Thus, he might learn something important about his behaviour, or assumptions, or motivations, or fantasies, or unconscious thoughts, or how he comes across to co-members, or why he behaves the way he does, or how he got to be the way he is. The scope for learning is obviously wide, but each patient enters therapy to learn about matters germane to himself. Implied here is the possibility, for example, that the lesson to be learned is an understanding of early conflicted family relationships through the development of transferential ties with one or more group members, including the therapist. In this instance, transference is more accurately defined as a condition for change, that is, in order for a certain form of self-understanding to proceed—the therapeutic factor involved—a particular pattern of relating is necessary (see Chapter 2 for a more comprehensive account of this topic).

A third alteration we made to previous classifications was to distinguish between two forms of expression: the release of feelings, such as anger, grief, or sorrow, which have been difficult or impossible for the patient to ventilate; and the patient's revelations about his life outside the group, his past, his problems, or his fantasies, all of which he regards as private and personal. The first is labelled catharsis; the second self-disclosure. Although the two commonly occur together, we think it useful to tease them out in terms of the primary effect they each exert. In catharsis, the chief therapeutic effect is the relief experienced by the patient upon releasing what are usually pent-up, intense feelings. Whereas in self-disclosure, the effect is intimately bound up with the experience of becoming more honest and open; this in turn enables the patient to explore himself more freely and genuinely.

The final change we made to previous classifications concerns interaction. We conceive this as the **attempt** by the patient to relate constructively and adaptively within the group, either by initiating some behaviour or responding to other group members, and the learning associated with this endeavour. The name we have given to this factor, learning from interpersonal action, is intended to convey its two interrelated dimensions—actional first, cognitive thereafter. As in the case of self-understanding, the range of potential behaviour within the framework of interaction is vast—relating more sensitively, intimately, assertively, and so forth. The particular actions tried out obviously depend on the patient's particular problems in the interpersonal realm, and his associated goals.

The remaining six factors in our scheme are the familiar ones of universality, acceptance, altruism, guidance, vicarious learning (the term it replaces, spectator therapy, conveys too passive a picture of the patient's involvement), and instillation of hope.

To avoid repetition, we defer consideration of the further evolution of the concept of therapeutic factors to later sections. Chapter 9, in particular, contains some noteworthy theoretical developments that have occurred in recent years.

Methods of study

Our final task in this introductory chapter is to describe briefly the customary methods of study that have been utilized in examining the subject. They are: the observations of clinicians, the formulations of theorists, and the systematic research of investigators.

The observations of clinicians

Psychotherapy has since its inception relied to a considerable extent on the close observation by its practitioners of clinical phenomena emerging during the course of treatment itself. Observation has yielded what we can conveniently refer to as clinical lore—a body of traditional knowledge regarded as offering valuable and useful insights into the processes of therapy. The content of the lore derives from observations made repeatedly and consistently, and which therefore appear to have a measure of face validity.

Clinical lore permeates all forms of psychotherapy. In group therapy it comprises a series of widely agreed observations on aspects of the group process that seem to exert a beneficial effect. Earlier we discussed the phenomenon of acceptance—the benefit derived from feeling valued and supported by fellow group members. This has been noted by clinicians for decades and has thus become firmly established as traditional knowledge. In the chapters that follow, we look at observations of the group process relevant to therapeutic factors which have found favour with group therapists and contributed to a greater understanding of these factors (about ten per cent of the literature under review).

The formulations of theorists

Observation alone cannot confirm the validity of the phenomena under study, although they may serve as the foundation for another form of study. To the theorist, an observation may trigger a formulation about some facet of the group's process, or the observation may fit into a pre-existing schema and so help to buttress it. A series of independent observations may be assembled together because they appear to be interrelated, and derived from this exercise may emerge a theoretical framework. Whatever mode of theorising is pursued, the purpose is similar—an attempt to explain the phenomena under consideration. We examine theories regarding specific therapeutic factors in Chapters 2–8; in Chapter 9, by contrast, we look at contributions by theorists who have produced formulations incorporating a constellation of factors (about 30 per cent of the literature under review relates to theory).

Systematic research

The clinician, both as observer and as theorist, serves to guide the systematic research investigator about the most suitable questions he should study. The investigation may take many forms, from a rigorous detailed scrutiny of a group phenomenon (e.g. ascertaining how often fellow members and therapist serve as models for the patient to imitate) to the testing of a hypothesis in order to refute or confirm a theoretical concept (e.g. that self-disclosure of personal information in group therapy is associated with clinical improvement). Let us now briefly consider the principal methodological approaches adopted by investigators.

The individual case study As discussed earlier, one approach is a natural extension of observation—the individual case study. In group therapy this becomes translated into the individual group study (although a particular patient within a group may obviously be focused upon). Therapists or independent observers carefully and methodically note how a group operates in order to detect its therapeutic ingredients. The method has not been widely used because the findings it yields are not readily generalizable or replicable. On the other hand the case study has one clear advantage—its respect for the uniqueness of a therapy group. Its chief utility lies in potentially generating new hypotheses for testing by other types of research. If, for example, a case study reveals a pattern whereby members of a group tend to indulge in greater self-disclosure following a series of self-disclosures by their therapists, a hypothesis might be erected that a group led by a 'transparent' therapist will be more self-revealing than a group led by an 'opaque' therapist (see Chapter 5).

The experimental method This brings us conveniently to the experimental method in which contrasting conditions are set up in such a way that a specified hypothesis can be tested. Ideally, two or more groups of patients, matched in as many respects as possible, such as diagnosis, sex, severity of condition, and motivation, are treated under contrasting conditions, and the effects of each set of conditions noted. The investigator can then answer the question of whether treatment condition X produces an effect which is different than treatment condition Y.

A study of an aspect of catharsis by Liberman[23] (see Chapter 6) serves as a good illustration of the experimental method. He set out to test the hypothesis that patients in group therapy led by a therapist who encouraged their expression of hostility towards himself would achieve greater improvement in their dependency problems than would patients led by a therapist who did not. Two therapists with similar training and experience and matched on a personality check-list, each led a group weekly for nine months. The two groups, formed from the waiting-list of an outpatient clinic, were matched on such variables as age, sex, marital status, social class, diagnosis, and record of previous therapy. Thus, impressive matching was achieved in respect of both therapist and patients (a relatively uncommon feature of experimental research on therapeutic factors).

In one group—the experimental condition—the therapist was instructed and trained to increase the expression of hostility directed towards himself, through specific processes of prompting and reinforcing. In the other group—the control condition—the therapist was advised to follow his usual 'intuitive' style. This difference in leadership style was subsequently confirmed by ratings made on transcripts of taped sessions. Although the experimental therapist was found to influence the timing and amount of hostility directed to himself, the hypothesis was not confirmed, i.e. expression of hostility was unrelated to outcome.

Apart from exemplifying the basic design which typifies the experimental approach, Liberman's work also serves to illuminate some pertinent aspects of methodology. The need for a control condition is obvious. Many forms of control are available to the investigator. They include: no treatment control, in which patients receive no treatment at all; waiting-list control, in which patients receive treatment only at the end of the experiment; attention–placebo control, in which patients are seen periodically but not given specific treatment; patient as own control, in which the effects on the same person of periods of therapeutic intervention and non-intervention are methodically monitored; and the 'missing ingredient' control, in which the control group receives the same treatment as the experimental group save for one or more key ingredients regarded as especially potent (Liberman used this form of control in the experiment described above). The last is particularly apt in research on therapeutic factors where, commonly, the goal is to tease out the relationship between a factor and another process variable or to examine the factor's effect on outcome.

The application of a control condition immediately raises another methodological issue—matching. In the most rigorous experimental design, experimental and control patients are drawn only from the population that the particular treatment is designed to help, and their assignment to treatment or control conditions is entirely random. The latter is usually difficult to achieve in therapeutic factor research especially because of the desirability to carry out randomized allocation of all patients at the same time so that factors which might change with time do not confound the experimental variables. In practice, the usual compromise is to employ a matching procedure whereby sets of patients are matched on as many features as possible and thereupon allotted at random to either experimental or control conditions.

As we noted in Liberman's study, the experimental and control conditions centred on an aspect of the therapist's style of leadership. The two therapists were matched on several variables but differentiated on one feature regarded as pivotal in exerting a specific effect on group members and in turn influencing their outcome. Such differentiation requires validation, namely objective evidence that the therapists did differ in respect to the feature under scrutiny. In Liberman's study, for example, validation was two-fold—through ratings of therapists' style from taped sessions and through a battery of measures of relevant behaviour of group members. Without validation there can be no assurance that the intended conditions have been achieved; and without some attempt at matching of groups—both patients and therapists—the possibility exists that other differences between experimental and control groups may have accounted for the findings. As we shall see, these desiderata are often not satisfied in their entirety and we point this out when necessary.

The correlational study Less informative than the experimental approach is the correlational approach. Here, the investigator does not distinguish between independent and dependent variables. Instead he notes how two or more phenomena relate to one another through the statistical procedure of correlation. This form of research is less illuminating since no causal relationship can be assumed. For example, X (insight) and Y (improvement) may be found to be associated with each other but to establish whether X is the cause of Y requires an additional experimental procedure.

On the other hand a correlational study has the advantage of being easier to carry out than an experimental one, and can yield useful data. More importantly, it can serve as a stepping stone to a comprehensive experiment by providing pointers to what would constitute the optimal design. The study by Kapp[24] and his colleagues on group cohesiveness illustrates the above point (see

Chapter 4). Members of several discussion and therapy groups completed a questionnaire at the end of their group programme; they rated their own levels of change and of involvement in the group, and assessed the degree of group cohesiveness they felt had been attained. A correlational analysis revealed significant associations between the three measures. These results, the authors suggested, demonstrated that cohesiveness might be an important factor in promoting change. They could not really claim more than this. Moreover, the correlational exercise was weakened by the fact that all measures were obtained from the same source. A member who perceived the group as cohesive and therefore felt a sense of belonging, might have been apt, as a result, to regard himself as a beneficiary. Far more desirable would have been the evaluation of outcome by an independent source. But even if that had been done and a positive correlation with perceived cohesiveness found, little could have been said other than to conjecture about a possible causal relationship. Kapp *et al.* would then have had to conduct a definitive experimental study in which cohesiveness was enhanced by specific procedures in some groups but not in others, the groups otherwise matched *vis-à-vis* patients, therapists, and mode of treatment. The difference in degree of cohesiveness between experimental and control groups would have required validation; outcome would ideally have been assessed by independent judges, naïve about the experimental design.

One could argue that the correlational 'prelude' is superfluous. Why not embark on a definitive experiment from the outset? Such action may well be appropriate when the investigator can confidently erect a hypothesis and reasonably expect to confirm it. In the case where the relationship between variables under study is not clear and few clues are available from clinical observation, a correlational approach can be deployed as a form of pilot investigation.

The analogue study Throughout our discussion of the experimental and correlational approaches we have referred to patients as the target of study. But as will become evident, a sizeable proportion of the research done on therapeutic factors involves non-clinical samples, such as members of sensitivity-training groups and volunteer subjects. In the case of the latter another research approach has been commonly adopted—the analogue study. Because of the many hurdles facing the investigator in his study of aspects of group therapy process as they occur, he has resorted to research designs that attempt to simulate the therapeutic situation. The analogue study facilitates the acquisition of an adequately sized sample (a perpetual problem in group therapy research of any kind) which in turn allows for well-controlled experimental conditions and the detailed analysis of the relationships between a variety of variables.

Consider an analogue experiment devised by Ribner[25] (dealt with more fully in Chapter 4). Interested in the effect on group cohesiveness and mutual liking of a specific contract on group members to divulge personal information about themselves, he studied ninety-six student volunteers. This large sample enabled him to form twenty-four groups, composed of either high- or low-scoring self-disclosers (evaluated by a self-administered questionnaire) or a mixture of both. Half these groups had an implicit contract which encouraged self-disclosure, the others were merely instructed to become acquainted. All groups met for a single, one-hour session. Taped segments thereof were rated for frequency and depth of self-disclosure. Members thereafter rated their liking for one another and for their group. Pertinent here are the various questions that can be posed and answered by the experimental design. Did the contract affect students' self-disclosure? Did the contract encourage cohesiveness or mutual liking? Were students' pre-group self-disclosure scores relevant? Was group composition in terms of students' self-disclosure scores relevant?

Despite the considerable advantages of an analogue study, as illustrated by Ribner's experiment, predictable objections to it are based on the obvious fact that group therapy *per se* is not studied directly, and that the results cannot therefore be extrapolated to it with any degree of confidence. The first point is indisputable, the second debatable. We would argue that since the intrinsic advantages of the analogue approach are sufficiently impressive, and the realistic limitations of direct research on the therapy group so problematic, both have a place in the study of therapeutic factors. Moreover, we would support Strong[26] in his advocacy of a complementary approach to research in psychotherapy generally: 'An integrated programme of research that begins with analogue studies and systematically extends to ongoing psychotherapy, using both experimental and correlational methods, would be an ideal approach.' Research on therapeutic factors would unquestionably be the poorer if the results of analogue studies were ignored. We have therefore had little hesitation in reviewing those that strike us as shedding light on the therapy group or which could with minor modification be replicated in a clinical context.

In our discussion of systematic research methods, we have focused on topics immediately relevant to the chapters that follow and intentionally avoided several issues, such as the specification of variables, the measurement of outcome and process, the uniformity myth, the ethics of research, the relevance of research, and so forth. These would take us well beyond our purpose and we refer the reader to other texts which cover this ground admirably.[27, 28]

Having spelled out the development of the concept of therapeutic factors, the efforts to classify them, and the methods for studying them, we can now embark on our detailed consideration of each of the ten we have selected for inclusion. We begin with an account of insight or self-understanding.

References

1. Frank, J. D. Therapeutic components of psychotherapy. *Journal of Nervous and Mental Disease* **159**, 325–42 (1974).
2. Bloch, S., Crouch, E., and Reibstein, J. Therapeutic factors in group psychotherapy. *Archives of General Psychiatry* **38**, 519–26 (1981).
3. Parloff, M. Group dynamics and group psychotherapy: the state of the union. *International Journal of Group Psychotherapy* **13**, 393–8 (1963).
4. Moreno, J. L. Psychodrama. In *American handbook of psychiatry* (ed. S. Arieti). Basic Books, New York (1959).
5. Pratt, J. H. The tuberculosis class: an experiment in home treatment. In *Group psychotherapy and group function* (eds. M. Rosenbaum and M. Berger). Basic Books, New York (1975).
6. Dreikurs, R. and Corsini, R. Twenty years of group psychotherapy. *American Journal of Psychiatry* **110**, 567–75 (1954).
7. Lazell, E. The group treatment of dementia praecox. *Psychoanalytic Review* **8**, 168–79 (1921).
8. Marsh, L. C. Group therapy and the psychiatric clinic. *Journal of Nervous and Mental Disease* **82**, 381–92 (1935).
9. Burrow, T. The group method of analysis. *Psychoanalytic Review* **14**, 268–80 (1927).
10. Wender, L. Dynamics of group psychotherapy and its application. *Journal of Nervous and Mental Disease* **84**, 54–60 (1936).
11. Slavson, S. R. *Dynamics of group psychotherapy* (ed. M. Schiffer). Jason Aronson, New York (1979).
12. Wolf, A. Psychoanalysis in groups. In *Group psychotherapy and group*

function (eds. M. Rosenbaum and M. Berger). Basic Books, New York (1975).

13. Foulkes, S. H. *Therapeutic group analysis*. Allen and Unwin, London (1964).
14. Bion, W. *Experiences in groups*. Tavistock, London (1961).
15. Ezriel, H. A psychoanalytic approach to group treatment. *British Journal of Medical Psychology* **23**, 59–74 (1950).
16. Corsini, R. and Rosenberg, B. Mechanisms of group psychotherapy: processes and dynamics. *Journal of Abnormal and Social Psychology* **51**, 406–11 (1955).
17. Hill, W. F. Further considerations of therapeutic mechanisms in group therapy. *Small Group Behaviour* **6**, 421–9 (1975).
18. Hill, W. F. Analysis of interviews of group therapists. *Provo Papers* **1**, 1 (1957). (Cited in reference 17)
19. Berzon, B., Pious, C., and Farson, R. The therapeutic event in group psychotherapy: a study of subjective reports by group members. *Journal of Individual Psychology* **19**, 204–12 (1963).
20. Yalom, I. D. *The theory and practice of group psychotherapy*. Basic Books, New York (1975).
21. Bloch, S., Reibstein, J., Crouch, E., *et al.* A method for the study of therapeutic factors in group psychotherapy. *British Journal of Psychiatry* **134**, 257–63 (1979).
22. Popper, K. *Conjectures and refutations*. Routledge and Kegan Paul, London (1963).
23. Liberman, R. A behavioural approach to group dynamics: II. Reinforcement and prompting hostility to the therapist in group therapy. *Behaviour Therapy* **1**, 312–27 (1970).
24. Kapp, F. T., Gleser, G., Brissenden, A., *et al.* Group participation and self-perceived personality change. *Journal of Nervous and Mental Disease* **139**, 255–65 (1964).
25. Ribner, N. J. Effects of an explicit group contract on self-disclosure and group cohesiveness. *Journal of Counselling Psychology* **21**, 116–20 (1974).
26. Strong, S. R. Social psychological approach to psychotherapy research. In *Handbook of psychotherapy and behaviour change* (eds. S. Garfield and A. Bergin). Wiley, New York (1978).
27. Garfield, S. L. and Bergin, A. E. (eds.) *Handbook of psychotherapy and behaviour change*. Wiley, New York (1978).
28. Gurman, A. S. and Razin, A. M. (eds.) *Effective psychotherapy: A handbook of research*. Pergamon, New York (1977).

2 Insight (self-understanding)

Group therapy has for the most part inherited from individual psychotherapy the notion that insight is at the heart of the therapeutic process. A wide range of terms—greater self-knowledge, enhanced self-awareness, greater self-understanding, among others—are used by therapists to reflect a cognitive or intellectual process. But with regard to what should be learned in group therapy and how that learning should occur, there is considerable variation in both theory and practice.

A fundamental question is whether insight is a requisite for clinical improvement. In the behavioural therapy tradition, at least until recently, insight has not been regarded as relevant; instead, the sufficiency of symptomatic change has been averred. Many clinicians would question whether insight necessarily leads to behavioural change. It is not appropriate for us to enter the fray although we will look later at some empirical work which relates to these questions. For the moment we proceed on the assumption that group therapy does constitute a process of learning, though the form and content of this learning may vary considerably.

In this chapter we will be concerned with (1) an attempt to define insight; (2) theoretical contributions (we focus on psychogenetic, interpersonal, and existential aspects); and (3) empirical research, chiefly along two strands—the relationship between insight and clinical change, and the role of feedback in promoting insight. Throughout, we will consider the implications of the systematic research for group therapy practice. For convenience we will refer to the term 'insight' since it is the one most customarily used.

Definition

The elusiveness of a precise definition probably stems from the intricacy of the concept and because so many elements comprise it. A convenient starting point, however, is the review of therapeutic factors by Corsini and Rosenberg.[1] A brief reminder that they identified statements in the literature reflecting therapeutic mechanisms and reduced these to nine factors. One of their nine factors was labelled intellectualization and defined as the '. . . process of learning or acquiring knowledge in the group. Intellectualisation leads to insight, which itself we consider not a mechanism, but a result of intellectualisation.' This definition is derived from statements which refer, *inter alia*, to intellectualization, understanding, intellectual comprehension, learning, re-education, and re-learning. Other statements refer to explanation, interpretation, analysis of dreams, and analysis of resistance.

We note immediately that the latter fall into a different class and are better conceptualized as techniques or strategies whereby learning occurs. For example, a therapist may make an interpretation or offer an analysis of a dream, or a patient may explain some aspect of a fellow member's behaviour, but none of these operations will have therapeutic import unless the recipient actually registers the information and reflects on it. A second point is that some of the above terms reflect new learning or discovery of previously unknown material whereas others are concerned with learning afresh matters that were previously learned in a distorted, unrealistic, or erroneous way. We do not regard Corsini and Rosenberg's own distinction between intellectualization and insight as crucial. Obviously insight is an end product. But if we insert the words 'gains' or 'acquires' it is clear that the knowledge a group patient attains is the result of a process of learning. Indeed, intellectualization is a poor term because it is commonly applied to that defence mechanism in which a patient employs intellectual means to protect himself from unpleasant or threatening emotions.

Corsini and Rosenberg also included the statement 'awareness of interpersonal relationships' in their list. This implies that the focus of insight concerns the nature of relating to others. It contrasts with a process of self-understanding, namely, gaining insight into intrapsychic processes, such as conflicts, roots of problems, or the unconscious determinants of behaviour. We shall return in detail to this topic later.

Before leaving Corsini and Rosenberg, a further distinction must be made between their factor of intellectualization and three others in their classification allied to it. The first is universalization; becoming aware that one is not unique and that one's problems are shared by others (see Chapter 8). The second is spectator therapy; learning about oneself through the observation of others, either by imitating some desirable aspect in them or by identifying with them (see Chapter 8). Lastly, reality testing: the patient tests himself in a relatively safe forum where he bumps up against reality. This is regarded by Corsini and Rosenberg as an 'actional' factor, whereas intellectualization, universalization, and spectator therapy are grouped together as 'intellectual' in type.

The efforts by Yalom[2] to define insight are important because of his ideas about *interpersonal insight*. He argues that this form of learning is more relevant in group therapy, compared to insight about the psychogenesis of symptoms. Of the twelve therapeutic factors in his classification, two relate to insight—*self-understanding* and *interpersonal learning—input*. By examining his questionnaire on therapeutic factors based on this classification, we get an idea of what these two represent.

Firstly, self-understanding. The five items that comprise it can be broken down into two groups. The first contains the single item 'discovering and accepting previously unknown or unacceptable parts of myself'; these parts may be positive qualities, strengths, and assets. This item represents a general process of self-discovery coupled with a behavioural component, implying that the patient acts on the knowledge he gains. The second group includes three items concerned with an appreciation by the patient of the influence of his personal and family history, thus: (1) learning that current feelings for a person are to do with past experiences with other people; (2) learning that current reactions to people or situations are associated with earlier periods in life; and (3) learning that feelings and behaviour are related to childhood and development.

This group also includes a fourth, closely related, item i.e. that the patient learns the cause and sources of his problems. The emphasis in this quartet is on the historical perspective, in particular, the link between contemporary behaviour, events, experiences, and memories of childhood. Also relevant is the patient reaching an understanding of how a problem, symptom or personality trait developed. We can see the obvious influence of psychoanalysis, with its emphasis on the past. 'Discovering and accepting previously unknown or unacceptable parts of myself', by contrast, is related to the present and falls into a different clinical tradition.[3]*

Yalom's other factor related to insight is interpersonal learning—input. (Its companion, *interpersonal learning—output*, is not primarily a learning factor but is concerned with action—the patient trying out various new behaviours with other group members.) This is composed of five items, all concerned with some form of feedback which the patient receives from his peers in the group; the therapist is not cited as such, but implicated only as a group member. The items show considerable overlap: the group teaching the patient about the impression he makes; the patient learning how he appears; the group telling the patient what they think of him; the group pointing out habits or mannerisms that annoy them; and the patient learning that he sometimes confuses others by not saying what he really thinks.

Interpersonal learning—input clearly differs from self-understanding. The patient learns what others feel about him; how others see him in the here-and-now of the group. There is neither an intrapsychic nor a historical component—for example, the patient does not learn about the sources of the mannerisms pointed out to him or the origins of any other observations proffered.

In our own work on classifying therapeutic factors, we treat insight broadly on the premiss that: (1) what the patient learns varies considerably and is to an important extent individualized to him; and (2) he learns about himself in many different ways.[4] This multidimensional view holds that learning in group therapy is an individual affair. Each patient enters the group requiring to develop new perspectives and see himself afresh, to gain knowledge about his specific problems or conflicts or dilemmas. How he will learn depends on what he needs to learn. Some learning will result from the feedback provided by fellow members about his overt behaviour. Other learning will follow interpretations about the underlying meaning of problems and behaviour made by the therapist or by other group members.

From this preamble, it follows that our definition is all-embracing: *The basis of insight is that the patient learns something important about himself*. This can come about as a result of feedback (direct or

*It is not surprising that in a study by Yalom[2] and colleagues of twenty highly improved patients in group therapy, the above five items were poorly correlated with each other. It is also of interest to note that the first item was chosen as most important by this group of patients.

indirect) and interpretation from other group members, both patients and therapists. Insight operates when the patient

(a) *learns something important about himself:* this learning may cover overt behaviour, e.g. he is detached, sensitive, envious, competitive, and the like, which can be readily observed by others; assumptions he holds about himself, e.g. that he is unlovable or inferior; motivations that underlie his behaviour, e.g. he acts in a detached way out of a fear that he will be rejected or is monopolistic to gain attention; fantasies, e.g. that a recurrent, frightening dream is linked to professional insecurity; unconscious thoughts—that he was completely unaware of before they surfaced in the group, e.g. that his pressure to achieve stems from a long-standing need to win his father's approval;
(b) *learns how he comes across to the group* (this is comparable to Yalom's 'interpersonal learning-input' and is mainly achieved through feedback by other members);
(c) *learns more clearly about the nature of his problem* (this refers to a more comprehensive understanding of a particular problem, e.g. discovering that keeping people at a distance is associated with a wish not to be hurt through rejection);
(d) *learns why he behaves the way he does and how he got to be the way he is* (this can be labelled as psychogenetic insight inasmuch as the patient learns about the mechanisms underlying his behaviour and about their origins).

The advantage of our operational definition is that the several different facets of insight are not collapsed together into an oversimplified account. To reinforce this point we cite examples of insight obtained from the 'most important event' questionnaire. (See reference 5 for a brief description of this questionnaire.)

Charles, a quiet shy member, told the group that it was up to others to help a person through depression. The group disagreed, pointing out that this placed an unfair burden on others; also that it was not adult-like for the depressed person to abdicate all responsibility. It was then mentioned by the group that Charles's reticence in the meetings was similarly unfair to them. While seeming to resist their arguments at the time, these did appear to have given him insight into how he affected others. His group participation increased greatly following this event.

For a few weeks Oliver seemed to be trying to mimic the therapist: his participation was limited to interpretations and judgements about other patients. He never showed any of his own feelings or problems. Other members ultimately reacted by ignoring him, behaving as if he were not there. This forced Oliver to drop this behaviour. He thus came face to face with the fact that this pose was a defence against his greatest problem: resentment of others in authority.

I became very antagonistic to the female therapist saying that she had not been at all helpful to me. I did not see any point in coming to the group any more. The therapist pointed out that, since my mother died when I was very young, I seemed to be searching for a substitute mother, and I seemed to want her to be my 'super-mother'. I felt this struck a chord in me and it helped me to explain much about my difficult relationship with women.

Martin had been conspicuously withdrawn for most of the meeting, which mainly focused on Peter. Since Martin was usually a voluble, demanding member, his withdrawal was keenly felt. Other group members felt manipulated as he feigned first boredom, then sleep. The other members finally turned on him remarking that he was selfish and obviously unable to give the meeting over to someone else who might benefit from his participation. Martin was startled by this confrontation, having no idea that others had found him demanding and selfish.

I became very cross when someone accused me of being 'cold'. Another member pointed out that my anger was typical and that it seemed that I wanted only praise from others. All my relations seemed to revolve around that desire. Although I did not respond well at the time it was very important for me to learn this about myself and it later clarified much for me.

Theoretical aspects

The psychoanalytic approach

In the previous chapter, we commented on the application during the 1930s of psychoanalytic theory to the therapy group. This is a good starting point to examine how insight is conceptualized by various theorists of group therapy.

The psychoanalytic pioneers in this regard are undoubtedly Trigant Burrow, Louis Wender, Paul Schilder, and Samuel Slavson. Wender,[6] for example, reported in 1936 on his then six years' experience of psychoanalysis in groups. He suggested that through a synthesis of intellect and emotion, the patient could comprehend those emotional reactions which would enable him to 'meet new situations with greater awareness and skill'. The role of insight is implied in such terms as intellect, comprehension, and awareness. Schilder[7] wrote of his experience at Bellevue Hospital, where he combined individual and group psychotherapy. Like Wender, Schilder incorporated psychoanalytic thinking on insight into his group work; as he commented: 'Psychoanalytic insight was utilized in this group treatment. In every case the life history of the patient was discussed and elucidated in detail and early infantile material was particularly studied.' The psychoanalytic group method sought to provide the patient with 'a deeper insight' into his personal life-history, problems, and expectations for the future. Typical psychoanalytic procedures, such as free association and the analysis of dreams, were advocated to achieve this insight.

Alexander Wolf[8] elaborated on these early developments. He began to experiment in 1938 and before long had five groups in progress. He imitated analytic methods explicitly—free association, analysis of dreams and fantasies, and the working through of resistance and transference were all to the fore. Wolf's purpose was unambiguous—the patient should achieve psychogenetic insight. To quote him: 'Psychoanalysis in groups entails an understanding of unconscious processes and motivations. It seeks out the historical basis for current behaviour in order to resolve its persistence in the present. It requires the working out and working through of repetitive and compulsive psycho-pathological manoeuvres.' Through free association, the patient enjoys the freedom to express any thought, fantasy, or feeling. By focusing on the 'there-and-then', he notes how historical determinants of behaviour persist in the present; and by tracing out the links between present and past, he is 'able to understand and cope with transferential distortions'. Transference, in Wolf's approach, is both vertical—the irrational association between patient and the therapist representing parental figures; and horizontal—distorted relationships developing between patients, which reflect old sibling ties.

Notwithstanding his adherence to psychoanalytic methods, Wolf did not discount the relevance of the interpersonal sphere. Although self-knowledge was stressed by him as a therapeutic goal, this was complemented by a major focus on interpersonal communication processes; both of these together, he believed, led to personality and social integration. The emphasis on the interpersonal is seen in his approach to free association. A particular patient begins to associate freely. His co-members soon join in with their associations so that participation is interdependent and reciprocal. For example, a patient presents a dream and his associations around that dream. Others associate in relation to his dream and then try to interpret the dream as well as the meaning of each member's associations.

Perhaps the most notable proponent of psychoanalytically orientated group therapy in the USA was Samuel Slavson.[9] He was even more bound to original Freudian tenets than Wolf, specifying that they could be applied directly to the group process. With regard to insight, he spoke of the 'uncovering, exploration and revelation of the content of the unconscious, regression to infantile traumas, and the evolution of insight and ego control ...' However, in a group, patients acted as mutual catalysts and this facilitated catharsis (by which he meant the free association of thought, feelings, and memory). A second difference with classical psychoanalysis was the dilution of the transference resulting in therapy less intensive and personality change less profound. This level of insight compared to individual analysis was limited: '... the potentials of individual treatment to plumb the depths of the unconscious and the past, and to unravel the profoundly disturbing and inadequately repressed associated feelings, are much greater than in group psychotherapy.'

In Europe, S. H. Foulkes[10] began, during the Second World War, to experiment with group analysis, and, like his American counterparts, advanced the idea that the group could accommodate the whole range of psychoanalytic concepts and procedures: 'All that psychoanalysis teaches us enters, in principle, fully into group analysis; structural, economic, and dynamic aspects of unconscious mental processes, the concepts of primary and secondary processes, of basic conflict, the emphasis on insight for revision of pathogenic reactions in the therapeutic situation.' The last phrase is particularly noteworthy. Group analysis enables a patient to participate in a free, spontaneous exchange of interaction and communication and, through the re-establishment of the original pathogenic conflict within the group, to achieve a greater degree of awareness. The therapist's tasks are to penetrate the presenting surface of the group material, and to translate unconscious phenomena into the conscious sphere through the analysis of resistance and defenses and by explaining the latent meaning of overt behaviour. Unlike Slavson, Foulkes saw advantages in the group method because transference was both vertical and horizontal—patient to therapist and patient to fellow patient—and thus yielded more data to observe and learn from. Here we see a close similarity with Wolf.

Yalom and interpersonal insight

All the theorists we have covered so far share one prominent view—that insight is the chief goal of group therapy. Moreover, insight of a particular kind—an understanding of the original cause(s) of present problems—most conveniently labelled 'psychogenetic'. In recent years, this position has been criticized by theorists, in particular Yalom[2] who, from the early 1960s developed an alternative model of group therapy based on the interpersonal theory of Harry Stack Sullivan.[11] This holds that psychogenetic insight is not the be-all and end-all of treatment. Instead, interpersonal insight is more relevant.

We noted the constituents of this approach when looking at Yalom's therapeutic factor of interpersonal learning-input earlier in this chapter. He differentiates four levels of insight that may occur in groups. At the first, a patient is informed by his peers or therapist how they see him or some aspect of his behaviour. The context is interpersonal and reliant on observation of overt behaviour. At the next level, the patient learns what he is doing to and with others over a longer time span; here the analysis is more detailed so that patterns of behaviour are noted and considered. The third level, 'motivational insight', examines why the patient behaves the way he does. This is not a historical question but psychosocial—what psychological and social factors in the patient influence his interpersonal style? At the fourth level, psychogenetic insight, the question is posed: How did the patient get to be the way he is or how did his problems originate in terms of his personal history?

A schematic example of one of our own cases serves to illustrate the four levels. A patient was observed by the group to be argumentative in a session. During succeeding sessions, the argumentativeness was seen to be an aspect of his rivalry with co-members. As he learned more about this interpersonal style, he came to understand that he competed in the group out of a fear that he might otherwise be completely ignored. At the psychogenetic level, it emerged that the patient's rivalry with a younger sibling to gain parental affection and attention was the antecedent, possibly the actual cause.

We readily note that the degree of speculation increases as we move from the first to the fourth level of insight. Yalom argues persuasively that it is conceptually erroneous to equate this greater speculation with a greater depth of self-knowledge. Though analytically orientated theorists aver that only insight into the origin of problems or personal traits yields substantial clinical improvement, Yalom argues that there is 'not a shred of evidence to support this contention', at least in group therapy. He questions the real value of the fourth level of insight, citing two clinical observations: a patient may gain a 'deep' level of insight but demonstrate no behavioural change; on the other hand a patient may improve clinically but without acquiring psychogenetic insight.

Elsewhere, Yalom comments forcibly on what he regards as the proper use of the past in group work. He is clearly opposed to the position that it is all-important but he does not discount the cogency of unconscious factors which, he reminds us, are not necessarily confined to the past. The future and the immediate present are important temporal frameworks too and deserve equal attention. Yalom also suggests that the past exists only as the individual constitutes it in the present and in relation to his view of the future. This notion is important for the achievement of insight: the process required is reconstitution, not simply excavation. It is no surprise in the light of these comments that Yalom's more recent energies have been devoted to existential psychotherapy.[12]

Psychogenetic vs interpersonal insight

We have now reached a point where, if we put aside the strictly behavioural view that insight is not a requisite for change, we have the choice of two opposing positions concerning insight—psychogenetic versus interpersonal. Some readers may argue that it is a question of emphasis rather than two qualitatively different camps. After all, both Wolf and Foulkes, as we have seen, displayed an interest in social processes that occur in groups and Yalom's approach does encompass such phenomena as transference and delving into the past if appropriate. None the less, if the classical position is adopted in both instances, the emphasis differs substantially.

Weiner[13] is sharply critical of Yalom's case and argues that he has set too much store by his therapeutic factor questionnaire and on the results of his study of patients achieving major improvement. In that study (which we consider in detail in Chapter 9), three of the top ten items rated as helpful by the sample were concerned with some aspect of learning how the patient comes across to others, i.e. interpersonal insight. The item regarded as most helpful concerned a broad aspect of self-understanding—'discovering and accepting previously unknown or unacceptable parts . . .' The psychogenetic items by contrast achieved relatively low ratings—positions 11, 15, 20, and 50 (there are 60 items in all). Moreover, items about transference (such as 'The group was something like my family, some members or the therapist being like my parents and others being like my relatives. Through the group experience I understand my past relationships with my parents and relatives.') were judged to be not at all helpful. Looking at it another way, if Yalom's twelve therapeutic factors are ranked in order of importance by these patients, interpersonal learning—input comes out top, self-understanding fourth, and family re-enactment—basically about transference—tenth.

Before proceeding with Weiner's criticism, we should note that although Yalom does devote considerable attention to the results of the study with his twenty improved patients it is clear that his views stem equally, probably more so, from theoretical and clinical sources. We can illustrate this with his approach to family re-enactment which he sees 'as part of the general horizon against which the group is experienced'. Family is the 'omnipresent spectre' and family experience determines, in great part 'the nature of his parataxic distortions [i.e. distortions in communication with others], the role he assumes in the group, his attitudes towards the group leaders, etc.'. On the other hand, he does caution against undue focus on 'those who are not present' and certainly eschews emphasis on such matters as 'Oedipal strivings' or on 'sibling rivalries'. Actually, one can detect quite evocative language in his qualification, which no doubt reflects his scepticism about the intrinsic value of such phenomena as transference and psychogenetic insight.

What does Weiner's criticism consist of? He claims that Yalom's questionnaire is loaded to support his own views since twice as many items concern interpersonal learning as any other factor; items that cover transference and its resolution (chiefly the family re-enactment items) are 'naïvely worded'; and one cannot expect a forced-choice questionnaire about conscious attitudes to reflect changes in unconscious processes, 'the resolution of which may manifest to the patient only as decreased discomfort'.*

The last point is crucial. Perhaps Yalom's patients gained symptomatically but they did not profit psychodynamically (see the work of David Malan[15] on this distinction in outcome evaluation) and never reached the point of exploring and understanding unconscious forces in themselves—the interpersonalist framework of the group simply did not give them the chance to do so. Weiner concludes that Yalom's research data, based as they are on his own biased questionnaire, do not constitute evidence that interpersonal insight is more valuable than psychogenetic insight. Interpersonal learning theory may be attractive but empirical research 'adds little valid support'.

Weiner does not let his argument rest there. Commendably, he proceeded with his own attempt to unravel some of the issues he raised.[13] He administered Yalom's questionnaire (despite his objections to it) to three groups, all composed of neurotic or personality-disordered patients.

1. One group of eight patients completed the questionnaire before embarking on long-term group therapy. All had had insight-orientated individual therapy previously. The purpose was to study their expectations. Does Yalom's questionnaire simply reflect patients' bias about what is of value in psychotherapy generally rather than cover factors specific to group therapy?
2. A group of nine patients in short-term group therapy completed the questionnaire following the ninth and penultimate session. This group's focus was on the here-and-now and on manifest behaviour.
3. Ten patients in a long-term group were given the questionnaire after, on average, two-and-a-half years membership. Genetic insight was a primary therapeutic factor in this group with free association, the analysis of dreams and defences, and the understanding of transference all featuring prominently.

Unfortunately, the results are only sketchily presented. But, in essence, it was found that members of the first group expected self-understanding and interpersonal learning—output to be helpful, but not so interpersonal learning—input and family re-enactment. In the

*We should note in this context that Jerome Frank,[14] when considering group therapy research, concludes that the covert meaning of behaviour or unconscious motivational processes are not major obstacles to empirical investigation.

second and third groups, interpersonal learning—input and self-understanding were regarded as the most helpful factors and family re-enactment judged unhelpful.

Weiner's interpretation of these results is that, with the exception of interpersonal learning—input, the factors favoured in group therapy correspond to those predicted by patients about to enter a group. The evidence is that interpersonal learning, both input and output, and self-understanding are consistently valued throughout the three groups. But, and this is crucial, Weiner lumps together interpersonal learning—input and output in his data analysis, unjustifiably. After all, they are quite different processes. Input refers to feedback and is directly concerned with interpersonal insight whereas output is 'actional' in quality and concerns the patient's efforts to relate more effectively with others. Thus, the fact that interpersonal learning—input was not predicted as helpful by patients about to enter a group, but was found to be so by both short-term and long-term group members despite the differential theoretical emphases in the two groups—here-and-how in the short-term and there-and-then in the long-term—indicates that the story is a complex one.

Indeed, Weiner is no more able than Yalom to resolve the question of whether interpersonal or psychogenetic insight is the more effective. The chief limitation is the reliance in both cases on the 'consumer' without any idea of the relationship between the choice of therapeutic factors and objectively assessed outcome. Yalom's study is somewhat more informative in this respect inasmuch as the twenty patients studied were all judged highly improved. But even here, we should note that there were only twenty in the sample; some were still in therapy at the time of assessment; the average period of group therapy was only sixteen months (it is questionable whether this is sufficient time for psychogenetic insight to be achieved); improvement was judged by therapists (there was an effort to confirm this judgement by considering the patients' duration of therapy—not a particularly potent criterion); independent ratings of outcome made by three researchers were prone to bias, the instruments used were not validated, and no data on reliability were provided; and the study was retrospective.

Without wishing to blur what is already a confusing picture, we note an interesting finding in a study of short-term encounter groups.[16] Here paradoxically, family re-enactment, which as we have seen covers transference in the main, was rated as 'somewhat helpful' by those participants judged six months later to have benefited from their group experience. Indeed, these learners, compared to those who were unchanged or who had a negative outcome, were three times more likely to regard as 'at least somewhat important in their learning', the group as analogous to family. Non-learners rarely referred to the group in this way. Although family re-enactment was still ranked as the least helpful therapeutic factor by the sample as a whole, thirty-six per cent of learners ranked it as most important or very important, compared to eleven per cent of those who were unchanged and a mere half per cent of those who had a negative outcome.

The existential view of insight

The issue of whether psychogenetic or interpersonal insight should be paramount does not apply to another theoretical position adopted in group therapy, the humanist-existential. Its approach to insight is radically different from either of the two forms we have just discussed. Under its rubric are a number of schools including Rogerian, existential and Gestalt. For the purposes of our discussion, these labelled therapies probably represent variations of emphasis rather than fundamental differences. We will thus consider the relatively pure existential view of the role of insight in group therapy. This is well described by Hora,[17] albeit with a measure of repetitiveness. (See also Helen Durkin[18] and, for a broader treatment of the theoretical basis of existential psychotherapy, Yalom.[12])

Hora firstly sets out the objectives of therapy. They are: to liberate the patient's creative potential; to enable him to relate to his fellows meaningfully; and to permit him to realize and come to terms with his finiteness and thus be relieved of the most basic of all anxieties, the dread of ever-imminent non-being. All these features are encompassed by the concept of the authentic personality. In the course of the group, members show their 'disturbed modes of being-in-the-world'. They act in such a way as to keep existential anxiety at bay. Neurotic anxiety intervenes to substitute for the more basic existential form; patients attempt to escape from the first and avoid the second. The omnipresence of existential anxiety also leads them to treat one another as objects and to use language manipulatively rather than as meaningful communication.

Insight, for the existential group-therapist, relates to this type of group behaviour and 'every group session becomes an experience of looking into a multi-faceted psychological mirror and discovering more and more details about one's own mode of being or failing to be-in-this-world due to a variety of defensive attitudes and strivings evolved in the course of a lifetime'. Further, the group process consists of '. . . a phase of self-discovery, followed by a gradually increasing amount of self-understanding, which then yields to a phase of experimentation in learning to let go of the defensive strivings. . . . Success in learning to accept one's anxiousness is an important step in the direction of accepting one's "thrownness" . . . and is rewarded by a new phase of discovering one's self as being-in-the-world in an authentic fashion.'

In order to achieve these insights, the group process has a number of distinct qualities. Its temporal focus is on the here-and-now. The group is unstructured; the content of the sessions relatively unimportant. Pivotal are the experiential aspects of interaction and communication. For example, the existential meaning of a dream presented by a patient is pursued in its 'basic climate, and only secondarily in its symbolic content'. The existential theory of group therapy eschews the importance of transference for the attainment of insight, on the grounds that it is a historical phenomenon and therefore avoids and denies the reality of the patient's current situation. 'To see transference . . . is to see his historical conditioning, rather than the human being as he really is.' Thus, an interpretation about transference only serves to objectify the patient and constitutes a pseudoscientific enquiry. Indeed, no interpretations are required since 'that which *is* speaks for itself, provided it is understood phenomenologically rather than interpreted in accordance with certain theoretical presumptions'. Instead, therapist and patient participate in a genuine encounter in which both are whole and the therapist's task is to understand his patient in an open-minded way from moment to moment. Durkin[18] captures the essence of this in a pithy description: 'Therapy becomes a clarifying, elucidating process rather than an analysis.' Another psychoanalytic tenet, the importance attached to the past, is discouraged. As Hora[17] puts it, such insight is tantamount to hindsight, that is, knowing one's self as one was, so as to be able to change to how one 'should be'.

In this account, we have quoted extensively because existential theorists tend to use language which does not lend itself well to paraphrase or précis. Indeed, some of the terminology resembles cliché and one cannot escape the feeling that there is an excessive lapse into repetitious jargon. Notwithstanding, it is clear from Hora's summary that insight is of a special transcendent quality and stems from a formulated philosophical theory (even though he and his colleagues may argue that their position is non-theoretical). They would probably also refrain from accepting the concept of insight as a therapeutic factor; this would constitute too reductive a view of a process perceived as an encounter between the therapist and his group members, an encounter typified by spontaneity and immediacy. Although sympathetic to this view, we suspect that existential theorists would enhance their formulations rather than detract from them were they to pin-point more explicitly the process of learning encompassed by 'genuine encounter'. In our view, there is no contradiction in pursuing clarity of the construct of insight in existential group therapy whilst remaining faithful to its non-reductive, non-objectifying position.

The eclectic approach—a solution?

Having covered the psychogenetic, interpersonal, and existential approaches to insight, we are inclined to conclude that an eclectic position is most desirable, one resting on the postulate that every patient has a unique personal history and set of needs when entering group therapy, and that the knowledge he requires should, therefore, be tailored to himself. The corollary is that psychogenetic, interpersonal, and existential forms of insight are all potentially relevant but the actual lessons the patient must learn depend on what ails him and where his particular area of dysfunction exists. The question then arises whether a single, general insight-orientated group can cover this spectrum of learning or whether patients with a certain constellation of problems should be directed to particular groups in which specific insights are striven for. In other words, a group led by Hora might be composed of patients who present principally a lack of purpose and direction, and a sense of emptiness and meaninglessness. A group led by Yalom would serve patients who mainly experience difficulty in their interpersonal life, such as an inability to trust, a fear of intimacy, a fear of expressing feelings, and general anxiety in social situations. A group led by a traditional analyst would suit those patients troubled by inner dilemmas and conflicts, for example, a sense of foreboding, pervasive guilt, doubts about self-worth, and confused self-concept.

The major snag in separating out these three groups is the substantial overlap between them. Many patients in group therapy commonly present a number of diverse problems. A homogeneous group geared towards one form of insight only, would seem inappropriate and not especially useful for such patients. But the quagmire of selection criteria for group therapy is well beyond our present remit.

Empirical research

As we mentioned at the outset, there are two strands to the empirical work on insight in group therapy: its relationship to clinical change; and the role of feedback in its promotion.

The few studies in the first area vary considerably in quality of method. Still, they are worth our attention if only to ascertain in what ways research could be improved. In the preceding section, we considered three types of insight a patient might strive towards. But we side-stepped the fundamental question of whether insight in any form is a necessary condition for clinical change. Insight is clearly unnecessary in treating certain disorders. For example, a phobia of spiders. It seems perfectly apt to apply desensitization or some procedure akin to it without exploring the patient's attitudes to his fear or its possible underlying cause. Similarly, the technique of response prevention in the case of compulsive behaviour does not call for the attainment of insight. In the middle of the 'insight spectrum' are a number of conditions, such as agoraphobia or sexual difficulties, where there is a growing trend for cognitive factors—attitudes and motivations—to be stressed. The current link between cognitive therapy and behaviour therapy, in particular, epitomizes the movement towards a double-barrelled approach and a recognition that what the patient thinks and feels about his problems are salient.

In the group therapies, it is likely that for some patients and for some problems a non-insight-orientated approach is perfectly suitable. Examples include long-term group-based supportive therapy;[19] behavioural modification in long-stay hospitalized patients to promote their socialization;[20] behavioural approaches in children for classroom discipline problems;[21] and social skills training.[22] For other problems dealt with in group therapy, it is likely on clinical grounds that insight plays a prominent role—confusion about sex role, fear of getting close to others, inability to trust, specific conflict with a significant other person, lack of spontaneity, sense of inferiority, undue dependence on others, chronic self-doubt, excessive sense of guilt, and the like.

The Meichenbaum study

One of the best of the few research studies in this area is by Meichenbaum and his colleagues.[23] The work is exemplary in design and methodology. The authors argue that in examining the role of insight in group therapy, it is imperative to choose a specific form of insight therapy and to subject it to a well-controlled test. They selected a treatment derived from Ellis's rational-emotive therapy,[24] in which the patient is made aware that his own self-defeating thoughts (or 'self-verbalizations') contribute to his maladaptive behaviour. This approach was compared with another therapy, in which insight plays no part, at least not intentionally by the therapist—systematic desensitization. Speech anxiety was selected as the clinical problem for treatment.

Volunteers were randomly assigned to matched groups and received one of four treatments: (1) insight—into their self-verbalizations in anxiety-producing situations; (2) desensitization—in imagination; (3) combined insight and desensitization; and (4) placebo—to control for non-specific factors, such as expectancy of improvement, group 'spirit', and the therapist–patient relationship; only neutral topics were discussed in this group. All groups met for eight weekly sessions. Participants were assessed at termination and three months later. This involved self-report measures to evaluate speech anxiety, including one reflecting the confidence to speak before an audience. In addition, a test speech was rated for performance anxiety by trained judges (the reliability of the latter was found to be satisfactory). To illustrate the methodological care taken by the researchers, we note that they also rated subjects free of speech anxiety in order to obtain a baseline measurement. Since a check for possible therapist effects was negative, the eleven therapists involved were combined in one analysis.

On all assessment measures, both at termination and follow-up, insight and desensitization groups achieved the greatest, and about equal, improvement followed by combined treatment and placebo. Additional findings are of great interest. Information from the participants suggested the existence of two subgroups. The first contained those whose speech anxiety was merely one element of a characteristic pattern of shyness that manifested itself in many social encounters. The second comprised those whose speech anxiety was the sole complaint, constituting a problem during public speaking alone. When these two groups were differentiated in terms of their pre-therapy measures, a significant interaction between treatment condition and type of client emerged. The single-anxiety group benefited significantly more from desensitization than the diffuse anxiety group. On the other hand, the insight and combined treatments were especially effective with generally anxious clients for whom desensitization alone was ineffective. Although these findings were derived *post hoc*, they demonstrate clearly that the role of insight is complex, even with a relatively straightforward problem like speech anxiety.

We have devoted substantial space to this study because of its exceptional merit. Noteworthy is the specification of the treatments, especially the insight condition. This is a decided improvement on a preceding investigation carried out by Paul and Shannon.[25] They also compared desensitization and insight in the treatment of speech anxiety, and although there was an explicit description of the former (which in any event is a well-known procedure), the insight treatment was left vague and ill-defined. Therapeutic strategies to promote insight were unspecified, as was the type of insight desired, and no validating data on the procedure were included.

Insight and interaction

In both the above studies, a comparison of an insight-orientated therapy was made with a behavioural treatment not intrinsically reliant on group process. Although we could assume that group factors, such as universality, vicarious learning, and instillation of hope operate in the latter, the behaviour therapist would contend that the main element of his therapy is a specific procedure, like desensitization. A more pertinent, but seriously flawed, study is that of Coons[26] in which he compared the effect of group therapy typified by interaction among group members with an insight-orientated approach. He randomly assigned hospitalized patients, mostly chronic schizophrenics, to one of three groups (similar in terms of age, sex, education, and socio-economic class). In one group, interaction was fostered without any effort to generate insight, self-disclosure was discouraged, and the atmosphere was warm and accepting. The therapist of the second group, by contrast, encouraged the development of insight through discussion of the nature of symptoms. The third group served as a control. Assessment, carried out before and after treatment, used the Rorschach test and an IQ test. The results showed that patients in the interaction group improved significantly more than those in the insight or control groups, with the latter two achieving comparable levels.

Coons[27] concludes: '. . . insight cannot properly be considered to be the crucial condition for behavioural change in psychotherapy . . . understanding is not enough to assure adaptive learning.' Instead, the patient needs the chance for 'interpersonal interaction in a consistently warm and accepting social environment'. He argues further that though the nature of acquired insight differs with various schools of psychotherapy, patients improve behaviourally. Since patients undergoing therapy of different schools share one experience, namely a warm personal relationship with an empathic therapist, it must be interaction in a non-threatening environment that accounts for change. Insight *per se* is unimportant.

Coons's conclusions are quite unwarranted and constitute a hopeless over-generalization. He makes too many assumptions. A counter-argument might run as follows. Many insights, despite different schools, could be shared, and indeed are. It is a common observation that therapists of different theoretical persuasion are often more convergent than divergent in their actual practice, and this could well apply to the way they deal with insight. Coons only considers the therapist–patient relationship (obviously crucial) but is unaware that there are several other non-specific factors which cut across schools of therapy. Jerome Frank,[28] for instance, mentions half a dozen. Among them is that of a rationale to explain problems and behaviour, shared by therapist and patient. What is crucial is an understanding by the patient, shared by his therapist, which makes sense and leads to a reduction in the patient's state of bewilderment.

What of Coons's own investigation on which he relies heavily? Compared to the study by Meichenbaum and colleagues,[23] it is poor in the extreme. The meaning of insight is not specified. The insight-treatment condition was not validated and we cannot assume that it was delivered in pure form. The sample was heavily biased in favour of interaction. Clinical observation would certainly suggest that chronically ill patients would be most unlikely to benefit from an insight-orientated procedure. On the contrary, they would probably have trouble grappling with the intellectual processes involved. Conversely, one might expect that such patients would find a warm atmosphere (as the interaction group was described) beneficial because of its predominantly supportive quality. Moreover, chronically hospitalized patients asked to face their problems more realistically would probably find this quite threatening. The outcome measures were decidedly inappropriate; the Rorschach test and an intelligence test cannot be regarded as satisfactory instruments for assessment. Finally, Coons should have included a combined insight-interaction treatment condition to ascertain whether both factors in tandem were advantageous over each on their own.

Roback[29] refers to Coons's work as 'an exciting piece of research' but also points out some of its limitations. Unfortunately, his own contribution remedies only some of them. We are left with an improved design and method but with persistent shortcomings which will become obvious as we describe the experiment. Again the aim was to compare the effectiveness of interactional and insight-orientated group therapy. The participants were in-patients, with an average eight years in their current hospitalization and mostly with the diagnosis of schizophrenia. Here lies the first problem. As with Coons, this sample would not be one's first choice to test the effect of insight. Patients were randomly assigned to one of four groups: (1) insight—patients' efforts at self-exploration were reinforced positively; (2) interaction—interaction on issues unrelated to patients' problems was encouraged; (3) a combined treatment; and (4) a control group in which films were shown. Each group met on thirty occasions over ten weeks, all led by the same therapist. Sessions were taped and assessed by blind raters to test the validity of the treatment conditions (the requirements of the experimental design were indeed met). Outcome was measured multidimensionally and included behavioural assessment, self-report, an intelligence test and length of time the patient was able to live outside the hospital—the last a poor criterion in view of the sample's chronicity.

Using analysis of variance, no significant differences were found between the groups. Rank-order differences on post-therapy measures were therefore examined, which revealed a superiority of the combined treatment over other groups. However, this statistical approach does not deal with the size of the difference and one must assume that it was small. In any event, Roback did demonstrate some superiority, which suggests advantages in the exploration of problems within a supportive atmosphere.

We can probably conclude from this work that interaction, which was largely conceived of as a warm, accepting environment, is a necessary condition for change but that insight, even in chronic patients, can serve some purpose. Obviously worthwhile is the application of a similar design to long-term out-patient groups since the effect of insight is more likely to emerge with a sample of neurotic and personality disordered patients treated over a longer period. The snag is that a purely interactional approach, which minimizes any potential for insight, is not customarily used in clinical practice and is also ethically dubious. A compromise is for short-term groups, say, 15 sessions, to be conducted in the context of Roback's design, or for the comparison in longer-term groups of therapeutic conditions that differ in degree, that is, high insight and low interaction versus low insight and high interaction, with these differences being validated.

Alternatively, group treatments which differ radically on the dimension of insight could be compared. Such an approach was adopted by Lomont and colleagues[30] in their comparison of insight-orientated group therapy and group assertiveness training. Two groups of in-patients were formed, matched approximately on intelligence and personality scores: one focused on exploration and interpretation of feelings with the aim of understanding the relationship between the past and current behaviour (although this condition was not validated); the other group received assertiveness therapy chiefly through the systematic practice of behaviour in various social situations. Outcome, without follow-up, was assessed using the MMPI and an interpersonal check-list. The assertiveness group showed greater change than the insight group on all MMPI scales but differences were not statistically significant. Similarly, no significant differences were found on the interpersonal check-list. The authors' own speculation is that patients in the insight group felt freer to acknowledge their psychopathology because they were encouraged to be more honest with themselves; such speculation is irrelevant however since the intergroup differences were so minor. In any event, this study suffers from several limitations, including unsatisfactory measures of outcome, non-validation of therapeutic conditions (especially required for the insight group), absence of a control group, and the small sample (only twelve patients).

Insight and psychological-mindedness

Our discussion earlier in the chapter suggested that the concept of insight is not at all unitary; the simple question of its value in group therapy is therefore probably ill-conceived. This point needs reiteration in light of the feuds that commonly take place between therapists who favour a central role for insight and those who wish to relegate it to a position of diminished priority. And, as we have seen, there are even those, such as Coons, who would welcome its demise. Indeed, it would be well to illustrate concretely how necessary it is to consider a comprehensive range of variables in any investigation of insight—the nature and content of the insight offered, to whom, by whom, when, and how. Two experiments lend themselves well to this exercise, one pointing to factors in the patient that may affect the utility of insight and the other to the issue of the type of interpretation emphasized in a group and its relationship to insight. Both come from the efforts of Abramowitz and colleagues[31, 32] and are based on the same basic design.

We noted in the Meichenbaum[23] clinical trial, the differential response of subgroups of patients. Insight was relevant to clients with speech anxiety as one feature of generalized social anxiety but not so to those with a circumscribed problem. Abramowitz and Abramowitz[31] looked at the influence of another quality in the patient—his psychological-mindedness. It comes as no surprise that they selected this variable for study. It has been a long-standing premiss that to benefit from insight-orientated therapy, the patient must be able to conceptualize in a particular way in order to understand the psychological constructs that typify such treatment.

In a cleverly designed study (albeit reported in turgid prose), 26 students participated in a group experience whose purpose was the 'enhancement of personal adjustment and relationship skills'. They were randomly assigned to one of four groups, all led by a counsellor with an eclectic but insight-orientated approach. In two groups, insight was to the forefront—designed to promote understanding of the causes of current feelings and attitudes. In the other two groups, insight was not so encouraged; instead, the leader facilitated an exchange of idea among members but links between therapeutic events and extra-therapy behaviour were totally ignored. Groups met for ten sessions over five weeks. Typically for Abramowitz, treatment conditions were validated, chiefly by independent judges rating the group transcripts. Levels of psychological-mindedness were measured using a test devised by Tolor and Reznikoff,[33] while outcome was assessed on a battery of self-report measures covering anxiety, guilt, shame, self-esteem, and personal control. The relationship found between psychological-mindedness, outcome, and type of group therapy was quite clear: only in the insight-orientated groups was psychological-mindedness associated with improvement. Such variables as previous therapy, sex, and age did not account for this difference. But there were shortcomings: outcome was measured only via self-report; the sample was small, homogeneous, and non-clinical; the therapy was short-term—only ten sessions; and all groups were led by a single therapist—biased to the provision of insight and also doubling as researcher. However, experimental conditions were validated and the results are reasonably convincing.

The work tells us that psychological-mindedness is advantageous for those participating in insight-orientated groups but is of no relevance in non-insight-orientated groups. Both facets are important. As we have seen, testing the value of insight in chronic, hospitalized patients will obviously not demonstrate much of significance because their limited (or absent) psychological-mindedness is likely to prevent insight from having any impact. On the other hand, the association between psychological-mindedness and outcome in the insight-orientated group echoes the common clinical observation that in long-term group therapy, psychological-mindedness is an important criterion of selection

Insight and interpretation

The second study, by Abramowitz (together with Jackson)[32] examined the effect on outcome of contrasting types of interpretation. As noted in the section on theory, psychoanalytically based group therapy stresses insight concerning links between present behaviour, thoughts and feelings, and family and developmental factors—commonly referred to as 'there-and-then' interpretations. In recently evolving group therapies—especially those derived from a humanistic or neo-Freudian tradition—greater emphasis is placed on experience in the present and on increased general self-awareness and insight about relationships with others. The past takes second place. Interpretations are correspondingly of the 'here-and-now' type. Of course, a middle position is held by some practitioners—that knowledge about past and present, and attitudes about the future (particularly in existential therapy), are all relevant.

How does one translate this into an experimental design? As in the previous investigation, Abramowitz and Jackson[32] had students participate in a group experience whose purpose was to improve personal adjustment and relationship skills. Twenty-eight students were randomly assigned to one of four groups, all led by the same therapist. In the here-and-now condition, members focused on intragroup feelings and behaviour, and interaction was regarded as important in itself rather than as a means to understand the past. The there-and-then group emphasized understanding of the relationship between past events and present behaviour. A combined group attempted to incorporate both approaches and an attention-placebo group provided a forum only for sharing concerns with no interpretations. All groups met for ten sessions.

Treatment conditions were validated as in the previous experiment and outcome was measured with similar instruments. Analysis of variance revealed no significant interaction between the variables; however, a ranking procedure (less potent and conceived *post hoc*) showed that the combined condition was consistently superior, followed by the attention-placebo group, the there-and-then group, and the here-and-now group. Since this ranking procedure is a particularly weak method of analysis, it is safe to assume that the content of therapists' interpretations did not significantly affect outcome. Moreover, because of an absence of differences between the three treatment groups and the control group, there is a question about the value of insight overall.

The authors highlight the fact that their research subjects were students and therefore probably more psychologically minded than the average population. Furthermore, the therapist was biased towards insight-orientated therapy. Thus, the insight treatments should, at least theoretically, have had more effect. But, we can readily identify several possible reasons for their finding. The sample was composed of volunteers, not patients; and they did not present with symptoms. Intelligence and psychological-mindedness are not necessarily synonymous; indeed, intelligent individuals may use intellectualization as a defence against genuine self-exploration. Although insight was found to be a feature of the three treatment groups, these were short term and a question remains about its depth and durability. The alleged control group may not have been a control group: its members were told to share concerns and although no therapist interpretations were made, there was a potentially powerful mode of learning through vicarious learning and universality (according to members' assessment via the insight test, only slightly more insight characterized the treatment groups).

We now return to the effect of different sorts of interpretations on outcome. Even if we were to put our reservations aside and accept that there was a trend for combined here-and-now/there-and-then interpretations to have enhanced outcome, we would support Abramowitz and Jackson's own speculation that the combination offered students a greater chance to express themselves, which in turn permitted more problems to be tackled in more diverse ways. We also agree with the authors' caution about generalizing the results to long-term, insight group-therapies. A handsome contribution would be replication of this research in long-term out-patient therapy, with a clinical sample, more than one group per treatment condition, and several therapists to act as group leaders.

The role of feedback in promoting outcome

Finally, in this review of empirical work, we turn to the process of feedback and examine its relevance in group therapy, and to outcome. Before proceeding we should try to sort out differences between feedback and interpretation. The two processes stem from distinctly different sources. Interpretation is essentially a psychoanalytic concept and commonly applies to a technique used by the therapist 'to make unconscious motives, attitudes, and feelings conscious in order that the patient can learn more about himself'.[34] Insight comes into operation whenever some unconscious source of behaviour—in all its dimensions—needs to be explained. Classically, the psychoanalytically orientated therapist interprets in four areas—transference, defences, dreams, and resistance.

We noted in the section on theory that in the transfer of psychoanalytic principles to group work, interpretation by the therapist remains a central task. But, to a greater or lesser extent, this is coupled with interpretations made by fellow members, which are subject to the same principles, goals, and techniques that typify the therapists' role. It is a common clinical observation that patients can, with the attainment of experience of group processes and knowledge about their co-members, reach a position of some authority which enables a mutual offering of interpretations.

Feedback differs from interpretation in one crucial way, in that it is concerned with what can be seen and observed; no inferences are involved. The difference becomes more clear if we look at the source of the concept. Feedback is derived from cybernetics and refers to 'the feeding back of parts of the output to the input at the proper phase' (Webster's dictionary; 2nd ed.). The social psychologist, Kurt Lewin, applied the concept to the behavioural sciences in his research on groups in the 1940s. Feedback then became one of the chief planks of the sensitivity-group movement. It was subsequently defined by leading figures of the movement in the following way: 'Feedback . . . signifies verbal and non-verbal responses from others to a unit of behaviour provided as close in time to the behaviour as possible, and capable of being perceived and utilized by the individual initiating the behaviour.'[35] Group therapy is unique in providing a forum for the mutual exchange of honest, explicit feedback. By contrast, feedback in individual therapy can only come from an authority figure—a radically different type of source than a patient's peers. There are few social settings where direct feedback is offered: perhaps a close friendship and a well-integrated family are the only other two; but even here, constructive, unimpeded feedback may be a rare phenomenon.

The role of feedback is conceived differently by various theoreticians. It is held to be particularly important by neo-Freudians—Sullivan is the most prominent respresentative of this group—who stress interpersonal insight as the dominant goal of treatment. We discussed this in some detail early in the chapter and noted in the work of Yalom (the foremost proponent of the interpersonalist approach) his therapeutic factor of interpersonal learning-*input*. We may remind ourselves that this factor covered such items as the impression a patient makes on others and his response at having his habits and mannerisms pointed out to him. Such items highlight the ahistorical quality of feedback—patients are seen by their fellows in the present and in the context of the group; the frequently used term 'here-and-now', is especially accurate in this regard.

Let us consider feedback in more clinical terms before examining the research that has been done on it. We can distinguish two basic categories. On the one hand, one or more group members feed back to a co-member information about some aspect of his behaviour in the group, for example, he interrupts repeatedly, reacts sympathetically, clowns each time he contributes, reveres the therapist, and so forth. On the other hand, group members may reveal their personal reactions to an aspect of another patient's behaviour, for example, 'I get irritated when you . . .', 'I admire your . . .', 'I feel optimistic when you . . .', and so forth.

These illustrations clearly demonstrate how varied feedback can be, but the two categories can be distinguished: the first examples are basically 'behavioural'—'this is what an aspect of your behaviour is like'; the second are personal emotional reactions—'this facet of your behaviour makes me feel such and such'—with emphasis on the respondent's feeling.

The examples also show that feedback can vary enormously in content. Obviously there is no limit to what group members will reveal about themselves, explicitly or implicitly, and therefore no limit to the range of corresponding feedback. Feedback may be given directly or indirectly. All the examples provided are of explicit feedback but frequently in group therapy it is given indirectly. For example, humour may be used to disguise feedback that the giver hesitates to offer because it is critical, or alternatively, an expression of affection. Feedback may be verbal or non-verbal. The verbal form is obviously shown in the examples. But facial gesture, tone of voice, posture, nod of the head, and so on, may be powerful messages, provided the intended recipient notes them. There is certainly nothing more explicit than slumping and dozing off in the face of a boring group member or squirming with embarrassment in response to a patient's indiscretion. Feedback may be positive or negative. Positive feedback is essentially complimentary—pointing out an admirable quality or expressing affection. Critical feedback brings to the receiver's attention an undesirable aspect of behaviour or personality trait but differs from a moral judgement.

Aside from these various features, other factors can exert a cogent influence on feedback, especially on its reception, an obviously crucial factor. To generate an effect, it must be registered, understood and appraised; if found credible, it must be accepted and acted upon. One important issue is timing. If feedback is not given in context, it will have little impact. If given too early in the development of a group, before a trusting milieu has evolved, it may be rejected because it is sensed as threatening. Another aspect is that feedback seems more valuable if it arrives close in time to the particular situation that has generated it. Related to timing is sequence—there is some question whether feedback is more effective if a positive statement is followed by a negative one or vice versa. We will return to this particular aspect later.

An important question is whether feedback is consensual or not. Feedback from a single fellow member is bound to be perceived differently to that offered by the group unanimously. In the first instance, something idiosyncratic in the deliverer may be more relevant than the content, for instance, envy of the target. Moreover, if the whole group or most members concur in their feedback, it is likely to be more objective and therefore more accurate (except where there is obvious scapegoating). Source of feedback in a group is another factor to consider. Therapist, co-therapists, the members, or, as we shall see shortly, audiotape or videotape are all potential sources. Clinical observation suggests that feedback from the authority of the therapist may be perceived quite differently to that received by peers. In the case of audio or video playback, the individual can take note of his own recorded behaviour. Such feedback is relatively concrete. This brings us to the final clinical observation, namely, that the more explicit the feedback, describing a particular pattern of behaviour or aspect of personality, the more readily understood and influential it seems to be. Conversely, feedback couched in esoteric terms and referable to some vague abstract context is usually a source of obfuscation rather than illumination.

Empirical research on feedback

With these general comments, mostly stemming from the clinical literature, and having dealt with theoretical issues earlier in the chapter, what can we learn from the empirical research literature?

The most substantial contribution by far is that of Alfred Jacobs and his colleagues. The chief question examined by them has been how feedback can best be provided. In this work they make the assumption, admittedly large, that feedback is an important means to self-understanding. But they tend to disregard the relationship between feedback and outcome and concentrate on the process itself. This is a reasonable approach particularly when so little empirical knowledge is available regarding the most effective way of delivering feedback.

Jacobs *et al.*[36] distinguish different forms of feedback, with a general definition as 'the process by which group members inform each other as to how their behaviour is perceived and reacted to by others'. Categories they are concerned with include: *valence*—positive (complimentary) or negative (critical); and *behavioural* (identifying an aspect of the recipient's behaviour) or *emotional* (an emotional reaction of the deliverer of the feedback), or a mixture of both. They have also considered the effects of different sequential patterns of these categories. The dependent variables in their studies have included the recipient's self-report on (1) credibility—'I think this feedback is inaccurate or accurate'; (2) desirability—'I find being described this way undesirable or desirable'; and (3) impact—'I react to the feedback weakly or strongly'.

In examining the research done by the Jacobs team, we should note that all their investigations were far removed from the clinical scene. The subjects were volunteer students; they participated in a sensitivity group lasting a matter of hours during a single day; the experience consisted of structured exercises punctuated by the administration of questionnaires; and the participants' feedback was limited to a list devised by the researchers.

Cataloguing these features does not constitute a list of criticisms but merely serves to remind us that the experimental findings may not have a bearing on therapy groups. Yet, in the absence of such work on clinical samples, we may be able to extrapolate, reassured by the ingenious experimental designs and sound methodology.

The first study looks at feedback in terms of valence and sequence.[36] The authors contrast three positions that have been advanced in this context. The first contends that negative feedback is most effective when delivered in an atmosphere of trust.[37] This implies that positive and negative feedback given in conjunction is the most effective form. The second position suggests that negative feedback 'unfreezes' the recipient by disrupting his customarily held self-concept; he is then provoked to think about himself afresh. The third position, stemming from the work of Carl Rogers,[38] holds that positive feedback should precede negative feedback: the recipient is more likely to accept complimentary comments initially, which will then pave the way for his preparedness to accept more critical information.

In order to examine these positions, students were randomly assigned to sensitivity training groups in which they spent the first four hours in two structured exercises designed to produce conditions for the mutual exchange of feedback. Three experimental treatments were compared. In the first students gave and received negative feedback after the first exercise and positive feedback after the second; in the second treatment the order was reversed; and in the third both positive and negative feedback were given and received after each exercise. Students delivered feedback to other group members from a list of descriptions of behaviour provided by the researchers. Following this exchange, all students rated the feedback they had received for credibility and desirability. The results are consistent and clear. Feedback, both negative and positive, was rated as more credible and desirable when the negative form was given first and the positive form second, compared to the reverse order. Students given a mixture of feedback rated it less credible and desirable than either of the other groups rated positive feedback; they also evaluated the experience less enthusiastically overall. Throughout, positive feedback was assessed as more credible and desirable than negative feedback, with ratings of mixed feedback between the two. These findings thus support the second theoretical position, namely, that initial negative feedback unfreezes the recipient and makes him more willing to consider and accept criticism. It is certainly not unexpected that students overall found positive feedback more desirable.

Unfortunately, these clear-cut results were not replicated in a subsequent study. Schaible and Jacobs[39] found exactly the opposite! There were some changes in design (summarized in the appendix (see p. 277)) but the basic approach was similar. On this occasion positive feedback first, followed by negative feedback, was rated as more credible and desirable than the reverse order. The authors speculate about the contradictory findings of their two studies but not very convincingly. For example, the longer group session in the first study may have allowed for more interaction, but this does not seem a crucial factor. In the second study each student only received feedback from one co-member compared to feedback from several in the first study; perhaps in the latter case, students rated the most credible negative feedback offered to them thus accounting for the smaller difference between positive and negative forms at the end of the first exercise.

We are left with a question mark hanging over the issue of sequence which can only be answered by further studies.

Moving on from the question of optimal sequence, Jacobs and his associates[40] incorporated another dimension of feedback into their experiments—behavioural versus emotional—in order to study its interactive effects with valence (positive versus negative) on the credibility, desirability, and impact of feedback. Interest is focused here on the important issue of whether feedback should be informative (i.e. behavioural) or evaluative (i.e. emotional) or some combination of the two. The authors note the lack of consensus in the literature. For example, Stoller[41] argues that feedback about concrete behaviour is more valuable than when it is inferential. In the encounter movement, a commonly held notion is that feedback that stresses the feelings of the deliverer is superior to behavioural feedback.

The specific research questions posed were: which pattern of feedback is most credible, most desirable, and has maximum impact—behavioural, emotional, or combined behavioural–emotional; and what influence does valance exert?

The research design used was similar to the first experiment save for the treatment conditions which here were: (1) behavioural positive—each student received two items of positive behavioural feedback from each of his co-members; (2) emotional positive—students received two items of positive emotional feedback; (3) behavioural–emotional positive—each student received one item of positive behavioural feedback and one item of positive emotional feedback; (4) behavioural negative; (5) emotional negative; and (6) behavioural–emotional negative.

The findings are most illuminating. As throughout their research, positive feedback is rated as more credible and desirable and as having greater impact than negative feedback. Positive emotional feedback is most credible, negative emotional least credible. Interestingly, positive behavioural feedback is enhanced by the addition of positive emotional feedback ('you were very helpful to group members [behavioural] and that makes me feel warm towards you' [emotional]). By contrast, negative behavioural feedback is best given alone ('you talk too much in groups' [behavioural] is more effective alone than when coupled with '. . . and that makes me angry' [emotional]).

A further experiment[42] involved one crucial change: feedback was given anonymously. Once again, positive feedback emerges as more effective than negative feedback but now—in complete contrast with the preceding study—negative emotional feedback is rated as the most credible of the negative feedback conditions and positive emotional the least credible of the positive feedback conditions. Listed from most to least credible in the study were: positive behavioural; positive behavioural–emotional; positive emotional; negative emotional; negative behavioural; and negative behavioural–emotional.

Subjects also rated the change they had made as a result of the group experience, using such criteria as ability to relate, sensitivity to others, and risk taking. Those receiving behavioural feedback reported greater change compared to their counterparts who got emotional or behavioural–emotional feedback.

The implications of feedback research for group therapy

What can we make of these assorted results? Firstly, to summarize, people prefer to receive positive than negative feedback, and behavioural appears to be more effective than emotional feedback. Furthermore, positive behavioural feedback is enhanced by associated positive emotional feedback whereas negative behavioural feedback is best given alone. Anonymous feedback permits negative emotional feedback to be accepted more readily than when the source is known. Negative feedback followed by positive was more effective than vice versa in one study but the reverse applied in a follow-up study. The implications of these results on group therapy, we recall, are qualified because of the nature of the experiments but they are:

1. Patients probably benefit—via positive feedback—when they are helped by co-members to recognize or rediscover assets, strengths and positive qualities; rare is the patient entirely devoid of worthwhile attributes.

2. Patients probably profit from behavioural compared to emotional feedback because it is more objective (since it is observable). Emotional reactions are, by contrast, prone to bias on the part of the deliverer. However, the therapist should probably promote a

norm whereby a deliverer of positive behavioural feedback supplements it with a positive personal reaction, as reinforcement. Conversely, negative behavioural feedback is perceived as punitive and threatening when supplemented by a negative emotional reaction; the latter should thus be discouraged. Also, negative behavioural feedback is likely to be more effective than negative emotional feedback.

3. The therapist could under certain circumstances—for example, when group members resist open exchange, including necessary mutual critical feedback—engage them in an exercise in which negative emotional feedback is written down and given anonymously via the therapist to the recipient.

4. Although positive feedback is generally more effective than negative feedback, there is necessarily a place for both. How could patients ever determine those undesirable qualities that, by group consensual validation, are deemed to be in need of modification, if negative feedback were banned? The sequence of these two forms however remains in doubt. It appears that negative feedback should precede positive feedback and so generate a state of dissonance in the recipient, and with it, an increased preparedness to hear and accept criticism. However, in a new group where a trusting environment has not evolved, such a sequence may prove too threatening.

5. Last, and certainly not least, the group therapist must remain aware of the multidimensional nature of feedback. Instead of adopting a rigid stance, either proclaiming its worth unreservedly or deriding it as worthless, the wise therapist will incorporate feedback judiciously and selectively.

The above are possible guidelines for the clinician. For the researcher on therapeutic factors, the work by Jacobs *et al.* demonstrates that they can be systematically investigated, their elements can be teased out, imaginative experimental designs that do not become esoteric and clinically irrelevant are available, and research can be cumulative with one set of findings serving as a foundation for succeeding experiments.

Unfortunately, the work at West Virginia came to an end by the mid 1970s presumably because the team disbanded. The obvious next step of transferring the methodology to therapy groups failed to materialize. Since then, in fact, little research has been devoted to feedback. However, brief mention should be made of the results emanating from the Stanford encounter group project.[16] On a questionnaire of perceived learning mechanisms, feedback was rated as the most helpful factor. The 'most important event' questionnaire[5] also showed the value attached to feedback, regardless of outcome. Surprisingly, there were no significant differences between the proportion of learners, unchanged members, and those with a negative outcome, specifying events in which feedback provoked a positive feeling or generated some cognitive learning. But students with a negative outcome recorded more events involving feedback as negative, i.e. 'hurtful rather than helpful'. The authors speculate that the lack of any difference between the three groups on feedback leading to cognitive learning could be ascribed to the notion that cognitive mastery through one's own actions (for example, through self-disclosure) is a different experience compared to learning through the actions of others (in this case, through the passive reception of feedback). However their data cannot substantiate this hypothesis and it must remain speculative.

Indeed, the important question of the link between feedback and outcome remains shrouded in ignorance. The Jacobs work did not really tackle this aspect and the rest of the literature on feedback is uninformative. The odd study pops up occasionally but is invariably non-clinically based. For example, Miles[43] found in a study of the effects of a two-week group experience on school principals that their feedback ratings scored for clarity, relevance, and helpfulness) had an inconsistent relationship with their level of change (e.g. sensitivity to others, skills in communication) assessed through self-report and by the trainers. There was no correlation between the two variables mid-way through the programme but it shifted to a significantly positive one by the end of the experience. High learners assessed their feedback as clear, strong, and helpful. Valence, whether positive or negative, was not relevant. At follow-up, eight months later, the association between feedback and change had disappeared. It would thus appear that feedback played some role in learning during the programme but that its effects were not enduring. Miles speculates about the possibility of a 'warm up' effect with feedback only exerting an influence after some delay. This could well be related to the achievement of a greater sense of trust following an initial phase of uncertainty and insecurity.

The place of video and audio playback in the provision of feedback

The effect of feedback on outcome has also been investigated in the context of video and audio playback in therapy. Before considering these studies, a brief introduction to the topic seems appropriate.

The advent of inexpensive video technology in the 1960s heralded its widespread use in various group settings (audio tape has never attained the same popularity, presumably because the feedback it provides is much more limited). Several clinical reports were published describing the possible uses of video playback, and the relevant techniques. Alger, for example, has been a keen proponent and, with Hogan,[44] notes the impact of video-recording on insight—both the awareness of inner reactions and the understanding of relationships with others. Several clinical examples are provided to illustrate how video feedback can promote insight into faulty patterns of communication (such as inattention to the other's message), into inner thoughts and feelings, and into aspects of the self and others. The authors claim that video feedback can help patients to gain awareness into hitherto elusive aspects of themselves and that it tends to reduce defensiveness. Technique is also covered. For example, short segments of therapy are played back immediately after recording. During the playback, the tape can be stopped at any point so that patients may assess their own reactions and the behaviour of co-members. This is then integrated into ongoing therapy.*

As is so often the case with therapeutic innovation, therapists rush in enthusiastically and try this and that technique; zeal soon wanes with the result that no systematic knowledge stems from their clinical experience. The contribution by Stoller[41] therefore is commendable. Although overlong and wordy, he offers a theoretical schema for the application of video feedback in groups, and draws up a series of hypotheses for systematic testing. He advances the notion that group therapy provides the patient with an opportunity for self-confrontation. The social microcosm of the group enables the patient to observe himself and his impact on others. A major element in this process is the feedback given by co-members as they point out their reactions to specific instances of the patient's

* A wide range of techniques is available in the use of video recording but this is not the place to discuss them. See Milton Berger's *Video tape techniques in psychiatric training and treatment*;[45] also recommended is the review article by Bailey and Sowder.[46]

behaviour. The group format allows each patient to play a wide range of roles and thus to display the scope of this behaviour. The patient must become aware of this behaviour and regard his peers as agents from whom he can learn. Video feedback is a natural extension of this process, and moreover, can sometimes be superior in effect to verbal feedback.

From his theoretical formulation, Stoller derives the following hypotheses:

1. The effectiveness of video feedback depends upon its acceptance by the therapist (including his own self-confrontation as a form of modelling), and upon the members learning how to give and take feedback. The equipment must be regarded by the group 'as a tool for use *by* group members, not *on* them'.
2. Video feedback is more valuable when directed by patients rather than by the therapist alone since it fosters a sense of altruism and mutual help. For example, a patient who suggests video feedback for a peer and cites his reasons for this, contributes to his own personal growth as well as to the potential recipient.
3. Information gleaned through video feedback arises from a relatively neutral source and is therefore more objective and less distorted than feedback coming from co-members.
4. The effectiveness of video feedback depends upon its relevance to what has actually taken place between the recipient and other group members; he must perceive an obvious link between group events and the information presented to him on the tape.
5. 'The closer the video feedback to the behaviour that is relevant, the more helpful it will be.' Stoller argues the case for immediate playback on the premiss that a paramount quality of group therapy is its immediacy—it works optimally in the present moment.

Obviously Stoller, while persuaded by clinical experience that video recording has an important role in the provision of feedback, also wants confirmation of its value through empirical investigation, hence his five hypotheses. However, the subsequent dozen years have shown little endeavour in this field. Jacobs,[47] in a review of the topic, commented on the paucity of studies, which were virtually all on non-clinical groups. Incidentally, of ten studies he mentions, four showed the positive benefits of video feedback, the other six had no effect or a negative one. Let us examine samples of this literature.

The most noteworthy investigation is that done by Robinson and Jacobs.[48] They predicted that more adaptive change would occur in behaviour on which video feedback had been focused. Forty in-patients—diagnosis and other clinical data were not provided—met on six occasions over a two week period. All sessions were video-taped. In three experimental groups, each therapy session was followed immediately by an hour of focused video feedback. The group reacted to the taped segments with the therapists pointing out adaptive and maladaptive behaviour. We should note that one co-therapist selected segments for replay according to observations he had made while the televised therapy session was in progress. The other therapist provided feedback to a particular patient or group of patients directly involved in the segment. This is opposite to Stoller's first, second, and third hypotheses (see p. 61). The members were however encouraged to respond to what they had viewed. In three control groups, a discussion period without video playback followed each therapy session.

Subsequently, independent judges rated patients' adaptive behaviour by observing the first and fifth videotapes. Patients also rated themselves on this dimension. The average change score in experimental patients was almost three times greater than in the controls. However, patients' self-ratings did not differ significantly. The authors explain this discrepancy by arguing that behavioural change (obvious to external raters) could result from an action-orientated procedure such as video playback with attitudinal changes following later after the patient 'has accepted the beneficial consequences of his behavioural changes'. This seems possible but not very likely. Robinson and Jacobs also concede that the behavioural change noted by the judges may have been superficial and not representative of the typical goals of insight-orientated therapy; possibly so, but the researchers appears to be displaying some confusion here about what they were trying to achieve with video in this experiment—changes in adaptive behaviour or fully-fledged insight into the nature of maladaptive behaviour? We suspect their patients, who only had six sessions of therapy, benefited somewhat from behavioural change without associated insight but we cannot judge without more information about the characteristics of the clinical sample.

Despite the difficulty in interpreting the results, the study was well conceived and methodological desiderata, such as the use of independent raters and the measurement of reliability of ratings, were taken into account. More work of this kind is needed using special patient groups in both short- and long-term therapy, and a comprehensive battery of outcome measures. Such studies should not suffer the gross limitations that typify Bailey's examination[49] of the effectiveness of feedback with audiotape of Danet's study[50] of the value of video playback on group process (they are both summarized in the table, see p. 271).

Danet's report includes mention of the hampering effect of video playback on some patients he studied. He speculates that the technique may generate defensiveness in the recipient with possible regression or denial. Similarly, Alkire and Brunse[51] in a study of the use of video playback in a married-couples group found negative effects on both individual members and relationships. This brings us back to Stoller's first hypothesis, namely, that the group must see video feedback 'as a tool for use *by* them, not *on* them'. The choice of the term 'tool' is significant for, as Yalom[2] points out, 'videotaping is but a technique, to be employed only insofar as it facilitates the operation of the basic curative factors'. We should also be wary, he cautions, of exaggerated claims. As we have seen, the technique is still far from having been adequately evaluated; its proper role in group therapy remains a matter for careful reflection.

Conclusion

Notwithstanding that this chapter is one of the lengthiest, we leave the subject of insight with some degree of dissatisfaction. It would seem that the complexity of the factor has precluded its clear definition, led to inconsequential debate about how it is best conceptualized, and hampered systematic empirical research. We are thus left with a body of knowledge, both slim and discouragingly inconsistent.

We conclude that the inherent nature of insight leads inevitably to the adoption of a broad, multidimensional approach to its study. We cannot escape from the notion that what a patient learns about himself and his interpersonal world will vary substantially—depending in great measure on the nature of the problems he brings to treatment and the therapeutic goals he sets for himself. Similarly, the pathways to his achievement of insight and the most appropriate ways and methods of learning will also vary considerably.

This multidimensional view need not necessarily interfere with the proper theoretical and empirical study of insight. The aforementioned work of the Meichenbaum and Jacobs teams, for instance, demonstrates convincingly that the subject is amenable to potentially effective and illuminating investigation.

References

1. Corsini, R. and Rosenberg, B. Mechanisms of group psychotherapy: processes and dynamics. *Journal of Abnormal and Social Psychology* **51**, 406–11 (1955).
2. Yalom, I. D. *The theory and practice of group psychotherapy*. Basic Books, New York (1975).
3. See: Bloch, S. *What is Psychotherapy?* Oxford University Press, Oxford (1982) pp. 77–85, for a summary of this tradition.
4. Bloch S., Reibstein J., Crouch E., *et al.* A method for the study of therapeutic factors in group psychotherapy. *British Journal of Psychiatry* **134**, 257–63 (1979).
5. The questionnaire for patient-respondents reads:

   'Of the events which occurred in the last THREE meetings, which *one* do you feel was the *most important for you personally?* Please describe the event; what actually took place; the group members involved; and your reaction.'

   '*Why was it so important for you?*'

   A comparable version for therapist-respondents reads:

   'During the last three meetings, what from *your* point of view has been the most important event for: (specified group member)? Please describe the event: what actually took place; the group members involved; the patient's reaction; etc. (Note: Select the event that *you* consider most important, not what you think the patient regards as most important.)'

   '*Why do you think this event was the most important?*'

   See reference 4 for more details about the 'most important event' questionnaire.
6. Wender, L. Dynamics of group psychotherapy and its application. *Journal of Nervous and Mental Disease* **84**, 54–60 (1936).
7. Schilder, P. Results and problems of group psychotherapy in severe neuroses. In: *Group psychotherapy and group function* (eds. M. Rosenbaum and M. Berger). Basic Books, New York (1975).
8. Wolf, A. Psychoanalysis in groups. In: *Group psychotherapy and group function* (eds. M. Rosenbaum and M. Berger). Basic Books, New York (1975).
9. Slavson, S. R. *Dynamics of group psychotherapy* (ed. M. Schiffer). Jason Aronson, New York (1979).

10. Foulkes, S. H. *Therapeutic group analysis*. Allen and Unwin, London (1964).
11. Sullivan, H. S. *The interpersonal theory of psychiatry*. Norton, New York (1953).
12. Yalom, I. D. *Existential psychotherapy*. Basic Books, New York (1981).
13. Weiner, M. F. Genetic vs. interpersonal insight. *International Journal of Group Psychotherapy* **24**, 230–7 (1974).
14. Frank, J. D. Group psychotherapy research 25 years later. *International Journal of Group Psychotherapy* **25**, 159–62 (1975).
15. Malan, D., Balfour, F. H., Hood, V. G., *et al*. Group psychotherapy. A long-term follow-up study. *Archives of General Psychiatry* **33**, 1303–15 (1976).
16. Lieberman, M. A., Yalom, I. D., and Miles, M. B. *Encounter groups: first facts*. Basic Books, New York (1973).
17. Hora, T. Existential psychiatry and group psychotherapy. *American Journal of Psychoanalysis* **21**, 58–73 (1961).
18. Durkin, H. *The group in depth*. International Universities Press, New York (1964).
19. Bloch, S. Supportive Psychotherapy. In: *An introduction to the psychotherapies* (ed. S. Bloch). Oxford University Press, Oxford (1979).
20. See for example: Tracey, D. A., Briddell, D. W., and Wilson, G. T. Generalization of verbal conditioning to verbal and non-verbal behaviour: group therapy with chronic psychiatric patients. *Journal of Applied Behaviour Analysis* **7**, 391–402 (1974).
21. Abramowitz, C. V. The effectiveness of group psychotherapy with children. *Archives of General Psychiatry* **33**, 320–6 (1976).
22. Falloon, I. R., Lindley, P., McDonald, R., *et al*. Social skills training of out-patient groups: a controlled study of rehearsal and homework. *British Journal of Psychiatry* **131**, 599–609 (1977).
23. Meichenbaum, D. H., Gilmore, J. B., and Fedoravicius, A. L. Group insight versus group desensitization in treating speech anxiety. *Journal of Consulting and Clinical Psychology* **36**, 420–1 (1971).
24. Ellis, A. *Reason and emotion in psychotherapy*. Lyle–Stuart, New York (1962).
25. Paul, G. L. and Shannon, D. T. Treatment of anxiety through systematic desensitization in therapy groups. *Journal of Abnormal Psychology* **71**, 124–35 (1966).
26. Coons, W. H. Interaction and insight in group psychotherapy. *Canadian Journal of Psychology* **11**, 1–8 (1957).
27. Coons, W. H. The dynamics of change is psychotherapy. *Canadian Psychiatric Association Journal* **12**, 239–45 (1967).
28. Frank. J. D. Therapeutic factors in psychotherapy. *American Journal of Psychotherapy* **25**, 350–61 (1971).
29. Roback, H. B. Experimental comparison of outcomes in insight and non-insight-oriented therapy groups. *Journal of Consulting and Clinical Psychology* **38**, 411–17 (1972).

30. Lomont, J. F., Gilner, F. H., Spector, N. J., *et al.* Group assertion training and group insight therapies. *Psychological Reports* **25**, 463–70 (1969).
31. Abramowitz, S. I. and Abramowitz, C. V. Psychological-mindedness and benefit from insight-oriented group therapy. *Archives of General Psychiatry* **30**, 610–15 (1974).
32. Abramowitz, S. I. and Jackson, C. Comparative effectiveness of there-and-then versus here-and-now therapist interpretations in group psychotherapy. *Journal of Counseling Psychology* **21**, 288–93 (1974).
33. Tolor, A. and Reznikoff, M. A new approach to insight: a preliminary report. *Journal of Nervous and Mental Disease* **130**, 286–96 (1960).
34. Crown, S. Individual long-term psychotherapy. In: *An introduction to the psychotherapies* (ed. S. Bloch). Oxford University Press, Oxford (1979).
35. Benne, K. D., Bradford, L. P., and Lippit, G. The laboratory method. In: *T-group theory and laboratory method* (eds. L. P. Bradford, J. R. Gibb, and K. D. Benne). Wiley, New York (1964).
36. Jacobs, M., Jacobs, A., Gatz, M., *et al.* Credibility and desirability of positive and negative structured feedback in groups. *Journal of Consulting and Clinical Psychology* **40**, 244–52 (1973).
37. Schein, E. H. and Bennis, W. G. *Personal and organizational change through group methods*. Wiley, New York (1967).
38. Rogers, C. R. *Client-centered therapy*. Constable, London (1951).
39. Schaible, T. D. and Jacobs, A. Feedback III: sequence effects. Enhancement of feedback acceptance and group attractiveness by manipulation of the sequence and valence of feedback. *Small Group Behaviour* **6**, 151–73 (1975).
40. Jacobs, M., Jacobs, A., Feldman, G. *et al.* Feedback II: 'the credibility gap'. Delivery of positive and negative and emotional and behavioural feedback in groups. *Journal of Consulting and Clinical Psychology* **41**, 215–23 (1973).
41. Stoller, F. H. Videotape feedback in a group setting. *Journal of Nervous and Mental Disease* **148**, 457–66 (1968).
42. Jacobs, A., Jacobs, M., Cavior, N., *et al.* Anonymous feedback: credibility and desirability of structured emotional and behaviour feedback delivered in groups. *Journal of Counseling Psychology* **21**, 106–11 (1974).
43. Miles, M. B. Changes during and following laboratory training: a clinical experimental study. *Journal of Applied Behavioural Science* **1**, 215–42 (1965).
44. Hogan, P. and Alger, I. The impact of videotape recording on insight in group psychotherapy. *International Journal of Group Psychotherapy* **19**, 158–64 (1969).
45. Berger, M. *Videotape techniques in psychiatric training and treatment*. Brunner/Mazel, New York (1970).
46. Bailey, K. G. and Sowder, W. T. Audiotape and videotape self-

confrontation. *Psychological Bulletin* **74**, 127–37 (1970).

47. Jacobs, A. *The use of feedback in groups*. In: *Group as an agent of change* (eds. A. Jacobs and W. Spradlin). Behavioural Publications, New York (1974).
48. Robinson, M. and Jacobs, A. Focused videotape feedback and behaviour change in group psychotherapy. *Psychotherapy: Theory, Research and Practice* **7**, 169–72 (1970).
49. Bailey, K. Audiotape self-confrontation in group psychotherapy. *Psychological Reports* **27**, 439–44 (1970).
50. Danet, B. N. Videotape playback as a therapeutic device in group psychotherapy. *International Journal of Group Psychotherapy* **19**, 433–40 (1969).
51. Alkire, A. A. and Brunse, A. J. Impact and possible casualty from videotape feedback in marital therapy. *Journal of Consulting and Clinical Psychology* **42**, 203–10 (1976).

3 Learning from Interpersonal Action (Interaction)

Interaction and learning

Interaction with one or more persons is obviously inherent in any form of psychotherapy. With no therapist for the patient to relate to, individual therapy could not proceed except of course through self-analysis. Group therapy would certainly be a nonsense without other patients to interact with. How can we then refer to interaction as a therapeutic factor? In fact, we should not. It is more logically to be viewed as a condition for change. But there is a fundamental therapeutic factor which is a direct consequence of interaction, variously labelled as interpersonal learning[1] and learning from interpersonal action.[2] As these labels imply, we are concerned with a learning process in which the emphasis is on learning from actual experience; more specifically from new efforts—tantamount to experimentation—at relating to others.

In this chapter our focus will be on this 'actional' factor but we will also necessarily examine aspects of its associated condition for change—interaction. Inevitably there will be some overlap with the section in Chapter 2 on transference and interpersonal insight. But we regard this as essential in order to distinguish learning as a result of interpersonal action and insight (or self-understanding). Let us begin by looking at the efforts to define learning from interpersonal action (LIA).

Definition of LIA

The early pioneers of group therapy, preoccupied as they were with their didactic role, were virtually oblivious to the potential advantages of promoting interaction, either between group members themselves or between members and the therapist. Following the application in the 1930s of the psychoanalytic model to groups, interaction did come to occupy a prominent place but this was largely confined to the relationships that evolved between the group analyst and each patient individually. Group treatment was regarded as comparable to individual analysis, with attention paid to analysis of transference, working through of resistance unearthing of psychogenetic factors from the patient's past, and so forth.

Thus, by the time Corsini and Rosenberg[3] conducted their review of the literature and produced their classification of therapeutic factors, transference had established itself as an identifiable entity for inclusion. However, its dimensions were substantially wider than obtained in classical psychoanalysis—a patient's 'strong emotional attachment' was possible not only to his therapist but also to one or more co-patients or to the group as a whole. By contrast, a separate therapeutic factor, dubbed interaction, was enveloped in obfuscation. Corsini and Rosenberg conceded that it was the most difficult factor to understand and classify. Their effort at definition illustrates this. The first part—that interaction 'relates to relationships of unspecified nature within the group'—is decidedly vague, and the second part—that 'any interaction engaged in by a therapeutic group manages to have beneficial results'—is nothing less than an *ex cathedra* statement and contains no definitional properties at all.

We should not be surprised at the limitations of this definition. Corsini and Rosenberg relied on scattered writings, mainly from the 1940s. Clinicians were then only beginning to perceive that relating between group members, including the therapist, might carry therapeutic potential above and beyond transference. Such terms as interaction, relationship, contact with others, and interstimulation had made their appearance but their conceptual basis was ill-understood and rudimentary. However, in the 1950s, humanistic psychology and the human-potential movement developed from the work of neo-Freudians such as H. S. Sullivan, Karen Horney, and Erich Fromm.[4] These approaches emphasized interpersonal issues and consequently the subject of interaction was tackled head-on and its qualities identified. At the same time, the strict Freudian mould that had been applied to groups began to soften. Transference was not the sole form of relating in group therapy; other forms existed alongside it and were of equivalent importance.

We see these developments crystallizing in the work of I. D. Yalom, and specifically in his concept of interpersonal learning.[1] We dealt with aspects of this in the previous chapter in our discussion of interpersonal insight (see p. 33). Pertinent in the present context is the form of interpersonal learning referred to as 'output'. The five items constituting this therapeutic factor in Yalom's questionnaire all point to its intrinsic nature. The group provides a forum in which the patient can benefit from his various efforts at relating to his fellow members: by enhancing his social skills; developing greater trust; learning to approach others; sorting out any difficulties in relating to a particular co-member; and learning about the ways he relates generally within the group. This factor excludes that form of learning which stems from the evolution and exploration of transference (which is embedded elsewhere in Yalom's classification).

The present concept of LIA

We have taken Yalom's concept further by stressing the behavioural or actional quality of interpersonal learning. Our modification of his term to 'learning from interpersonal action' is not a reflection of semantic pedantry but a way of highlighting the relevance of the patient's actual behavioural efforts in the sphere of relationships. We define LIA as 'the *attempt* to relate *constructively* and *adaptively* within the group, either by initiating some behaviour or responding to other group members'.[2] More important than the reaction of other members is the patient's attempt to modify his own mode of relating. Since patients receiving group therapy present with a wide range of difficulties in relationships, the definition is couched in terms which imply that learning can arise from a variety of interpersonal actions, the particular dimension being tied to an individual patient's specific needs. We have elaborated on LIA in our Manual on Therapeutic Factors (see ref. 2) as follows:

'This factor operates when the patient (a) tries out new, potentially positive ways of *initiating behaviour* with other group members. These ways can include:

(i) expressing oneself to co-members to clarify one's relationship with them;
(ii) making an explicit, overt effort to develop a more honest, open relationship with one or more co-members;

(iii) expressing oneself in a more constructively assertive fashion;
(iv) expressing oneself to achieve intimacy with other group members.
And when the patient (b) tries out new potentially positive ways of *responding to* other group members, such as being more sensitive or accepting valid criticsm.'

We go on to distinguish between LIA and three other factors with which it overlaps—self-disclosure, catharsis, and altruism.

Illustrations of LIA Examples of LIA elicited by use of the 'most important event' questionnaire are:

I felt miserable at the beginning of the meeting. Finally I told the therapists that I had felt unjustifiably criticized in the previous meeting's summary.* I felt good that I could confront the therapists with my firm and honest opinion.

Shaun had looked tense and had been silent during the previous few meetings. Two members complained about his non-participation. Shaun reflected on this and then shakily volunteered that he had been afraid that he might have been ridiculed about—what he felt to be—his relatively insignificant problems. Consequently, he had not spoken. He had also felt, quite honestly, that no one cared for him. However, he was touched that others did care, and was glad they showed it. This event was most important for Shaun because he tends to keep himself aloof. This admission meant that he was fostering a closer and more caring and more honest relationship with the rest of the group.

I got out my anger towards Beverley through role playing, with Mary taking the role of Beverley. Afterwards, Beverley and I were much more relaxed with one another. I was very pleased I could work out this block in my relationship with her.

Tim talked about problems with his homosexual lover. Previously Ken would feign boredom or grow impatient whenever Tim brought up the topic of homosexuality. This time Ken listened with patience and even offered appropriate comment. This event was important because Ken needs to develop more sensitivity and responsiveness to others in general, and has found it most difficult to do, especially with Tim.

Gerald barged in with one of his own problems during the silence, following

*A summary prepared by the therapists was distributed each week to group members—see Yalom *et al.*[5] for a detailed account of this procedure.

a difficult revelation by Zena. The therapist pointed out that by his actions Gerald had ensured that Zena felt abandoned. Gerald responded by saying that the therapist was right, and that it was because he had felt inadequate to respond to Zena that he had butted in. This event was important because he had responded to the therapist's criticism without getting defensive. Previously his responses to such criticism had been either melodramatically apologetic or self-righteously rejecting.

The above elaboration of our definition and the five illustrative 'events' help to demonstrate the miscellany of problems that may be tackled through the mechanism of LIA, and perhaps also serve to explain why Corsini and Rosenberg[3] had so much trouble in pinpointing the therapeutic gist of interaction. They were also handicapped at the time of their taxonomic endeavour by a dearth of theorizing about the nature of the factor. Since their work, the picture has substantially improved. We now focus on the theoretical advances that have been made over the past three decades or so.

Theoretical Aspects of LIA

In considering theoretical contributions on LIA, two main conceptual models can be distinguished though we will see a good deal of overlap: one focuses on the relationship that evolves between the therapist and each of the group members; the other highlights the relationships that develop between the members themselves. A third, but relatively less important model in this context, involves the relationship between the therapist and the group as a whole. In this section we discuss the first two models, their differences and the features they have in common. We also mention briefly the third model in our discussion of non-therapeutic aspects of interaction.

The transference model

The member-to-therapist model—derived exclusively from psychoanalytic theory—may be conveniently labelled the transference model since it is each member's transference relationship to the therapist that serves as the target for analysis, and hence of learning.[6] As in individual analytic therapy, each member of the group interacts with the therapist on a level typified by the experiencing of unconsciously derived and irrational feelings, attitudes, and fantasies. The evolution of the transference paves the way for the elucidation and understanding of key, conflict-laden relationships experienced in the past, but still exerting a potent, deleterious effect in the present. These are usually relationships involving parents and/or siblings. The resultant insight offers the group patient an opportunity to alter aspects of his hitherto maladaptive behaviours, including those in the interpersonal sphere. Such behavioural changes may initially find expression within the relatively safe confines of the group, and later be replicated elsewhere.

We may summarize the psychoanalytic position by quoting one of its foremost proponents, Samuel Slavson. Interaction is, in his view, only a preliminary to the 'essential psychotherapeutic dynamics'. For it to be productive, interaction must occur within a framework of reflection that 'loosens the rigid defensive armour and leads to inversion and introspection, retracing and recalling of the past, and the uncovering of forces that operate in current feelings and conduct'.[6]

This brief quotation clearly reflects the orthodox psychoanalytic position *vis-à-vis* transference. But even the most traditional group analyst has come to accept that transference cannot be identical to that taking place in classical individual analytically based treatment. The presence of fellow-members inevitably impinges on the individual association between the therapist and each of them. Moreover, the characteristic features of a group's development also necessarily influences individual transference relationships. The contributions of Stein[7] and Farrell[8] illustrate these respective issues.

Although Stein stresses that transference to the therapist is 'one of the essential dynamic factors in the group', he adds the qualification that group conditions lessen or dilute its intensity. This leads to transference being split and directed towards other patients as well. The picture is further complicated by a specific group dynamic: with transference to the therapist left uninterpreted, group tension escalates and 'intensified inter-member transference reactions' ensue. Patients unwittingly both act out, and try to inveigle their peers into acting out, certain transference roles. Thus, one patient relates to another at an unconscious transference level, the latter responds, and an interaction gets under way between the pair. Stein now shows his basic allegiance. Interaction of this type is the means whereby transference patterns are studied; interpretation (by therapist or fellow-patients) is the tool, and insight is the goal sought. In other words, interaction serves as a vehicle for the understanding of transference, and insight of the psychogenetic variety (as we described it in the previous chapter) is the key mechanism for change. We should add, incidentally, that Stein recognizes other forms of interaction which serve other purposes. For example, in non-insight-orientated groups, like those in Alcoholics Anonymous, interaction is a means whereby members support one another and satisfy infantile needs. Although transference is basic to this process, it is never explored with the patient.

For Farrell,[8] the concept of transference is a cardinal feature of group therapy. He is critical of those theorists who emphasize formulations supposedly unique to group therapy, as setting themselves apart from individual therapists; the concept of transference is thereby devalued. Moreover, Farrell argues that transference is not only the fundamental therapeutic experience in individual treatment but also plays a similar and equally crucial role in group therapy. Transference reactions between all members constitute the group's therapeutic culture. He charts graphically how these reactions operate in terms of the group's development. Firstly, notwithstanding a sense of isolation and insecurity, compounded by resentment about being treated in a group, patients have a positive rapport with their therapist. During this initial stage, they hesitate to express any of these feelings openly. But, by adopting a relatively passive stance, the therapist coerces members into grappling with their feelings among themselves. Anxiety consequently mounts, culminating in pent-up dissatisfaction and irritation which reveals itself in patients' complaints about how they have been exploited by others in their everyday lives. This becomes fused with attacks on the therapist, arising in part because he is failing to fulfil the group's expectations of him as leader.

An awkward phase follows, typified by silences and recrimination. Scapegoating and the emergence of a leader from the group's ranks may occur. These processes lead patients to recognize their own, unarticulated anxiety about group therapy. They then conclude that the therapist is responsible for subjecting them to this anxiety and he becomes a feared object. An effort is made to enlist the therapist's help, but frustratingly so. Patients also offer one another help, revealing as they do, a great deal about how they use others to satisfy their own needs. When this becomes apparent, resentment between members is experienced—resentment of a type previously felt in relation to significant others, such as family members or authority figures. Patients turn once again to the therapist, now for relief of their hostile feelings. Instead of providing this, he attempts to carry exploration beyond confrontation, to an understanding of its roots.

The group, however, wishes to remain at the level of re-enacting the conflicts rather than examining them. Collective resistance occurs; hostility is now vented against the therapist. Coupled with it is the revival of positive ties between the patients. The therapist accepts the hostility without reprisal and positive feelings towards him return. Ultimately, the therapist succeeds in gaining acceptance for his interpretations that link current intra-group feelings with past conflict-laden relationships, and a great deal of the distortion of interpersonal relationships in the group is thereby resolved. The group thus personifies and dramatizes the unconscious conflicts of its members, while the therapeutic process frees them from the crippling, maladaptive ties to which they have been subjected because of their infantile perception of their relationships with significant others.

In summary, Farrell defends the purity of the concept of transference as applied to group therapy and painstakingly dissects the component parts of the evolving transference to the therapist. The therapeutic thrust of this approach is cognitive in nature, but depends entirely on the evolution of an emotional tie between patient and therapist. The patient's growing awareness of what underlies this tie and the ultimate understanding of links between intra-group, interactional behaviour and problems with significant others in everyday life, constitute the learning process.

We have spelled out in some detail Farrell's exposition of the interactional processes underlying the theory of transference in groups as contrast for the views of other theorists who, while also aware of the relevance of transference, do not apportion so much weight to it. George Bach's[9] contribution is especially noteworthy. In comparing psychoanalytic processes operating in individual and group therapy, he suggests that the concept of transference may be insufficient to describe the complex interchanges that take place in a group. Although a group member is apt to perceive his peers in some respect as their real selves, they also come to represent other figures derived from the patient's own life. The result is a process labelled 'set-up operation'. This refers to the patient's efforts to entice his co-members—by setting them up—into behaviour which fulfils his own here-and-now needs. Illustrations of this phenomenon are seen in Bach's concept of 'unconscious symbol assignments' and 'role maturation'. According to the first, group members unconsciously allocate roles to one another based on their perceptions of appearance and behaviour. For instance, an attractive female member may be looked upon as a sex symbol while a large burly male patient who talks volubly may be assigned the role of aggressor. Role maturation refers to a developmental process whereby each group member moves through four roles. As 'novice', the new member sets up the group as a supporting object to satisfy all his unrealistic wishes and to deal with his neurotic anxieties. Then, the patient enters the 'sophomore' role and uses others to encourage his own expression of newly-discovered emotional needs. Moving into a 'junior' role, he becomes self-analytic. Finally, as a 'senior', there is acceptance of the self and of its interdependence with others. With the assistance of the therapist, patients are able to deal with each other's set-up operations as well as learn about the nature and origins of their own.

Set-up operations are examples of interaction that clearly bear a resemblance to transference reactions occurring between members. Inter-member transference may be a more accurate term yet Bach's terminology is vivid and the processes he describes will be readily recognized by therapists whatever their theoretical inclinations. The essential difference between his formulation and that of Farrell's revolves around the type of relationship emphasized as providing the main source of learning about the interpersonal sphere. For Bach, it is clearly member to member, for Farrell it is member to therapist.

The dynamic interactional model

As we can see, the locus of learning is obviously salient in theories about the role of interaction, but another dimension must now be added to our account which we can conveniently label the cognitive-behavioural. The theorists we have considered thus far may differ in the relationships they regard as the chief source of benefit but they are more or less agreed that the process involved is inherently cognitive in type. Here we trespass on territory covered in the previous chapter concerning insight (see p. 25). Another mode of learning is more behavioural in nature and entails a patient's actual efforts at altering some facet of his interpersonal style. We alluded to this in the section on definition when referring to our own term of 'learning from interpersonal action', a term intended to stress this behavioural component. The therapy group is utilized as a forum for interpersonal experimentation.

As mentioned early in the chapter, I. D. Yalom[1] is a foremost exponent of this approach to interaction, readily evidenced by the name he applies to it—*dynamic-interactional.* With H. S. Sullivan's[10] interpersonal theory of psychiatry as the backbone—that psychiatric symptoms and problems originate and express themselves as disturbed interpersonal relationships—Yalom has formulated a theoretical position which emphasizes two concepts: (a) the group as a social microcosm; and (b) the corrective emotional experience.

Social microcosm is the term applied to a group whose members interact freely and in ways that closely resemble their customary, everyday social functioning. In so doing, patients tend to manifest their faulty, maladaptive patterns of interpersonal behaviour, the very patterns that will become the targets for change. To Yalom, the social microcosm is '. . . of paramount importance . . . [it] constitutes a keystone upon which our entire approach to group therapy rests'.

The corrective emotional experience is a concept derived from the work of Franz Alexander.[11] It is summarized by Yalom as follows: the patient takes the risk, emboldened by the group's supportive structure, of expressing some strong emotion to one or more group members—including, perhaps, the therapist. Within the context of the here-and-now, the protagonist is able to reflect on the emotional experience he has just undergone and to become aware, with the aid of fellow-members, how appropriate his reactions were. This awareness paves the way for an improvement in interpersonal relating.

If we combine the interpersonal theory of Sullivan, the notion of the group as a social microcosm, and the concept of the corrective emotional experience, we are well placed to appreciate the basic features of Yalom's factor of interpersonal learning. Schematically, the model has the following steps:

1. The patient's symptoms are derived from disturbed interpersonal relationships. At the same time, such symptoms often adversely affect interpersonal functioning and the major presenting problem is therefore some form of difficulty in relating to others.
2. The group provides a social microcosm wherein the patient experiences and manifests relationship difficulties similar to those

he has in his day-to-day world.

3. The therapist promotes a climate within which the patient becomes cognizant of faulty interpersonal patterns of behaviour.
4. Awareness leads to the possibility of change, which is more likely if the patient is motivated, committed to the group, and sufficiently flexible.
5. The patient experiments with new interpersonal behaviour in the group. Combined self-observation and feedback from other members, including the therapist, enable him to judge the effectiveness and appropriateness of his experimental efforts.
6. The learned behaviour is subsequently tried out in the patient's everyday life and such experimentation reported back to the group for validation.
7. An 'adaptive spiral' is set up which severs the previous circular link between symptoms and disturbed relationships. More adaptive interpersonal behaviour generates greater self-esteem. The capacity for rewarding relationships improves and this further boosts self-esteem, promoting yet more change.

LIA: psychoanalytic versus interactional schools

Although a cognitive mechanism is clearly involved in interpersonal learning as we have outlined it (the term itself suggests that), the stress is on behavioural experimentation. This is in contrast to the traditional psychoanalytically orientated view of interaction. Moreover, as we saw in the previous chapter, the quality of the insight sought by dynamic-interactional therapists is also different. Psychogenetic insight (the understanding by the patient of *how* he came to be the way he is) is considered less cogent than interpersonal insight (his understanding of *what* it is that makes him relate poorly).

Glad and Durkin[12] have helpfully identified the distinctions between the analytic and interactional theoretical schools by depicting what each of their representatives stress in therapy. The group analyst, for example, encourages his patient to acquire insight—by discovering the influence of past experience on current behaviour through examination of transference—within the framework of emotional interaction. The 'interactionalist', on the other hand, emphasizes 'reciprocal action or influence' between members and argues that interaction is the chief agent for change. Although in both schools the therapist is regarded as a central figure, there is a difference in how his optimal role is formulated. The interactionalist views himself as a relatively transparent catalyst and model; the analyst sees himself as a relatively opaque neutral observer. In a temporal sense, the interactionalist works mostly in the present, in the here-and-now; the analyst makes liberal uses of historical data and therefore focuses readily on the there-and-then. Finally, the interactionalist lays much store on making the group experience a positive one from the outset whereas the analyst believes that resistance to learning must first be removed before patients are capable of benefiting from positive experience.

Elsewhere, Durkin[13] has summarized the distinction even more succinctly: '. . . in analytic group therapy, emotional interaction is the necessary context for insight; in experiential [interactional] group therapy, it is the major therapeutic agent . . . this confidence in spontaneous experience in the here-and-now as the mutative factor stands in contrast to the analytic reliance on analysing the resistance, working through, and using history'. Durkin concludes: '. . . the two schools may remain good neighbours but marriage is out of the question because of the religious differences!' Is she correct?

Indeed not, according to Ruth Cohn.[14] While she concedes that differences do exist between analytic and experiential models, especially in relation to the therapist's role and the temporal framework, these differences do not, in her view, constitute a dichotomy. Hypothesizing that many diverse therapeutic interventions can exert beneficial effects, Cohn advances the view that the therapeutic process can be spurred on by, *inter alia*, 'interpretation to promote insight' as much as by a 'realistic encounter geared towards a curative experience'. Moreover, the therapeutic process involves both interactional here-and-now experience plus the 'totality of the there-and-then of past and future'.

Following a clever and lively case illustration in which she compares the likely therapeutic experiences of a patient treated by a group analyst on the one hand and by an experiential group therapist on the other, Cohn argues that the latter (assuming that psychodynamic concepts form the basis of his work—a rather large assumption in fact) has not deviated from the analyst's approach so much as extended his role and functions. Thus, the experiential therapist builds on the Freudian concepts of transference and resistance by 'intensification of personal communication and exploration of the immediate encounter'. This encounter is characterized as open and authentic, and involves the therapist 'revealing his personal experience of the patient to him'.

General systems theory: a synthesis?

Cohn, it may seem, wants to have her cake and eat it. For an analytically orientated therapist to act as transparently as an experiential therapist and continue to make interpretations about transference is a tall order both clinically and theoretically. We suspect that Durkin comes closer to the truth than Cohn when she contends that despite any overlap, the nature of the therapist-patient relationship in the two approaches differs markedly. But the question then arises as to whether aspects of each may be moulded into a completely new theory, a theory in which interaction retains a prominent place. Boris Astrachan[15] has tackled the matter through deployment of general systems theory. His contribution is important in breaking new ground and deserves careful attention.

Astrachan starts from the premiss that all three major models of group therapy which stress some form of interaction, namely those which focus predominantly either on the relationships between members and the therapist or between the members themselves or between the group as a whole and the therapist, neglect important interactional patterns. In the patient-therapist model, the therapist's behaviour precludes the evolution of a peer culture. The result is obvious. While patients may learn about their relationships to authority, they miss out on the opportunity to improve their capacity at relating to their peers. Conversely, in the member to member model, more effective interpersonal relationships may develop, but dealing with authority figures will not be tackled.

Attempts to overcome this compartmentalization have, in Astrachan's view, been only partially successful. For example, Eric Berne's[16] approach, which attends both to patients' relationships to the therapist as an authority figure and to interaction between patients in the context of the here-and-now, is flawed in that power is retained exclusively by the therapist, in determining whether the group is working effectively at the peer interactional level or whether transference issues are dominant and warrant exploration. The result is a group dependent on its leader, with obvious implications for an abiding child-like transference. Whitaker and Lieberman[17] are also cited as theorists who have attempted to establish a bridge between transference and inter-member interaction through their 'group focal conflict' theory. But Astrachan's criticism is again that the group's focus is disproportionately on the members' links with their therapist; this at the expense of interaction at the inter-member level.

An additional limitation of the basic three models, according to Astrachan, is that they do not reveal the relative influence in determining a patient's behaviour of factors inherent in the patient, his interactions with a particular group, and the therapist style. The solution he offers for all these deficiencies lies in general systems theory, an approach regarded as sufficiently comprehensive to facilitate an understanding of how the patient and the group interact with, and change, one another. Aspects of the group's structure, function, and organization are integrated in order to achieve this understanding. The therapist plays a pivotal role through 'functioning as a central regulatory agent'. Among his tasks is to define and maintain the boundaries of therapy—what is pertinent for the group's agenda, what is in the group and what is outside of it, and how patients relate to one another. Thus, the therapist influences to a considerable degree the relationship of the group to its environment as well as the interaction of various parts of the group system with each other. He does so in the knowledge that a change in any one part of the system will have an impact on all other parts.

The advantages claimed of a model based on general systems theory are in essence the converse of Astrachan's criticisms of the three models it would supersede. The therapist appreciates the many diverse aspects of his role as regulatory agent and is attuned to all parts of the therapy system. He is therefore well placed to modify his regulatory posture in the light of the system's specific needs at a particular time. Simultaneously, he recognizes the likely repercussions on the system of the regulatory behaviour he adopts. Moreover, the therapist also attends to systems other than the therapy one, which are relevant to the patient. Since the therapy system is open with permeable boundaries, he is aware of the potential changes that may occur in, for example, the patient's marriage, his family, and work and how these may in turn affect the patient's experience in treatment. We could say, in summary, that the therapist is flexible in his role as group leader because he is not bound by a segmental view of the therapeutic process *vis-à-vis* the learning that stems from interaction. All forms of interaction are potentially useful, none deserving priority over the rest.

Astrachan's arguments are persuasive, his own theoretical contribution impressive. And in his espousal and advocacy of general systems theory, he is sturdily supported by several prominent theorists such as Kernberg,[18] Fried,[19] Skynner,[20] and Durkin.[21] The boundaries of this chapter do not permit a more extended account of the theory. Suffice it to say that it serves group therapy well and is particularly apt with regard to interaction. But whether Astrachan's solution to the problem of a segmental view of interaction is workable or not remains untested. Specifically, can the therapist toss away his oft long-standing predilection for a more circumscribed model of interaction (whether its focus is transference or peer relationship)? Furthermore, does not the role of regulatory agent carry with it a tendency, unless most assiduously monitored and checked, for the therapist to convey an image of the authority figure to his patients, and therefore a bias towards interaction of the transference type?

The detrimental effects of interaction?

In our discussion of theory thus far, there has been an implicit assumption that interaction is intrinsically therapeutic. Is this indeed always the case? Slavson[6] has raised the possibility that interaction may not always be helpful. For example, he cites interaction occurring on a plane of querulousness and tension, though this does not negate for him the potential benefits of negatively toned interaction. Operating from the premiss that 'all human contact initially activates some degree of uncertainty and anxiety', Slavson[22] points out the potential for heightened discomfort in the interactions between members as a function of the group's facilitation of their idiosyncratic patterns of response; this concept is similar to the 'group as a social microcosm' that we commented on earlier. For instance a customarily aggressive person is likely to manifest his aggressiveness in the group, much to the discomfort of those of his peers who are temperamentally timid and diffident. Provided the therapist is aware of and manages these group dynamics appropriately, their therapeutic effects will predominate by serving as the basis for the acquisition of insight.

The implication here is of potentially anti-therapeutic effects as a consequence of certain forms of aggressive interaction. One form that springs readily to mind is the scapegoating of a patient by his peers. For example, classical work by Lewin and his associates[23] has demonstrated how authoritarian handling of a group of boys (in an activities centre) caused discontent among its members. This discontent was dealt with in part by the hostile, unwarranted victimization of an innocent group member.

Other forms of anti-therapeutic interaction are not necessarily aggressive in type. Bion,[24] for instance, has suggested that anxiety among group members may lead to the unconscious adoption of certain assumptions about how the group functions (the so-called basic assumption group) and prevent it from becoming a 'work group' in which the therapeutic task is faced. Whereas members of a work group unite in collaborative endeavour, aware of reality and tolerant of frustration, members of a basic assumption group resort unconsciously to primitive strategies which deny reality and are irrational, even magical in quality. In one such strategy, *dependency*, patients relate to one group member (not necessarily the therapist), as if he were omnipotent and omniscient. All interactions revolve around their dependent status as they attempt to inveigle the chosen leader into taking responsibility for the group's welfare. As the embodiment of wisdom, he will provide the solutions to the group's problems. In another form of basic assumption, *pairing*, responsibility is delegated to a pair of members. Their relationship—a form of collusive subgrouping—is promoted in the hope that out of the union will arise the answers to all their difficulties. Subgrouping may occur for diverse reasons but, whatever its source, it is a form of interaction likely to exert a deleterious effect on the group.

Bion's work is the pioneering contribution to the third paradigm of interactional learning cited earlier. The focus here is on the association between the group as a whole and the therapist. In raising it in the context of non-therapeutic interaction we follow Bion himself. He did not postulate his model of group dynamics as therapeutic but set out rather to identify factors which serve to disrupt the purposeful work of a group. Although patients might, with the aid of the therapist's interpretations, discover the nature of their group's 'basic assumptions', this would be sought primarily to enable the therapeutic enterprise to take place. Thus, the value of Bion's contribution lies in his theorizing about anti-therapeutic forces, including those based on undesirable patterns of interaction, that block a group's progress.

Clinical experience points to a variety of counter-productive interactional patterns. Apart from the aforementioned—dependency, scapegoating, and subgrouping—other examples are rivalry, overt aggression, submissiveness, and withdrawal. These patterns are topics for study, either in their own right or in the context of an inherently therapeutic interaction going awry. The need for innovative theoretical contributions is obvious.

Empirical research

In contrast with the above theoretical work, systematic research has been disappointing both in amount and quality. Probably because of the complexity of the process of LIA, investigators have tended to concentrate on its more straightforward components. The few studies done have tackled the relationships between interaction and various personality factors of group members, and between interaction and therapist behaviour. The link between interaction and outcome has barely been touched. Before considering this work, we briefly look at the efforts to measure patterns of interaction, an obvious requisite for the proper study of LIA.

Measurements of interaction

As they stand, these contributions on measurement do not have a direct bearing on LIA, but it is conceivable that links to it will be forged by future research. For example, it may be that patients who relate in particular ways in a group are more able to profit from LIA than their counterparts who show other patterns of interaction.

The topic has been well reviewed by McPherson and Walton.[25] They have also conducted a neat study in which experienced clinicians observed a therapy group and then described the members' interactional patterns using a repertory grid technique. Analysis of the grids revealed three main independent dimensions which differentiated patients' behaviour: (a) assertive/dominant versus passive/submissive; (b) emotionally sensitive versus emotionally insensitive (to peers); and (c) aiding versus hindering the attainment of the group's goals. These dimensions seem valid and thus warrant more attention. We would support McPherson and Walton's notion that they may provide an empirically derived framework for the observation and measurement of interaction in therapy groups.

A more comprehensive classification of interpersonal behaviour has been offered by Lorr.[26] He postulates no less than nine dimensions of relating. He applied his classification to a study of forty-five groups, containing a total of nearly 200 patients with either neurosis, or psychosis in remission. Four meetings of mature groups were sampled by observers who rated patients' interpersonal behaviour on a schedule of 75 items. A factor analysis was then performed to determine the extent to which items could be grouped into Lorr's previously hypothesized dimensions. Eight factors emerged: dominance; hostility; leadership role; supportive role; help-seeking; submissiveness; withdrawal; and disorganization. A second-order analysis yielded four factors: activity level; submissiveness/disorganized; supportive role; and leadership role. This work is potentially relevant to the study of interaction but the observer ratings may have relied too heavily on subjective judgements.

Another approach to the measurement of interpersonal behaviour devised by William Schutz[27]—fundamental interpersonal relations orientation (FIRO)—is based on a hypothesis that man's chief social needs are three in number, and involve his inclinations concerning control, inclusion, and affection. A self-report measure covers these three areas and calls on the respondent to rate: his need to control others or be controlled by them; his wish to be included in or excluded from, the activities of others; and his wish to get close to or retain a distance from others. Because the FIRO scale is self-administered, and its construction not directly associated with groups, its applicability to the study of interaction in group therapy is probably limited (see Chapter 4 for its relevance to the study of compatibility and cohesiveness).

It will be obvious from this brief account that the measurement of interaction in groups is no easy matter. The rudimentary quality of the work attests to the conceptual and methodological hurdles facing the researcher. To establish the key dimensions of relating is fraught with difficulty. Then we have the problems of how to identify them in a group and how to rate their importance. Yet, measurement is a *sine qua non* for the effective study of interaction, and the need to wrestle with it remains a high priority.

The relationship between interaction and personality factors in the patient

We have found two studies in which the relationship between

interaction and personality factors is examined. Ryan[28] opted to focus on a quality he labelled the 'capacity for mutual dependence' (CMD). CMD contains two elements: (a) the potential to 'give', encompassing the ability to empathize, form relationships, delay personal gratification, and act altruistically; and (b) the potential of a person to handle his wishes for others to gratify his own needs. A Rorschach-based scale was designed to assess these elements. On the first, a person might be 'giving' or 'non-giving'. On the second, he might show 'dependence-flexibility' (i.e. be able to handle both dependence and independence appropriately), 'dependence-acceptance', or 'dependence-denial'. A high score on the CMD scale reflects a pattern of being able to give and be dependence-flexible. Applying the measure to twenty-five patients in group therapy, Ryan found that those with a high capacity for mutual dependence were more involved in the group (assessed through therapist's ratings and length of stay in the group).

Although full details of the study are unavailable (it was published only as a dissertation abstract), its evident limitations should lead us to be cautious about accepting the result. The sample was small; the personality variable under scrutiny was measured using a dubious scale; and the rating of group members' involvement was not independent (indeed, therapists may well have been biased by their impression of the very personality factor under examination). The conception of the study is also questionable. Presumably Ryan regards CMD as a predictor variable—of a patient's level of involvement in group therapy. Does this mean that a patient with a low CMD score is unsuitable for treatment? It could equally be argued that such a patient is especially appropriate, since the group format provides an opportunity for him to learn how to be more 'giving' and 'flexible' with regard to dependence-independence. However, Ryan's concept of CMD is an interesting one, and deserves more attention.

The complex way in which interaction is influenced by personality factors is revealed in an analogue study by Lee.[29] He set out to elucidate how interaction is related to sex, preparedness to take risks, and the degree of structure imposed on a group. Students, chosen on the basis of their extreme scores on a risk-taking scale, were assigned randomly to a simulated first session of group therapy. This consisted of practice trials for training in three prescribed behaviours—self-disclosure, feedback, and confrontation—all aspects of interaction in the context of the experiment. Groups were run either as high, moderate, or low in terms of structuredness. Lee demonstrated that a structured session fostered a greater level of interaction between members but that there was a differential effect involving both sex and willingness to take risks. Thus, structured groups were more effective in promoting the prescribed behaviours than less-structured groups except in the case of high-risk-taking men. The behaviours were greatest overall amongst men and high-risk-taking subjects.

Why these particular patterns should emerge is difficult to explain. At least they demonstrate an interplay of factors leading to interaction, and we see, as common sense suggests, that a preparedness to take risks is generally conducive to the development of interaction. This latter observation is supported by the findings of another experiment, very similar in type but which did not differentiate between the sexes.[30] But extrapolation to clinical groups is not wise. The effects were noted over the course of a single session only. It is unlikely that interactional patterns would be amenable to such elaborate study in the first session of a therapy group.

Interaction and the therapist's role

While covering the effects on interaction of personality factors we cited the relevance of group structure. Obviously, the therapist can attempt to manipulate the level and direction of interaction between members of his group, including interaction with himself. The precise pattern sought would no doubt relate to the therapist's theoretical preference. Thus, the therapist adhering to a dynamic-interactional approach would coax his group members into relating actively among themselves, whereas the classical group-analyst would be more interested in the interaction between his patients and himself.

Are therapists able to direct their groups in this way? A study by Heckel and his associates[31] suggests that this is possible. The therapist of a small group of psychiatric in-patients which met on six occasions was trained to refer back to them any comments directed to himself. This he did during the first three sessions. In the second three sessions he desisted, as a control condition. Statements by the therapist and patients were subsequently coded from audiotapes; the therapist's as redirection versus non-redirection; the patients' as therapist-directed or inter-member interaction. A clear association was found between the therapist's actions and the patient's interactional pattern: the more often he redirected (and the less he contributed in terms of his overall number of comments) the greater was the level of interaction between patients.

In a similar study, again of in-patient group therapy, Salzberg[32] used four modes of relating between therapist and patients. These were: silence (contributing only when clearly necessary); talking (contributing when conversation lags); redirecting (responding to a patient's comment or question by involving another patient); and directing (addressing the patient directly, without reference to any other members). Four combinations of these modes were deployed in fifteen-minute segments of each group session, namely silence-redirection, silence-direction, talking-redirection, and talking-direction.

Patients' responses were coded in terms of their frequency, form (interactive or not), and content (the last is not pertinent here). Correlations obtained were generally as expected. The therapist's silence led to more interaction, his talking to less. Redirecting had no specific effect on the form of the patients' responses but did lead to significantly more of them. In the light of these findings, Salzberg suggests the following role for the therapist: when a group is new and its members strangers to one another, he might provide a sense of structure by talking and directing and thus enable the patients to become familiar with one another's problems. Thereafter he could reduce his level of talking, and commence redirecting. Although a reasonable strategy, it does seem to represent an over-interpretation of his data. The picture in clinical practice is certainly more complex.

Salzberg raises the question of how these results might relate to outcome. A study by Land[33] attempts to deal with this by ascertaining the effect of the therapist's silence and redirection versus a more active, directive stance. The investigation was carried out firstly with a sample of chronic in-patients and then with acutely ill in-patients. In each case, two experimental conditions were compared in terms of their effects on both process and outcome. A control group was also included in the design. In one experimental condition, the therapist talked actively and directly to individual patients and initiated conversation to break silences; in the other condition, he remained silent until a question was directed at him, whereupon he referred it to another member. The discrepant findings that emerged in these two clinical samples point to the complexity of the relationship between therapist behaviour and interaction between group members. In the acutely ill group, the pattern resembled the results of Heckel *et al.*[31] and Salzberg,[32] namely interaction was more evident in the group in which the therapist redirected questions. But this effect was not noted among the chronic patients, possibly because, as Land suggests, they were too impaired to dispense with the therapist's leadership. His work thus reminds us that patients who participate in groups cannot be treated as if they were all alike. Clearly their capacity to interact varies according to the acute/chronic distinction and many other characteristics.

Land's attempt to examine the effects of therapist behaviour on outcome was unfortunately still-born, with neither treatment group showing substantial improvement on any of the outcome measures he used. His attribution of this non-response to inadequate treatment is probably valid. The programme was limited to ten sessions only, and the patients in both investigations were sufficiently ill to require hospitalization.

The quality of interaction

In the above studies, interaction is treated as if it were a unidimensional process, with the experimental objective confined to the test of whether its amount varies as a function of specific therapist behaviour. The question is rather facile. After all, patients may interact at a furious pace but the particular quality of the interaction may produce undesirable effects. For instance, in one group, members may relate well together in a warm, rosy, and supportive way. In another group, by contrast, every interaction may be hostile and destructive in nature; each patient is on the offensive. In the first group, everyone feels jolly comfortable but no one achieves any clinical change, and in the second group the patients' goal is mere survival. (We briefly discussed anti-therapeutic interaction in the section on theory.)

Flowers and his colleagues[34, 35] are certainly aware of this dimension of interaction. Their work is also noteworthy because of a rather ingenious, albeit intrusive, experimental method. Patients and therapists hand out a blue token to one another as a concrete accompaniment of a positive statement, and a red token to reflect a negative statement. The token makes obvious by visible means the quality of the communication. Two experiments conducted by the Flowers team are relevant to our discussion. In the first,[34] with a supportive group of severely disturbed out-patients, therapists and patients distributed tokens during the first twelve sessions of the experimental programme. As a control condition, the following six sessions weere conducted without tokens.

Patterns of interaction were noted and compared during the two phases. The exchange of tokens accurately reflected the proportions of positive and negative statements made. Secondly, their use was associated with an increase in interaction between patients, overall interaction within the group, and negative statements (critical feedback) made by therapists to patients. The findings suggest that particular patterns of communication can be facilitated by the token strategy.

Another experiment[35] demonstrates this even more clearly, although on this occasion the subjects were students participating in a short-term group. An ingenious experimental design was applied in which different proportions of positive and negative statements, accompanied by the corresponding tokens, were made by the therapists. Negative statements were found to correlate with increased interaction between members. But the level of intensity of these statements were also relevant. Group members felt more trust in their peers during sessions in which the negative statements made were of low rather than high intensity. In other words, the relatively gentle expression of critical comments by the group leader promoted interaction and trust between members. Another finding of interest was the reduction in the level of positive interaction between members during sessions in which the leader delivered more negative statements. The point here seems to be that he acted as a model for a particular pattern of interaction. A possible implication for the therapist is that he may need to maintain a careful balance between the expression of positive and negative statements in his efforts to promote interaction.

These two studies are full of interest for reasons already cited. The major drawback is the intrusiveness of the method. Quite conceivably, the use of tokens *per se* affected the nature of the interaction in both samples. For example, a low proportion of negative statements made by group members towards the leaders was noted, and this may well reflect a heightened self-consciousness induced by the tokens. Such inhibition might influence group development, since the emergence of the group's capacity to be critical of the therapist is probably an important element in its maturation. Another snag is the mechanical and dehumanizing aspect of passing tokens. One would also want to see the development and testing of hypotheses in clinical situations to clarify whether the 'token' is of any practical significance. Meanwhile, it remains an intriguing concept, and certainly worthy of more systematic attention.

Just as tokens may influence interaction, so may the *size* of the group. Grosz *et al.*[36] demonstrate this in their study of male in-patients. Patients met for, on average, five sessions in one of five groups of variable size (4–6 members). Although the main aim was the promotion of interaction between patients in all groups, the level of interaction, as reflected in the verbal responses uttered, was a function of the number of members therein. More inter-member interaction took place in the larger groups. Of course, the analysis corrected for the fact that group size was not distributed evenly. The finding that the experience of the therapist was also associated with the amount of interaction makes it difficult to reach confident conclusions. As the investigators themselves point out, some effects may have arisen in part as a result of the evolution of specific group 'cultures' during the initial sessions. Nonetheless, it is highly likely that the size of a group is a cogent variable in determining interaction. Thomas and Fink[37] have reviewed its significance and concluded that size affects a variety of group processes, including interaction. For the moment however, the question of the optimum size of a therapy group in promoting interaction remains open. On the one hand, as we noted in the section on theory, a group requires sufficient numbers to facilitate the development of a social microcosm whereby its members can interact with a variety of other members and learn from the variegated encounters that ensue. On the other hand, it can be argued that beyond a certain size, the individual member 'gets lost in the crowd' or may seek refuge in a subgroup. Despite the phenomenon of the 'large group',[38] it cannot be fortuitous that small group therapy is universally favoured by clinicians.*

Grosz *et al.*[36] conclude their article by commenting that: '... no

*The large group—for example, the 'community meeting' in a therapeutic community—is relatively little studied and we exclude it from consideration here.

generalizations about group interactions can be made from results obtained for a single therapist or one group of patients'. They then refer to the great complexity that typifies interactional processes and to their uniqueness in a particular therapy group. The researcher's task, in their view, is to identify factors which '... influence group processes in predictable directions'.

The Grosz team has followed its own recommendation and undertaken the investigation of some of these factors. In one pertinent study,[39] the effects on interaction of a regular change in group leadership, varying group composition, and the stage of the group's development, were looked at. In a weekly, open-ended group consisting of psychiatric in-patients and led in turns by three equally experienced therapists, the level of interaction between patients and between patients and the therapist was monitored by an observer/co-therapist. During the six months of the study the group's membership changed constantly as a result of discharge or drop-out and the admission of new patients. The findings are of considerable interest. Interaction between patients increased steadily during the first sixteen sessions and, on reaching a peak, remained at this level. In the first session, the average number of interactions by patients was 12; by the final session this had reached 104. Composition was also related to patients' interactional patterns. Stability of membership, i.e. having the same group of patients in a particular session as in the preceding session, was associated with an increase in interaction. A change in membership resulted in either an increase or decrease. Therapist effects were absent in this study, contrasting with the results of the aforementioned first experiment conducted by Grosz *et al.* This was perhaps because all three therapists in the second study were equally well experienced and had adopted the same leadership style.

The explanation provided by the researchers for the steady increase in interaction and its persistence, despite regular changes in leadership and membership, is entirely reasonable: therapists introduce and inculcate a norm that calls for interaction; patients learn what is expected of them; the norm becomes an established feature of the group's culture and is transferred from session to session since there are always '... members present in the group who will communicate and reinforce the therapist's expectation through their own behaviour'.

Interaction and outcome

Apart from the attempt by Land,[33] mentioned earlier, to examine the link between interaction and outcome, we have only managed to locate a solitary study on this important aspect, and that on a non-clinical sample. Using the Hill interaction matrix to measure the content and style of interaction, Kaye[40] focused on the relationship between such interaction and behavioural change, in a student sample undergoing a ten-day sensitivity-training group experience. Effective learning was found to be dependent on the development of interaction of a distinct form—member-centred and emotionally involving. However, the effects of this interactional pattern had waned at follow-up, eight months later. Kaye's own conjecture that long-term change required a more confrontational mode of interaction than had occurred in his groups is certainly a possible explanation for the evaporation of the benefits. But, the limitations of his investigation—small sample, non-clinical, concentrated group format (over ten days), among others—makes one cautious about applying either the findings or the conjecture to conventional group therapy. We should, however, note two strengths of the study—the use of a control group and the comparatively long follow-up.

An alternative explanation emerges from a well-executed study by Swarr and Ewing.[41] Although not directly concerned with the interaction-outcome association, it does shed light on the types of change that occur in a group and their respective timing. Their sample comprised forty-five student–patients with neurotic problems, treated in interactional out-patient group therapy for an average six months. The researchers demonstrated significantly positive change taking place in the first ten sessions but in specific areas only, such as lowered self-esteem and anxiety. Contrariwise, other problems, particularly poor interpersonal functioning and associated feelings of distrust, hostility, and lack of assertiveness, only showed significant improvement at the end of treatment, i.e. after an average of six months.

The study is defective in its lack of a follow-up but the data are sufficient to show that certain sorts of clinical change in group therapy necessitate a patient's participation in risk-taking interpersonal behaviour within the group in order to resolve longstanding problems in relating. Also, that the requisite learning necessarily takes place over an extended period. Swarr and Ewing's study also lends support to the relevance of group development and to the specific notion, widely held by group therapists, that the work done in a group is bound up with its stage of evolution. Clearly, there is scope for the investigation of the relationship between the timing of interaction and the benefits that accrue from it: when is the optimal phase for its deployment? Attempts to wrestle with this question would be potentially rewarding, and indeed are most necessary.

Conclusion

All practitioners of group therapy, of whatever school, would assent to the relevance of the phenomena which we have subsumed under the broad umbrella of LIA. This is shown by the substantial and intelligent volume of theoretical attention devoted to it. Disappointingly, the same cannot be said of the systematic researcher's endeavour—this has been relatively scanty and for the most part unsophisticated. The reason for the discrepancy is obvious. Most schools of group therapy have advanced theoretical formulations regarding the sort of learning that stems from interactional processes; but the task of identifying and measuring this learning has obviously proved difficult. Instead, researchers have opted to study the simpler construct of interaction *per se*, which is much more amenable to investigation.

What have we learned from the theoretical work in conjunction with the findings of systematic research? We have more than hinted that the theoretical contributions contain common themes despite what seems at first glance to be enormous conceptual differences. As pointed out, the chief gulf is between the psychoanalytic and dynamic-interactional approaches. The first emphasizes cognitive aspects of the interactional process with special regard to transference, whereas the second is more concerned with behavioural change in the interpersonal domain, starting with intra-group relationships. In recent years, a body of thought has developed which suggests the relevance of both cognitive and behavioural dimensions in interactional learning. In particular, Astrachan's application of general systems theory[15] shows promise.

Of the empirical studies we have cited, only that by Kaye[40] sets out to try to clarify some characteristics of therapeutic interaction. Future research could usefully be directed towards the experimental investigation of cognitive and behavioural aspects of interpersonal learning. Specifically, which aspects are associated with good outcome and in what sort of patient? Do patients learn best from practising new forms of interpersonal behaviour or from their appreciation of the nature and source of their relationship difficulties? Does such a factor as psychological-mindedness influence the picture, i.e. do psychologically minded patients benefit more from a cognitively-based process and non-psychologically-minded patients from a behaviourally orientated process?

Whatever answers to these questions ultimately emerge, we surmise that on the basis of current knowledge, the therapist should not be unduly bound by the theoretical model he follows or stress one aspect of interpersonal learning to the exclusion of others. He may also take note of the systematic research that demonstrates the influence of the therapist's behaviour on interaction between group members. For example, the redirection responses studied by Heckel *et al.*[31] and by Land[33] clearly promote interaction among certain types of patient. This work supports clinical impression as far as it goes, but it would be most useful to gather more information from empirical studies. Thus, we need to know whether redirection responses promote ultimately profitable interactional behaviour, to what degree such responses should be used, and how their application should vary with different clinical groups. Land's results shed light on the last issue and suggest the need for flexibility in the therapist, namely that he must adopt different strategies for groups of different composition to enable beneficial interaction.

References

1. Yalom, I. D. *The theory and practice of group psychotherapy.* Basic Books, New York (1975).
2. Bloch, S., Reibstein, J., Crouch, E., *et al.* A method for the study of therapeutic factors in group psychotherapy. *British Journal of Psychiatry* **134**, 257–63 (1979).
3. Corsini, R. and Rosenberg, B. Mechanisms of group psychotherapy: processes and dynamics. *Journal of Abnormal and Social Psychology* **51**, 406–11 (1955).
4. See, e.g. Brown, J. A. C. *Freud and the post-Freudians.* Penguin, Harmondsworth (1961).
5. Yalom, I. D., Brown S., and Bloch, S. The written summary as a group psychotherapy technique. *Archives of General Psychiatry* **32**, 605–13 (1975).

6. Slavson, S. R. Interaction and reconstruction in group psychotherapy. *International Journal of Group Psychotherapy* **16**, 3–12 (1966).
7. Stein, A. The nature and significance of interaction in group psychotherapy. *International Journal of Group Psychotherapy* **20**, 153–62 (1970).
8. Farrell, M. P. Transference dynamics of group psychotherapy. *Archives of General Psychiatry* **6**, 66–76 (1962).
9. Bach, G. R. Observations on transference and object relations in the light of group dynamics. *International Journal of Group Psychotherapy* **7**, 64–76 (1957).
10. Sullivan, H. S. *The interpersonal theory of psychiatry*. Norton, New York (1953).
11. Alexander, F. *Psychoanalysis and psychotherapy*. Allen and Unwin, London (1957).
12. Glad, D. D. and Durkin, H. E. Summary of panel discussion on interaction and insight in group psychotherapy. *International Journal of Group Psychotherapy* **19**, 279–80 (1969).
13. Durkin, H. E. Concluding remarks of panel discussion on interaction and insight in group psychotherapy. *International Journal of Group Psychotherapy* **19**, 288–91 (1969).
14. Cohn, R. C. Psychoanalytic or experiential group psychotherapy: a false dichotomy. *Psychoanalytic Review* **50**, 333–45 (1969).
15. Astrachan, B. Towards a social systems model of therapeutic groups. *Social Psychiatry* **5**, 110–19 (1970).
16. Berne, E. *Principles of group treatment*. Oxford University Press, New York (1966).
17. Whitaker, D. S. and Lieberman, M. A. *Psychotherapy through the group process*. Atherton, New York (1965).
18. Kernberg, O. F. A systems approach to priority setting of interventions in groups. *International Journal of Group Psychotherapy* **25**, 251–75 (1975).
19. Fried, E. Building psychic structures as a prerequisite for change. *International Journal of Group Psychotherapy* **32**, 417–30 (1982).
20. Skynner, A. R. *One flesh, separate persons*. Constable, London (1976).
21. Durkin, H. E. Change in group psychotherapy: therapy and practice: a systems perspective. *International Journal of Group Psychotherapy* **32**, 431–9 (1982).
22. Slavson, S. R. The anatomy and clinical applications of group interaction. *International Journal of Group Psychotherapy* **19**, 3–15 (1969).
23. For a summary of this work, see: Whiteley, J. S. and Gordon, J. *Group approaches in psychiatry*. Routledge and Kegan Paul, London (1979).
24. Bion, W. R. *Experiences in groups*. Tavistock, London (1961).
25. McPherson, F. M. and Walton, H. G. The dimensions of psychotherapy group interaction: an analysis of clinicians' constructs. *British Journal of Medical Psychology* **43**, 281–90 (1970).
26. Lorr, M. Dimensions of interaction in group psychotherapy. *Multivariate Behavioural Research* **1**, 67–73 (1966).

27. Schutz, W. *The interpersonal underworld.* Science and Behaviour Books, Palo Alto (1966).
28. Ryan, W. Capacity for mutual dependence and involvement in group psychotherapy. *Dissertation Abstracts* **19**, 1119 (1958).
29. Lee, S. T. The effects of sex, risk-taking, and structure on prescribed group behaviour, cohesion, and evaluative attitudes in a simulated early phase of group psychotherapy. *Dissertation Abstracts International* **36**, 4695–6 (1976).
30. Evenson, P. and Bednar, R. L. The effects of specific cognitive and behavioural structure on early growth development. Cited in: *Handbook of Psychotherapy and Behavioural Change* (eds. S. L. Garfield and A. E. Bergin). Wiley, New York (1978).
31. Heckel, R. V., Froelich I., and Salzberg, H. C. Interaction and redirection in group therapy. *Psychological Reports* **10**, 14 (1962).
32. Salzberg, H. C. Effects of silence and redirection of verbal responses in group psychotherapy. *Psychological Reports* **11**, 455–61 (1962).
33. Land, E. C. A comparison of patient improvement resulting from two therapeutic techniques. *Dissertation Abstracts* **25**, 628–9 (1964).
34. Flowers, J. V., Booraem, C. D., Brown, T. R., *et al.* An investigation of a technique for facilitating patient to patient therapeutic interactions in group therapy. *Journal of Community Psychology* **2**, 39–42 (1974).
35. Flowers, J. V. The effect of therapist support and encounter on the percentage of client–client interactions in group therapy. *Journal of Community Psychology* **6**, 69–73 (1978).
36. Grosz, H. J., Stern, H., and Wright, C. S. Interactions in therapy groups as a function of differences among therapists and group size. *Psychological Reports* **17**, 827–34 (1965).
37. Thomas, E. J. and Fink, C. F. Effects of group size. *Psychological Bulletin* **60**, 371–84 (1963).
38. Kreeger, L. C. (ed.) *The large group: dynamics and therapy.* Constable, London (1973).
39. Grosz, H. J. and Wright, C. S. The tempo of verbal interaction in an open therapy group conducted in rotation by three different therapists. *International Journal of Group Psychotherapy* **17**, 513–23 (1967).
40. Kaye, J. D. Group interaction and interpersonal learning. *Small Group Behaviour* **4**, 424–48 (1973).
41. Swarr, R. R. and Ewing, T. N. Outcome effects of eclectic interpersonal-learning-based group psychotherapy with college student neurotics. *Journal of Consulting and Clinical Psychology* **45**, 1029–35 (1977).

4 Acceptance (Cohesiveness)

We can all identify groups to which we belong—social groups, groups at work, groups devoted to particular hobbies, and so forth. Indeed, individuals who do not belong to groups of any kind are labelled as 'socially isolated', or stigmatized as 'hermits'. So the sense of belonging which comes from membership of groups is a very familiar one. This sense of belonging has a number of components, which may include identification with the aims of the group, admiration of the group leader, and liking of the other group members. If we find a group an attractive place to be, we feel emotionally comfortable and the task in hand is that much easier. On the other hand if we feel ill at ease, then it is likely to be difficult to join in effectively.

This feeling of belonging is widely regarded as most important in therapy groups. Most therapists believe it essential that each member is accepted by his fellows and that the group develops into a cohesive entity. The group therapy literature abounds with terms, such as support, togetherness, solidarity, and belongingness, all of which reflect this notion. It seems important that group members are attracted to each other and 'gel' together. Common sense and clinical experience support the idea that a group will work more therapeutically if its members find it an attractive place to be. A cohesive group, in which members have an investment in its continued existence, provides an apt forum for the exploration of personal problems. Moreover, cohesiveness is the cement which keeps the structure of the group in place when stormy emotional weather is encountered.

Definition

Although cohesiveness has long been recognized by both social psychologists and clinicians, the concept remains rather blurred. This is more than evident in the variegated statements that Corsini and Rosenberg[1] identified from their 1955 survey of the group therapy literature. Representative are: *esprit de corps*, friendly environment; unification of the group; emotional acceptance; emotional support; loss of feeling of isolation; group reassurance; feeling of belonging; group identification; togetherness; permissive environment; the group's tolerance of the patient; the therapist's tolerance of the patient; acceptance by the group; and supportive relations.

Applying the generic label, acceptance, Corsini and Rosenberg noted that this was the most frequently cited therapeutic mechanism and amounted to 'respect for and sympathy with the individual', and implied a sense of belonging with a warm, friendly, supportive atmosphere in the group.

If we again peruse the representative list, it becomes clear that it contains at least three separate, albeit overlapping, dimensions: (a) *group cohesiveness* is encapsulated in the terms togetherness, *esprit de corps*, unification of the group, and group identification; (b) *acceptance* is reflected in feeling of belonging, loss of feeling of isolation, the group's tolerance of the patient, the therapist's tolerance of the patient, and acceptance by the group. Closely allied to acceptance is (c) *support*, embodied in such terms as emotional support, supportive relations, and group reassurance.

Obviously, group cohesiveness, acceptance, and support go hand in hand, as therapists would readily testify. Yet, a moment's reflection reveals that this pattern is not axiomatic. For example, a tightly cohesive group may be able to sustain the temporary absence of support in the face of a necessary and constructive phase of challenge and confrontation. This does not negate the existence in the past of a supportive framework (indeed, this is invariably so if confrontation is to be of value), and its continuing 'background' presence. Acceptance and cohesiveness do not necessarily occur in tandem. The group may be cohesive but one of its members may not enjoy the sense of being accepted by his peers and/or the therapist. For instance, a new arrival to a well-established group may have to weather an initial period of not feeling part of things. A patient may be delegated to act as a scapegoat so that the rest of the group can achieve a sense of cohesiveness; only with the aid of the non-accepted member can such cohesiveness materialize.

Cohesiveness

Even if we take the first dimension alone, closer inspection suggests that it is multidimensional. Bednar and Kaul[2] argue this point persuasively, suggesting that 'there is little cognitive substance to the concept' of cohesiveness. In their view, the common assumption that cohesiveness is a continuous, bipolar phenomenon is unwarranted. Instead, it should be regarded as an unstable, fluctuating, multidimensional process, incorporating such aspects as attraction to the group as a whole, attraction to peers within the group, attraction to the group leader, and agreement with the group's goals. They go so far as to advocate dropping the term cohesiveness entirely and replacing it with the various different factors embedded within it.

Bednar and Kaul are clearly influenced in this thinking by recent efforts to measure cohesiveness. For example, they cite the work of Silbergeld *et al.*[3] This team identified six subscales—spontaneity, support, affiliation, involvement, insight, and clarity—in its pursuit of the constituents of cohesiveness, making it abundantly clear that the phenomenon is multidimensional.

The recommendation by Bednar and Kaul to drop the term cohesiveness is unlikely to be accepted—it is too well established and too convenient a term. But the effort to define it would be eased by adopting their view of its multidimensionality and fluctuating nature. Perhaps the customary definition in the field of social psychology research—that group cohesiveness is 'the resultant of all forces acting on members to remain in the group'[4] is a good starting point. Then, as Cartwright suggests, we should invoke a set of forces which in conjunction *determine* cohesiveness—basically certain properties of the group and certain characteristics of its members—and effects that are the *consequences* of cohesiveness. We return to this important topic of determinants and consequences in the section on theory.

In the specific context of group therapy, detailed appraisal of the phenomenon of cohesiveness indicates that it is best conceived of as a *condition for change*. A group must be attractive to its members in order that therapeutic factors can operate. Consider the most obvious implication: an unattractive group would probably fail to exert a therapeutic effect as members drop out or lose their motivation to work at the required task. At the same time, we should bear in mind a well-recognized clinical observation, namely that cohesiveness is not invariably linked to productive therapy. As we shall mention later, a cohesive group may avoid therapeutic work because of its cosy, comfortable atmosphere in which the members can obtain gratification but avoid threatening, distressing, or otherwise discomforting matters.

Acceptance

In contrast to cohesiveness, acceptance refers more to an individual member's subjective experience (though it is clear from our allusion to Cartwright's comments that certain characteristics of group members contribute to the determination of cohesiveness). Yalom[5] does link the two by using the terms 'total group cohesiveness' and 'individual member cohesiveness' (i.e. acceptance) but he also highlights their distinctive qualities. The links and distinctions are reflected amongst the relevant items in his therapeutic factor questionnaire (categorized, somewhat misleadingly, as group cohesiveness), to wit: 'Belonging to a group of people who understood and accepted me'; 'Belonging to and being accepted by a group'; and 'Revealing embarrassing things about myself and still being accepted by the group'. Two other items refer to the move from a position of aloneness to one of being in close contact with others.

In our own work we have adhered closely to Yalom's criteria. Like him we find it useful to focus predominantly on such aspects as the sense of being understood, of feeling accepted, and of belonging. But we also include the interwoven experience of feeling cared for and supported by other group members. This covers the third dimension of *support* that we identified from the statements listed by Corsini and Rosenberg[1] at the outset of this section. We see support here as a patient not merely being tolerated by his peers and the therapist but also actively encouraged by them.

As a result, we have arrived at the following definition; acceptance operates when a patient:

(a) feels a sense of belonging, warmth, friendliness and comfort in the group;

(b) feels valued by other group members;
(c) values the support that the group offers to him;
(d) feels cared for, supported, understood, and accepted by other group members;
(e) feels unconditionally accepted and supported, even when he reveals something about himself which he has previously regarded as unacceptable.

The following examples illustrate acceptance elicited with the use of the 'most important event' questionnaire.

I had been silent and tense and was suddenly asked by the group to disclose what I was feeling. I exclaimed vehemently that I was feeling angry, particularly at my mother; I burst into tears and bolted from the room. When I returned, I felt embarrassed and upset, but the group showed much concern and assured me that I was welcome back, and supported me about my feeling angry in the first place.

Paul, absent from the group for two weeks, seemed tense, and eventually brought up the possibility that he might drop out. Others commented that they would feel very unhappy to see him go. One member even got angry, calling him selfish to consider leaving, as he was needed by the group. Paul relaxed and said that, following the group's responses, he was convinced he should stay.

I was having much trouble expressing what had been bothering me. It got so bad that at one point I began to give up and to withdraw from the group. Another member then tried to describe my trouble to me. As he was correct, I felt much better, and felt from then on that I could join in the rest of the group discussion. It was very good for me to be able to feel that I was part of the group again.

The most important thing that happened was the support I received from the group when my job was in jeopardy. I received help in some way from all group members. It was an opportunity to test others' opinions of the situation, but what happens when I no longer have the group to fall back on?

Simon had looked tense and had been silent the previous few meetings. Two members complained about his non-participation. Simon reflected on this, then shakily volunteered that he had been afraid that he might have been ridiculed about his—what he felt to be—relatively insignificant problems. Consequently, he had not spoken. He had also felt, quite honestly, that no one cared for him. However, he was touched that others did care, and was glad they showed it. This event was most important for Simon, because he tends to keep himself aloof. This admission meant that he was fostering a closer, more caring, and more honest relationship with the rest of the group.

These examples allow us to see acceptance operating as a therapeutic factor in relation to specific, identifiable group events. The notion of total group cohesiveness is, by contrast, much wider and more difficult to pin down and, as we shall see, research has suffered the all too familiar problem of vagueness and inconsistency of definition. We therefore have difficulty learning much of clinical relevance from the results unless we can identify occasions on which the defined therapeutic factor of acceptance applies. Then we have a basis for progress and can look at such basic questions as whether and in what circumstances it is beneficial for group members to feel supported and accepted by their fellows and whether confrontation and challenge are safer and more effective in groups where members enjoy a sense of belonging.

When we turn to the literature on acceptance/cohesiveness, we encounter an unsatisfactory state of affairs. Although the topic has received a reasonable amount of theoretical and experimental attention, there has been insufficient effort to distinguish between condition for change and therapeutic factor. Cohesiveness especially is referred to in vague terms in both theoretical and clinical contributions, and a variety of different types of measurement are used in experimental work, with little check on whether these relate to one another. Also, most experimental studies deal with laboratory and other non-therapy groups.

We have thus found it difficult to know what to select for review, specifically in discerning work on cohesiveness that relates to acceptance. In the end, we have chosen to consider a wide range of the cohesiveness literature because of the importance clinicians attach to this condition for change and because some of the findings have a bearing on acceptance.

Theoretical aspects

As Cartwright[4] points out in his authoritative review, group cohesiveness has achieved a prominent place in theories of group dynamics. Although the concepts he discusses stem in part from systematic work on non-clinical groups—such as industrial workers, students living in college residences, the military, and subjects participating in laboratory experiments—his contribution is relevant to therapy groups too. What follows is a distillate of various theoretical notions covered by Cartwright.

Determinants and consequences of cohesiveness

His use of the definition of cohesiveness as 'the resultant of all forces acting on members to remain in the group' leads him to discuss the nature of these forces. Fundamentally, a person's attraction to a group is a function of his appraisal of the desirable and undesirable effects of membership. He cites Thibaut and Kelley,[6] who see this evaluative process in terms of the rewards and costs involved in being a member. Thus, greater attraction will be associated with the expectation of favourable outcomes. Thibaut and Kelley go further by postulating the existence of a 'comparison level': in assessing the likely outcomes of membership, the prospective member applies a standard against which to compare these outcomes. This standard is derived from past experience of groups, and amounts to an average value of all the outcomes of which he is aware.

Central to the determination of a group's attractiveness are its 'incentive properties', for example, its prestige, objectives, activities, and the characteristics of its members. Consider the last as illustrative. A widely held assumption is the close link between members' liking for one another and the attractiveness of their group. Indeed, in their review of cohesiveness, Lott and Lott,[7] are so persuaded by this incentive property that they define cohesiveness in terms of it as the 'number and strength of mutual positive attitudes among the members of the group'. Another potential incentive property posited are the group's goals. The value of these goals for a member as well as their explicitness and the probability of their attainment are regarded by some workers as crucial.

Incentive properties and the expectation of favourable outcomes both intersect with yet another factor, namely the 'motive base' of the group members. This includes their need for security, affiliation, recognition, 'or other values that can be mediated by groups'.[4] For example, it has been demonstrated experimentally by Schachter[8] that the promotion of anxiety leads to an increased inclination for affiliation. Schachter speculates that the motive underlying affiliation in this context is the need to lessen anxiety as well as the need for self-evaluation, the latter helping the individual to work out an appropriate response.

The aforementioned factors are conceptualized as *determinants* of cohesiveness. The implication follows that cohesiveness also has *consequences*. Among these are thought to be: the maintenance of membership, i.e. a negative association between group attractiveness and attrition; the power established in a group to exert influence or pressure on its membership; increased participation in the group's activities; and an enhanced sense of security consisting of such feelings as acceptance, trust, and self-esteem.

Cartwright hastens to qualify the distinction between determinants and consequences. Since a consequence of cohesiveness can in turn also act as its determinant, he argues the need for a model that encompasses the 'circular processes' involved. The aptness of such a model is readily apparent through a couple of illustrations. Firstly, a cohesive group becomes increasingly able to satisfy its members' needs; this strengthens the group's incentive value, which in turn has a positive effect on cohesiveness. And secondly, personal security in the form of heightened self-esteem—an effect of cohesiveness—may lead to greater interaction between members and thus increase their mutual attraction to one another.

It is obvious from this that cohesiveness is the chief focus of attention for Cartwright and the social psychological tradition he represents. Acceptance enters the picture only in a subsidiary role. This may be reasonable considering the contributions covered are those of investigators primarily interested in group rather than individual processes.

Cohesiveness in group therapy theory

What, then, about the theoretical ideas of group therapists? One of the first to offer a systematic account of cohesiveness in therapy groups was Jerome Frank.[9] He argues that its development is a universal tendency reflecting man's innate gregariousness. Several factors are pertinent in the establishment of cohesiveness: the extent to which the group satisfies the members' personal needs; the attractiveness of members for one another; and the appeal of the group's activities. Various social forces are salient too, including the prestige of the group and the consequent desirability of belonging to it. Frank suggests a number of ways in which cohesiveness crucially supports the therapeutic process in clinical groups. The more a person is attracted to a group, the more influenced he will be by its norms. If these norms, for example, promote the open expression of feelings and honest attempts at self-examination; if communication is encouraged, even when leading to the exchange of uncomfortable feelings, such as anger; and if group members develop mutual respect—then cohesiveness is likely to lead to positive change.

By contrast, in a group where the predominant norms are suppression of feelings and strengthening of personal defences, then cohesiveness may prove anti-therapeutic because no one will feel able to challenge these norms. A cohesive group with appropriate norms both protects and promotes self-esteem in its members, reinforces beneficial change in behaviour and attitudes, helps members resolve inter-personal difficulties which lead to conflict in the group, and facilitates constructive release of feelings.

Frank returns to the same theme in his classic work, *Persuasion and healing*,[10] when pointing out that patients in group therapy derive support from a sense of belonging to their group. This feeling slowly evolves from a growing body of shared experience. In more directive types of group treatment, the therapist may actively cultivate belongingness to enhance the value of the group for its members. Another important point made by Frank, which appears elsewhere in the literature and which seems to form part of the 'shared wisdom' about therapy groups, relates to the effect of cohesiveness on members' feelings of personal power. The group is seen as representing an extension of the individual patient. In the cohesive group a sense of shared responsibility for the group's activities and welfare evolves, which promotes each member's feeling of competence—an experience that may generalize to the patient's everyday life. This increased sense of competence, Frank comments, may account for the observation that dependence in a group is apparently not as demoralizing to patients as dependence in individual therapy.

Some theorists see the evolution of cohesiveness in the context of the development of the group. Tuckman[11] exemplifies this view. In forming a new group, patients accept the idiosyncracies of fellow members and, because they want it to continue, the group becomes an established entity and generates its own norms. Harmony is an important aspect and conflicts are avoided in order to ensure this. Cohesiveness is an expression of this harmony between members.

Tuckman's account seems to underestimate the complexities of the phenomenon and should be set against the position of psychoanalytic writers, such as Slavson[12] and Wolf and Schwartz,[13] for whom cohesiveness is anti-therapeutic and non-productive in certain circumstances. We will return to their views later, but the point here is that a substantial difference exists between the acceptance of an individual member with all his flaws within a cohesive group, and a superficial harmony in which members evade and ignore conflict. Also, cohesiveness is not merely a developmental phase of the group but remains an important component at all stages. The benefit of acceptance *per se* as a therapeutic factor can be felt both at the initial stage, when the group member feels a sense of satisfaction, even relief, that here are people who are prepared to listen to him, and also later in the group's development, when he discovers that they still value him, even though they may have discovered unpalatable things that he dislikes so much about himself.

As we noted earlier, Yalom,[5] is careful to distinguish between cohesiveness and acceptance. He regards the former as the analogue of the therapist–patient relationship in individual therapy; it is not only a condition for change but also enhances the development of other desirable group processes. He emphasizes that cohesiveness may help a patient to overcome the sense of isolation from which he suffers—to such an extent that, after a few sessions, he may feel more at home in his group than in any other situation. This sense of belonging may be so strong as to be retained and valued long after the group experience is over (a form of introjection).

Yalom draws comparisons between the phenomena of cohesiveness and 'unconditional positive regard'—one of the attitudinal qualities in the therapist (together with empathy and genuineness) regarded by Carl Rogers as paramount in individual psychotherapy.[14] Yalom cites Rogers's view that acceptance of a member by his peers, together with the feeling of being understood, probably carries more power and meaning than similar acceptance and understanding shown by the therapist. The former is comparable with the benefit children derive from acceptance by their peers. An obvious clinical implication is that people who have grown up feeling rejected by their peers can experience this valuable form of social learning in a therapy group. This can in some way compensate for the lack of acceptance in their own childhood.

Quite commonly, Yalom notes, acceptance is slow to appear in a group and may be preceded by criticism for co-members, as well as feelings of self-denigration. Obviously, there is a link between acceptance by others and self-esteem, a quality often lacking in patients entering groups. We would add that ideally there is a reciprocal process, whereby a patient's self-esteem develops through acceptance by his co-members at the same time as his liking for them evolves. When this occurs the group becomes cohesive in a genuinely therapeutic sense, laying the ground for members to participate in the work necessary for change. Yalom also echoes Jerome Frank's point[9] that the more attached a patient becomes to his group and its norms (a criterion of the cohesive group), the more he will derive self-esteem through acceptance by his fellow members. This comment reflects the close link between the condition for change—group cohesiveness—and the therapeutic factor—acceptance. As Yalom puts it, 'Cohesiveness is both a determinant and effect of inter-member acceptance . . .'.[5]

Empirical research

In looking at experimental work on cohesiveness, we reiterate that we are surveying the field in a broad sense, and then relating this to the therapeutic factor of acceptance. To begin with, we return to Bednar and Kaul.[2] Commenting wryly that there is 'little cohesion in the cohesion research', they highlight how limited has been the attempt to distinguish between therapeutic factor and condition for change. In particular, methods to measure cohesiveness are poorly established, and there is only scanty recognition that different methods of measurement of supposedly the same construct do not yield equivalent results. However, they do conclude that research data suggest cohesiveness is helpful in group treatment.

In an earlier review by Bednar and others,[15] it is similarly concluded that empirically derived evidence is supportive of this notion and tentative conclusions are drawn about the ways in which cohesiveness may be promoted in groups. Thus, the therapist plays a part in its development by reinforcing group members' statements 'containing high cohesion content'—statements that reflect in some way the sense of belonging within the group. Furthermore, Bednar *et al.* suggest that the more compatible members are in terms of interests, attitudes, and personal qualities, the more cohesive their group. They conclude that provided the therapist encourages sustained interaction and self-disclosure amongst his patients then cohesiveness is likely to evolve.

Other reviewers also draw attention to the conceptual problems in measuring cohesiveness, highlighted by Bednar and Kaul.[2] For example, Lewis and McCants[16] stress the difficulty that arises in studies where an attempt is made to count and classify the number of 'cohesive statements' made by members during the course of a group, by listening to audiotaped sessions. The point here is that the wording of such statements as 'I really like this group' or 'Can nobody in this group say anything important?' is insufficient in itself to judge whether or not they reflect cohesiveness. Also needed are knowledge of the context and manner of delivery. The first statement above could be sarcastic and insulting or it could be an attempt to divert attention from a threatening topic; the second might be the effort of a committed member to spur the group into action and may therefore reflect a high degree of cohesiveness.

A comprehensive review of the empirical work on cohesiveness in a broad sense is provided by Lott and Lott.[7] Although it covers the years 1950–62 and is therefore somewhat dated, the research results are impressively appraised and discussed.

Briefly summarizing their conclusions, we find that cohesiveness has both antecedents and consequences (an obvious parallel with Cartwright's determinants and consequences[4]). The following are *antecedents*:

(a) interaction between group members; (b) a democratic atmosphere within the group; (c) mutual acceptance (of each others' problems and characters); (d) perceived external threat to the group; and (e) compatibility between members.

They identify, more tentatively, the following *consequences* of cohesiveness:

(a) tolerance for the expression of anger within the group; (b) increased attraction between members; and (c) increased communication between members who have a particular attraction for each other.

These conclusions confirm common clinical observations about therapy groups, but since they derive from a wide range of group types, caution must be exercised about thinking in the same terms about the clinical situation.

In the following sections we cover specific aspects of the systematic research work on cohesiveness, focussing particularly on sensitivity-training and therapy groups. We deal first with the relationship between cohesiveness and outcome.

Cohesiveness and outcome

The generally accepted view of cohesiveness among clinicians is that it favourably influences outcome. (The links between acceptance and outcome are apparently ignored, certainly by investigators.) Most therapists would regard it as self-evident that a group must develop a certain amount of 'bonding' to work at all. It is important to remember, however, that some therapists point to the possible anti-therapeutic effect of cohesiveness and place less emphasis on it in the development of the group's therapeutic work. This is a reasonable position: if cohesiveness is intrinsically a condition for change, then it is potentially a condition both for therapeutic *and* anti-therapeutic change. Certainly the picture is familiar of the group which clubs together in a manner excluding the therapist, and avoids therapeutic work. Using Bion's terminology, it is entirely credible that a 'basic assumption' group may be much more overtly chummy and cohesive than a 'work group'.[17] However, most therapists would no doubt agree that a certain level of attraction within the group is necessary in order that members will attend. The question is whether cohesiveness over and above this level is helpful. Unfortunately, relevant experimental work with therapy groups yields only fragmentary evidence. We have found three studies in which cohesiveness correlates, to a varying degree, with self-ratings of improvement. There is also one study which shows cohesiveness related to poor outcome, although its experimental design and methodology are unsatisfactory.

Kapp *et al.*[18] administered a group opinion questionnaire (GOQ) to forty-seven members of a number of discussion and therapy groups. The GOQ measures self-perceived change in personality, involvement in the group, and the respondent's assessment of the level of cohesiveness in his group. Self-perceived personality change correlated significantly with both the members' sense of involvement and with their assessment of cohesiveness. The researchers' conclusion that cohesiveness might be an important factor in promoting change must be regarded with caution; the design is weak, relying as it does on a correlation between two variables rated subjectively by group members. A welcome feature of the study, however, is that participants' ratings were obtained over long periods of membership of their groups—up to two years, though there was no follow-up after the groups had ended.

Yalom and his colleages[19] carried out an exploratory study aimed at identifying predictors of improvement among group therapy patients, and included among the variables measured a cohesiveness questionnaire. They studied forty patients in five out-patient groups for a year, administering batteries of questionnaires before and during therapy, and conducting a semi-structured interview at the end of the year. Cohesiveness correlated positively with self-ratings of improvement in symptoms and in overall functioning at the end of the study period, but the correlation did not hold when interviewer ratings of outcome were included. However, the related factor of an individual's popularity in the group, which is more akin to acceptance (and was measured at the sixth and twelfth sessions), did correlate strongly with both self- and interviewer ratings on all outcome measures. There was a high rate of attrition from the groups. Of the 20 who dropped out, 11 did so before the twelfth meeting and none after the twentieth meeting. All drop-outs expressed dissatisfaction with their group. 'Completers' often showed most of their improvement late in the year. The course of these groups, then, suggests that the initial phase was unstable, and was followed by a later, relatively cohesive stage, which was more conducive to members grappling with their problems. This pattern underlines the need to conduct studies in which outcome is measured over a sufficient period, to allow for evolutionary aspects of the group.

This study was carefully executed and shows welcome features in design. Newly formed out-patient groups of similar composition and from a specified patient population were conducted by therapists of similar experience and training who were closely supervised. Experimental measures were administered before therapy began and then again during the sixth and twelfth sessions. A semi-structured interview to assess outcome was carried out after one year of treatment and independent raters observed these interviews and rated them separately. The one limitation is the lack of a follow-up assessment.

A study by Weiss,[20] reported in abstract form only, is relevant in that it sets out to demonstrate relationships between cohesiveness, outcome, and aspects of group process in 12-hour marathon groups. The author studied six such groups, composed of student volunteers. The Hill interaction matrix was administered as a measure of interpersonal style before and after the experience; the students also completed a personal orientation inventory at these times as a measure of outcome. Audiotaped segments of the group sessions were rated for interaction; the participants completed two questionnaires designed to measure cohesiveness on several occasions throughout the experience. Cohesiveness was found to develop in a linear fashion as the marathon evolved, but no clear-cut relation with interaction was observed. The two measures of cohesiveness correlated with each other, though only one of them was associated, to moderate extent, with outcome. A study of such a short-term group with student participants rather than patients is unlikely to yield useful information about outcome (in fact, most subjects made no appreciable gain) and so we regard the link found between cohesiveness and outcome as of limited significance.

The results of the fourth study to examine the association between cohesiveness and outcome challenge the view that cohesiveness is advantageous. Roether and Peters[21] studied sex-offenders who had been compulsorily assigned to a programme of group therapy. Their aim was to study cohesiveness, the expression of hostility, and the relationship of these two factors to outcome. Cohesiveness was found to be associated with poor outcome. Successful treatment was linked to the cathartic expression of hostility to figures outside the group. This result demonstrates the tantalizing nature of some group therapy research. What would seem on the face of it to be an interesting result, one challenging accepted wisdom, loses its force because of reservations about its generalizability and about the design of the study itself. Firstly, the members were a highly specific category of patient who had not sought therapy. Secondly, the sole outcome criterion was the rearrest rate within one year of the start of treatment, certainly a relevant factor but still a crude measure of change. Thirdly, the therapeutic approach was unspecified and the measures of cohesiveness and hostility rough and ready. One is left intrigued by the study, but diffident about drawing valid conclusions which relate to group therapy generally.

Cohesiveness and therapeutic factors

Assuming that cohesiveness is a condition for change, it would be valuable to understand what relationships exist between it and various therapeutic factors other than acceptance. Several studies have demonstrated an association between *self-disclosure* and cohesiveness; these are covered in Chapter 5. Danet[22] found that the use of video-tape feedback (see Chapter 2)—showing patients a tape of themselves in earlier group sessions—increased group cohesiveness. But since his sample was small and the study not well designed, it is difficult to place reliance on this finding. Moreover, the method is obviously intrusive and would be expected to affect the group process considerably; indeed, Danet comments that the presence of the video camera influenced the course of meetings.

In a study of a short-term sensitivity-training group, Snortum and Myers[23] concluded that cohesiveness increased as a function of *interaction*. Unfortunately, here again the experimental design was inadequate to provide convincing support for this finding, which in any case is at variance with the result from the marathon groups studied by Weiss.[20] Work by Smith[24] also seems to lend support for the notion that interaction and cohesiveness are associated though few details of his experiment are reported.

Cohesiveness and other aspects of group process

We have been unable to find research literature on the relationship between cohesiveness in therapy groups and other aspects of group process, though this is conceptually an important issue. One interesting study of laboratory groups is, however, worth reporting. Rich[25] devised an ingenious experiment to test the hypothesis that communication to a member who holds deviant views from the rest of the group would be less hostile and more friendly in a cohesive group compared to a less cohesive group. The study appears in abstract form only and experimental details are thus not available. It appears that Rich composed two sets of laboratory groups of normal individuals; one set designed to be highly cohesive, the other to be low in cohesiveness. An extra member was then added to each group with instructions to express deviant opinions on a specified group task. Audiotape was used to record statements whose purpose was to change the opinion of the deviant member, and to assess their emotional quality as either hostile or friendly. In fact the results did not bear out the hypothesis: the high cohesive groups disagreed with the deviant member significantly more often than the low cohesive groups. Conversely, members of the low cohesive group voiced agreement with the deviant member more often than members of the high cohesive group.

Rich's result is interesting and the type of hypothesis formulated would bear exploration in therapy groups as it has implications for the extent to which members are prepared to be open and honest with each other. Certainly the finding in this particular experiment is in line with clinical experience that it is 'safer' for patients to confront each other in a secure, cohesive group.

This section and the previous one demonstrate the paucity of research on the association between cohesiveness and other process variables. It is worth noting, too, that because existing studies are correlational in type and small-scale, we have difficulty in drawing any conclusions from them. Only in laboratory-group studies, such as Rich's,[25] do we find the experimental manipulation of variables.

The therapist's role in influencing cohesiveness

The therapist's role in promoting a cohesive climate in his group is clearly an important matter. Liberman,[26] whose therapeutic approach is basically behavioural, has devoted considerable thought to what he regards as the two central problem areas dealt with by therapy groups: the distribution of affection (what he considers as cohesiveness) and the distribution of power (which he terms dependency). The therapist who promotes more cohesiveness within his group, he argues, will generate more personal growth in its members. Thus, he sees cohesiveness as an important condition for changc. He describes a carefully designed experiment in which the therapist was trained to prompt and reinforce patients' statements which reflected cohesiveness. (A second, linked experiment using the same system to prompt and reinforce the expression of hostility, and its association with dependency, is described in Chapter 6.) Comments made by group members which reflected attraction between them were noted by the therapist. He then explicitly praised the members for making their cohesive statements (reinforcing) or encouraged them to make additional cohesive statements if the situation seemed apt (prompting). Liberman refers to his method as 'verbal operant conditioning'.

The experiment was conducted on a small scale, with only one experimental and one control group, but it succeeds in demonstrating that these therapist strategies do increase cohesiveness. Additionally, the experimental group showed greater symptomatic improvement compared to the control group, both during the course of therapy and at a six month follow-up.

In his discussion, Liberman outlines several practical principles of leadership that emerge from the experiment. In order to maximize his effectiveness, the therapist should: respond to target behaviour as soon as possible; keep intervention simple in content; address the patient directly; use reinforcement more than prompting; and avoid satiation of the group through excessive comment. Because the experiment was limited in scale we must take care not to place too much reliance on the results, but the recommendations concerning therapist behaviour make a lot of sense.

Krumboltz and Potter[27] have taken up Liberman's observations in a theoretical contribution. They link the accomplishment of goals in groups to the development of trust and cohesiveness. It is possible, they note, to observe and rate different kinds of interaction between members who trust one another compared to those who do not. They then propose a list of behaviours indicative of trust, cohesiveness, and the accomplishment of goals. Krumboltz and Potter further suggest that if these behaviours are rated by therapists, feedback will be obtained on the effectiveness of their prompting and reinforcing which might then be used to modify technique. Apparently no one has yet taken up this suggestion in an experimental study.

Therapist style In a well-conducted study with adolescents participating in 'self-awareness' groups, Hurst[28] examined the relationship between style of leadership, cohesiveness, and attitudinal change (outcome). He demonstrated that a 'caring' style of leadership was an essential component of cohesive groups: leaders who showed such a style were more likely to promote cohesiveness than those who did not; furthermore, it was necessary for both leaders (they worked in pairs) to exhibit the caring style in order to promote cohesiveness. A related finding concerned therapists' 'self-expressiveness'; those who revealed their own emotional reactions were more likely to enhance cohesiveness.

The topic of group therapist style is obviously important. There are clear conceptual and clinical links between research on the style of the group leader and work, such as that of Rogers[14] and Truax and Carkhuff,[29] on the optimal style of therapists doing individual psychotherapy.

We know that therapist style is probably of import in all forms of psychotherapy (see, for example, Lieberman, Yalom and Miles[30] and the experimental comparison of psychodynamic psychotherapy versus behaviour therapy by the Sloane team[31] in which a considerable resemblance was noted between analytically orientated therapists and behaviour therapists). But the topic has received much less attention than it warrants. Moreover, research work, such as the studies cited above, has not been applied and extended as it deserves to be.

Group organization Cohesiveness is likely to be influenced not only by therapist style but also by the way in which he organizes his group. This has been recognized at a clinical level but has received little attention from the research investigator. Dies and Hess,[32] in comparing the development of cohesiveness in marathon and conventional groups, found that it developed to a greater extent in the former. This is as one might expect, though it would have been useful to extend the scope of the study by exploring the effects of the more rapid establishment of cohesiveness in the marathon groups. Marshall and Heslin,[33] using groups assembled to co-operate on a task, studied the effects on cohesiveness of group size, density and composition (single or mixed sex). Small-sized groups were more cohesive, as were mixed-sex groups; density—the degree of crowding in the experimental room—did not exert much effect. It is impossible to apply these data directly to therapy groups, but the issues raised are worth studying in the clinical setting.

A further aspect of the therapist's organization is pre-group instruction. This is commented on in more detail in the section on guidance (see Chapter 7), where it will be seen that there are some indications that instruction prior to a group's commencement may encourage cohesiveness. This is also supported by a study on self-disclosure, dealt with in Chapter 5. Ribner[34] demonstrated that explicit pre-group instruction designed to encourage self-disclosure, also fostered cohesiveness in a one-hour laboratory group.

Compatibility and cohesiveness

The related tasks of selection and composition can be regarded as aspects of the therapist's organization of his group. In the context of cohesiveness, an issue that has proven especially attractive to the investigator is the optimal level of compatibility between members. He has opted by and large to accept the notion that the more compatible patients are with one another, the more cohesive their group will be. At first sight, it is puzzling that compatibility has been such a popular topic for study. After all it is a rather vague concept, referring as it customarily does to the capacity of two or more persons to 'get along' with one another ('mutual tolerance' is a descriptive term commonly encountered). The popularity of compatibility is also puzzling when one considers that the effects on cohesiveness of a host of other variables, such as diagnosis, age, education, sex, and values, would seem not only attractive but also potentially useful subjects for study.

Another factor which should militate against a research interest in compatibility emerges from a review by Melnick and Woods[35] of research and theory on group composition. As the authors put it: 'laboratory and clinical researchers favour heterogeneity and conflict for interpersonal learning'. The therapy group as a social microcosm and the application of dissonance theory are relevant here. We discussed the first in the previous chapter where we pointed out the increased opportunities for learning, especially at the interpersonal level, that a heterogeneous group provides. A group composed in such a way as to enhance the social microcosm obviously increases the range of interpersonal styles, attitudes, personal qualities, psychopathology, and other factors to which a member is exposed. Dissonance theory holds that 'individuals will learn new behaviour patterns when their customary ways of behaving no longer achieve their aim'. That this is likely to occur more readily in a heterogeneous group, where challenge and confrontation are acceptable norms, is self-evident.

Fundamental interpersonal relations inventory-behaviour (FIRO-B) So, why has compatibility been a research front-runner? The answer probably lies in the fact that there has been a questionnaire available to measure it that is solidly researched both in theory and methodology. Indeed, this is an excellent example of empirical research arising out of the development of an effective measuring instrument, in this case, the fundamental interpersonal relations inventory-behaviour (FIRO-B).

We commented briefly on the FIRO-B in Chapter 3 but in order to appreciate its role in studies of the association between cohesiveness and compatibility, we highlight its chief features here. William Schutz[36] postulates the existence of three basic interpersonal needs that constitute a sufficient framework of interpersonal behaviour to explain interpersonal phenomena. The first, *inclusion*, is defined as the need to establish and maintain satisfactory interaction with others, a feeling of mutual interest; this is associated with a person's need to feel significant and worthwhile. The need for *control* refers to the handling of authority, influence, and power in relationships. The third dimension is the need to establish and maintain satisfactory relations in terms of *affection*—in other words to love and be loved.

FIRO-B is a self-report questionnaire of fifty-four items arising from the above postulates and measuring how a person behaves towards others with respect to inclusion, control, and affection, and how he desires the behaviour of others along the same dimensions.[36] Let us now turn to the five studies in which FIRO-B has featured prominently in the context of group cohesiveness.

Yalom and Rand[37] were the first to examine the relationship between FIRO-B-derived compatibility and cohesiveness. Five outpatient therapy groups with broadly similar composition were studied over their first twelve sessions. A group compatibility score was obtained by administering the FIRO-B to each member prior to the first session and computing the level of agreement on the three interpersonal need areas between all possible pairs. Cohesiveness was measured multidimensionally in terms of attendance, level of premature termination, rating of satisfaction with the group (completed after each session), and a cohesiveness questionnaire (administered after the sixth and twelfth sessions). The findings are consistent: groups showing greater compatibility also showed greater cohesiveness; premature terminators were less compatible with their peers than those who did not drop out; satisfaction with the group was rated lower by patients who were incompatible with at least one of their peers.

Yalom[38] was sufficiently persuaded by these data to advance the case, though tentatively, that compatibility as measured by FIRO-B might be deployed by therapists to guide them in composing their groups effectively. Five years later, in the second edition of his book on group therapy, he appeared to have deleted this suggestion and, indeed, advised caution about the results of his own work.[5] This followed the failure by Costell and Koran[39] to replicate the findings in a study conducted along the same lines. They used eleven outpatient therapy groups, comprising a total of eighty-seven patients (as opposed to Yalom and Rand's five groups with a total of forty patients), similarly followed for an initial dozen sessions. Group compatibility was not significantly correlated with cohesiveness, measured after the twelfth meeting or with premature termination. Convinced particularly by the absence of a relationship between cohesiveness and any of the three FIRO-B sub-scales, including the one measuring inclusion, Costell and Koran concluded that compatibility is not a reliable guide in group composition.

The picture becomes even more confusing if we consider two other relevant studies in which the FIRO-B was applied. In the study by Riley,[40] compatibility and cohesiveness were positively associated; in that by Bugen,[41] only a certain type of compatibility was so related. The work by these two researchers is possibly more illuminating than the previously cited investigations in that compatibility was treated as an independent variable and groups were compared in accordance with specified FIRO-B levels. The drawback, however, was the nature of the samples—students participating in sensitivity-training programmes rather than patients in therapy groups.

Riley[40] composed three groups, two of them relatively more compatible, and one relatively less so. The groups were then studied until termination nine months later. FIRO-B and measures of cohesiveness were completed before, during, and after the programme. The two more compatible groups showed greater cohesiveness, thus supporting Yalom and Rand (Riley found no indication of associated superior change in 'self-concept' in the more compatible groups). Another interesting finding, and indicating the care required in the use of FIRO-B, was the change of scores on the instrument as the groups proceeded, especially in the level of interpersonal behaviour desired in others. This obviously casts some doubt on the stability of the construct of compatibility, at least as measured with FIRO-B. One is reminded of another factor regarded as central in patient selection—motivation. Recently, it has been well argued by Crown[42] that we need to bear in mind to what an extent motivation may be influenced by a patient's experience during therapy. Compatibility is probably subject to similar change, dependent on how a patient experiences the initial developmental phase of his group.

Bugen's study is not directly comparable with those we have already discussed on two main counts—compatibility levels were derived from the inclusion sub-scale of the FIRO-B only; and an additional independent variable was included, a set of pre-group instructions stressing group cohesiveness. Nevertheless, the work is of considerable interest and still helps to shed light on the compatibility-cohesiveness relationship.

Bugen set out with the hypothesis that both homogeneous composition, i.e. compatibility in terms of FIRO-B scores, and pre-group orientation of a specific type would contribute to the development of cohesiveness. Four pairs of groups were composed according to scores on the inclusion sub-scale: one pair of groups comprised subjects with a high need for inclusion, one pair high-moderate, one pair moderate-low, and one pair with a low need for inclusion. One group from each pair then received instructions stressing cohesiveness whereas the other served as the control. A cohesiveness questionnaire was completed by all subjects at three points during the fifteen week sensitivity-training group programme.

The findings reveal the complexity of compatibility. Although all eight groups were homogeneous, in the sense that they contained members compatible with one another, cohesiveness developed differentially according to the nature of that compatibility. Thus, the two moderate-low inclusion groups were the most cohesive whereas the extreme high and low inclusion groups were the least cohesive. The high-moderate groups were intermediate. Pre-group instruction, by contrast, exerted very little effect on the development of cohesiveness.

Bugen has difficulty explaining these results. He is probably correct in inferring that the instructional variable was not sufficiently potent but he seems at a loss to explain the superior cohesiveness of the moderate inclusion condition. He prefers to leave this as a question for future research. We may speculate in the interim that group members with little self-reported inclination to associate with others, i.e. low inclusion need, will be true to their word and not exert much effort to become involved. Conversely, those with a high need to be included will not be satisfied whatever level of cohesiveness the group attains. This latter point shows up a weakness of this and some of the other studies discussed earlier—the use of a single measure of cohesiveness only, and then obtained from a subjective source. Desirable here would be a multi-dimensional assessment of cohesiveness, including independent judges as raters.

One final study, on which we comment briefly, again demonstrates the complexities that underlie compatibility. Edwards[43] headed directly to the compatibility-outcome relationship, and found that only certain aspects of the former (as reflected in FIRO-B scores) related to outcome, and then in opposite directions. The greater the need to exert control, the worse the outcome. Conversely, the greater the need for closeness and affection, the better the outcome. In general, however, compatibility had little consequence for patients' improvement.

Considering the above studies together is an interesting exercise. Allowing for differences in experimental conditions, there is a suggestion that compatibility contributes to group cohesiveness but that cohesiveness does not affect outcome. However, when we look deeper, we note Riley's finding[40] that FIRO-B scores change as the group evolves, and the finding by Bugen[41] that groups homogeneous on the FIRO-B inclusion sub-scale differ markedly in their development of cohesiveness. The likely implication of all this is that compatibility is not a unitary factor that can be directly measured and then correlated with other group processes or with outcome. None the less, compatibility is important in group therapy since it does appear to be relevant to the group's composition.

Thus far, group therapists have been apt to rely on clinical lore in composing their groups. While this source of knowledge has proved reasonably helpful, the potential guidelines that could emerge from continuing work on compatibility and related topics would be more than welcome. The reader is recommended to the critical review by Melnick and Woods[35] for an excellent analysis of the subject.

Conclusion

The point of the wry remark made by Bednar and Kaul[2] that 'there is little cohesion in the cohesion research' should be readily apparent by now. From the contributions on cohesiveness, what can we learn about the therapeutic factor of acceptance?

The first major point is that though acceptance as we have defined it is seen by most therapists as clinically important, it has not received attention from the research fraternity. This is probably because the crucial distinction between the condition for change and the therapeutic factor is obscured by the amorphous nature of the concept of cohesiveness. As clinicians, we witness the testimony of patients in many different group settings that they benefit from the sense of being valued. The sheer experience of feeling valued and accepted probably exerts a therapeutic effect in its own right.

Nevertheless, the question persists: is acceptance a real therapeutic factor or is it mediational—a condition for change. Can the feeling of being accepted contribute to improvement or is it merely a helpful step which must be built upon through the operation of other therapeutic factors? Unfortunately, any clues to the answer remain buried in the work on cohesiveness.

We turn therefore to total group cohesiveness as a condition for change and, recalling Bednar and Kaul's stricture, ask whether the available research provides any guidelines to the practitioner. One prominent theoretical position holds that the development of cohesiveness is central since it is the analogue of the relationship in individual therapy. The argument is confused however by the vagueness of the term cohesiveness and obscures the fact that all therapists accept the obvious need for group members to stay together in order to work effectively. This in itself indicates the occurrence of some sort of cohesion. At this level cohesiveness is clearly a prerequisite for change. However, it does not follow axiomatically that such cohesiveness leads to productive therapy; a cohesive group can just as easily evade the therapeutic task.

We have drawn the reader's attention to theorists who have made these particular points, but experimental research does not offer much guidance on this point. Although laboratory work suggests that cohesive groups work more effectively, the effects of neurotic resistance in these groups is likely to be minimal, especially where the aim is the performance of a task unrelated to members' personal difficulties. In therapy groups, resistance to work is commonly encountered and may assume the form of an anti-therapeutic cohesiveness. Though discussion of this issue appears in the literature, it is little reflected in systematic research. For example, though the study by Roether and Peters[21] illustrates a situation in which cohesiveness is anti-therapeutic, the result is suspect because of poor experimental method. In addition there is no attempt to explore why the result occurred as it did with the specific sample studied.

The most thoroughly documented recommendations for therapists regarding cohesiveness stem from theoretical contributions. For instance, Yalom's view[5] that it is comparable to the patient–therapist relationship in individual therapy is well argued and constitutes an essential ingredient of his approach to group therapy. Frank's[9] guideline, that therapists of supportive groups should promote a norm of shoring up patients' defences, whereas leaders of insight-orientated groups should encourage the dismantling of such defences, is widely accepted. He sees these therapeutic tasks made possible by a cohesive group. This point links with the well-established experimental finding, namely, that the therapist's behaviour can strongly influence this condition. Liberman's[26] techniques of reinforcement and prompting are clearly of relevance and the study by Hurst[28] illustrates the influence of the therapist's style.

References

1. Corsini, R. and Rosenberg, B. Mechanisms of group psychotherapy: processes and dynamics. *Journal of Abnormal and Social Psychology* **51**, 406–11 (1955).
2. Bednar, R. L. and Kaul, T. J. Experiential group research. In: *Handbook of psychotherapy and behaviour change* (eds. S. Garfield and A. Bergin). Wiley, New York (1978).
3. Silbergeld, S., Koenig, G., Manderscheid, R., *et al.* Assessment of environment-therapy systems: the group atmosphere scale. *Journal of Consulting and Clinical Psychology* **43**, 460–9 (1975).
4. Cartwright, D. The nature of group cohesiveness. In: *Group dynamics: research and theory* (eds. D. Cartwright and A. Zander). Tavistock, London (1968).
5. Yalom, I. D. *The theory and practice of group psychotherapy.* Basic Books, New York (1975).
6. Thibaut, J. W. and Kelley, H. H. *The social psychology of groups.* Wiley, New York (1959).
7. Lott, A. J. and Lott, B. E. Group cohesiveness and inter-personal attraction. *Psychological Bulletin* **64**, 259–309 (1965).
8. Schachter, S. *The psychology of affiliation.* Stanford University Press (1959).
9. Frank, J. D. Some determinants, manifestations and effects of cohesiveness in therapy groups. *International Journal of Group Psychotherapy* **7**, 53–63 (1957).
10. Frank, J. D. *Persuasion and healing.* Johns Hopkins University Press, Baltimore (1973).
11. Tuckman, B. W. Developmental sequence in small groups. *Psychological Bulletin* **63**, 384–99 (1965).

12. Slavson, S. R. *A textbook in analytic group psychotherapy*. International Universities Press, New York (1964).
13. Wolf, A. and Schwartz, E. K. *Psychoanalysis in groups*. Grune, New York (1962).
14. Rogers, C. R. *Client-centered therapy*. Constable, London (1951).
15. Bednar, R. L., Weet, C., Evensen, P., *et al.* Empirical guide-lines for group therapy: pretraining, cohesion and modelling. *Journal of Applied Behavioural Science* **10**, 149–65 (1974).
16. Lewis, P. and McCants, J. Some current issues in group psychotherapy research. *International Journal of Group Psychotherapy* **23**, 268–78 (1973).
17. Bion, W. R. *Experiences in groups*. Tavistock, London (1959).
18. Kapp, F. T., Gleser, G., Brissenden, A., *et al.* Group participation and self-perceived personality change. *Journal of Nervous and Mental Disease* **139**, 255–65 (1964).
19. Yalom, I. D., Houts, P. S., Zimerberg, S. M., *et al.* Prediction of improvement in group therapy. *Archives of General Psychiatry* **17**, 159–68 (1967).
20. Weiss, B. J. *Dissertation Abstracts International* **32,** 6065–B (1972).
21. Roether, H. A. and Peters, J. J. Cohesiveness and hostility in group psychotherapy. *American Journal of Psychiatry* **128**, 1014–17 (1972).
22. Danet, B. N. Videotape playback as a therapeutic device in group psychotherapy. *International Journal of Group Psychotherapy* **19**, 433–40 (1969).
23. Snortum, J. R. and Myers, H. F. Intensity of T-group relations as a function of interaction. *International Journal of Group Psychotherapy* **21**, 190–201 (1971).
24. Smith, J. E. The relationship of encounter group interaction, certain process variables and cohesiveness. *Dissertation Abstracts International* **31**, 1025–A (1970).
25. Rich, A. L. An experimental study of the nature of communication to a deviate in high and low cohesive groups. *Dissertation Abstracts* **29**, 1976–A (1968).
26. Liberman, R. A behavioural approach to group dynamics: I. Reinforcement and prompting of cohesiveness in group therapy. *Behaviour Therapy* **1**, 141–75 (1970).
27. Krumboltz, J. D. and Potter, B. Behavioural techniques for developing trust, cohesiveness and goal accomplishment. *Educational Technology* **13**, 26–30 (1973).
28. Hurst, A. G. Leadership style determinants of cohesiveness in adolescent groups. *International Journal of Group Psychotherapy* **28**, 263–79 (1978).
29. Truax, C. and Carkhuff, R. Correlations between therapist and patient self-disclosure: a predictor of outcome. *Journal of Counseling Psychology* **12**, 3–9 (1965).
30. Liberman, M. A., Yalom, I. D., and Miles, M. B. *Encounter groups:*

first facts. Basic Books, New York (1975).
31. Sloane, R. B., Staples, F. R., Cristol, A. H., *et al. Psychotherapy vs. behaviour therapy*. Harvard University Press (1975).
32. Dies, R. R. and Hess, A. K. An experimental investigation of cohesiveness in marathon and conventional group psychotherapy. *Journal of Abnormal and Social Psychology* **77**, 258–62 (1971).
33. Marshall, J. E. and Heslin, R. Sexual composition and the effect of density and group size on cohesiveness. *Journal of Personality and Social Psychology* **31**, 952–61 (1975).
34. Ribner, N. J. Effects of an explicit group contract on self-disclosure and group cohesiveness. *Journal of Counseling Psychology* **21**, 116–20 (1974).
35. Melnick, J. and Woods, M. Analysis of group composition research and theory for psychotherapeutic and growth-oriented groups. *Journal of Applied Behavioural Science* **12**, 493–522 (1976).
36. Schutz, W. G. *The interpersonal underworld*. Science and Behaviour Books, Palo Alto (1958).
37. Yalom, I. D. and Rand, K. Compatibility and cohesiveness in therapy groups. *Archives of General Psychiatry* **15**, 267–75 (1966).
38. Yalom, I. D. *The theory and practice of group psychotherapy*. Basic Books, New York (1970).
39. Costell, R. M. and Koran, L. M. Compatibility and cohesiveness in group psychotherapy. *Journal of Nervous and Mental Disease* **155**, 99–104 (1972).
40. Riley, R. An investigation of the influence of group compatibility on group cohesiveness and change in self-concept in a T-group setting. *Dissertation Abstracts International* **31**, 3277–A (1971).
41. Bugen, L. A. Composition and orientation effects on group cohesion. *Psychological Reports* **40**, 175–81 (1977).
42. Crown, S. Individual long-term psychotherapy. In: *An introduction to the psychotherapies* (ed. S. Bloch). Oxford University Press, Oxford (1979).
43. Edwards, W. F. Interpersonal relations orientation compatibility as related to outcome variables in group psychotherapy. *Dissertation Abstracts* **29**, 3909–10 (1969).

5 Self-disclosure

It may be stating the obvious that in the psychotherapies—at least those of the insight-orientated type—the patient must divulge to the therapist (and to other group members if he is participating in group therapy) a minimum body of information about himself. For example, he must disclose the problems for which he seeks help. It is inconceivable that a patient could sit in the therapist's room tight-lipped about himself and yet gain from the experience.

Even in treatment typified by a highly specific procedure—systematic desensitization for a simple phobia, for instance—a detailed analysis of the phobic pattern is needed to establish proper therapeutic conditions, and this involves revelations by the patient about the circumstances of his problem.

It was Freud's[1] discovery of free association that paved the way for the universal recognition among psychotherapists that self-disclosure is fundamental. Freud referred to a specific form of self-disclosure—the patient should reveal everything and anything that came into his mind without restraint or censure. Such was the way to reach that layer of consciousness normally unknown to the patient but relevant to his understanding of what underlay his symptoms. This form of self-disclosure predominated in the experimental application of psychoanalytic principles to group therapy—free association was posited as a cardinal feature.[2] For example, Foulkes[3] developed the concept of 'free group association'. He instructed his patients to associate freely in the same way as they might in individual therapy but noted that the associations produced were altered by the group situation. Foulkes subsequently applied the term 'free floating discussion' to this particular form of free association, which for him represented the unconscious aspects of the group's functioning.

Definition

Over the past two decades, self-disclosure in group therapy has assumed a more general form, and refers to a patient's direct communication of personal material about himself to other group members. The material invariably concerns intimate aspects of himself which would not be discovered otherwise. The patient divulges information which is often about previously hidden aspects of himself, conveniently described as long-held 'secrets'. The number of secrets is infinite and the range of self-disclosure unlimited. The content will thus cover a variety of events in the individual's life, either current or in the past, as well as fantasies and dreams. Self-disclosure also includes another dimension, more contemporary in nature—the feelings, attitudes, and thoughts (conveniently grouped under the rubric of the here-and-now) that a patient reveals in relation to the group or a particular member in it.

What it is not

Before proceeding to our own definition of self-disclosure, it may be helpful to state explicitly that self-disclosure is *not* any of the following:

(1) *Participation in the group*—a member may be active, even dominate the group's work, without necessarily disclosing anything personal or private. Indeed, such a member may monopolize the group as a defence against becoming known by his peers. Thus, simple volume of verbal expression is not the equivalent of self-disclosure.

(2) *A confessional*—the religious confessional bears some resemblance to the self-disclosure of group therapy in the sense that the confessor divulges much that is deeply private and which would not be discovered save for the confession. Moreover, the act customarily brings a measure of relief and emotional comfort. But typically, the confessional involves both purgation and cleansing on the one hand and a judgemental response on the other, whether it be some form of absolution or a more adverse reaction. Psychotherapeutic self-disclosure may involve revelations about some shameful deed but it is not done for the purpose of being absolved or judged. On the contrary, judgemental reactions are universally regarded by thera-

pists as counter-therapeutic and potentially harmful.[4]

(3) *Total, wholesale personal revelation*—therapeutic self-disclosure does not infer the complete stripping of the patient's defences or privacy. The basic need for privacy and others' respect for it is not a contradiction of the value of self-disclosure. There is a widely held assumption that a patient does not have to 'bare his soul' so that he is bereft of defensive manoeuvres.

(4) *A major, dramatic, single revelation*—although a patient may make some profound revelation which he has hitherto been unable to do, such an act is rarely sufficient to bring about the resolution of problems. Customarily, self-disclosure entails a shift in attitude, which allows the patient to share much of his private self with others in a new, constructive fashion, and to generally act more openly and honestly with himself and with others.

(5) *Abreaction or catharsis*—although in many instances of self-disclosure there is a mixture of both the sharing of personal material and a discharge of intense emotion, these two aspects are distinguishable from one another and their therapeutic effects are specific. We consider the therapeutic factor of catharsis in Chapter 6 but can anticipate here by noting that catharsis involves primarily the release of strong feelings, such as despair, shame, guilt, envy, anger, and frustration, which is followed by a palpable sense of relief.

What it is

In our own classification of therapeutic factors in group therapy, we define self-disclosure as *the act of revealing personal information to the group*. We suggest that the factor operates when the patient: reveals information about his life outside the group; or his past; or his feared, embarrassing, or worrisome problems; or his fantasies, which he regards as private and personal—even though such revealing and sharing may be difficult or painful.

Examples from our work using the 'most important event' questionnaire are:

Sam revealed to the group that he had masochistic fantasies which upset him very much. Until then he had felt that he could not tell anyone about them and this included his wife. He felt he had been harbouring guilty, painful secrets. He decided that he was being less than honest with the group by avoiding these fantasies when they were indeed a pressing problem. Therefore, it was important for him that he was able to share this problem.

I was able to open up to the group for the first time about my problems in relating to men. I revealed that I characteristically run away from relationships. For the first time I felt ready to share these problems with the group and was glad that I did.

I disclosed to the group my personal problems and feelings. Before this, I had settled into the role of interested spectator-therapist to hide myself but I felt members of the group turning their attention to why I was not revealing myself. I began to talk about myself on a personal level, nervously at first. When I had finished there was a silence, which I appreciated. I felt better for having talked, but emotionally drained. I had overcome the first hurdle, which had loomed large, in my group therapy.

Peter began talking about how hard he found it to show his feelings towards people, especially affection. He often wanted to turn a friendly relationship with a woman into a more intimate one, but said that he rationalized, telling himself he might spoil the friendship if he took the risk of showing his affection. It was the first time Peter was really able to share his fears, and after that he was able to say more about his feelings in the next session.

I revealed to the group that I tend to put up a blank wall to people and will not, if I can help it, reveal much about myself. Perhaps after revealing this, I will feel more able to show my true feelings to people.

Theoretical aspects

The theoretical basis for postulating self-disclosure as a therapeutic factor in contemporary psychotherapy, individual and group, is dependent predominantly on work of the American psychologist, Sidney Jourard.[5] He began his diligent examination of self-disclosure in the mid-1950s and was obviously influenced by the then burgeoning interest in humanistic psychology and the human potential movement.[4] Jourard himself claimed to be strongly influenced by the existential-phenomenology school of psychology and he acknowledged the importance of Husserl, Heidegger, Sartre, Buber, and Laing in his thinking. He set out with the premiss that self-disclosure is a central feature of psychological health and well-being, and also serves as a means of attaining an integrated personality.

More specifically, the chief purpose of self-disclosure is that it facilitates heightened self-awareness, which in turn paves the way for authentic being. The authentic person has the capacity to make himself fully known to at least one significant person in his life. More generally he is being himself, honestly, in relation to his fellows. The adage 'Know thyself' is superseded by 'Make thyself known, and thou shalt then know thyself'.[5] By contrast, the person who hides his true self from others is alienated from himself, does not know who he is, and as a consequence, cannot allow himself to grow and develop emotionally.[6]

How much self-disclosure?

Jourard did not hold the view that self-disclosure and psychological health were directly correlated with each other. Instead, he proposed a curvilinear relationship between them. To Cozby,[7] who conducted an excellent review of Jourard's contribution and of the large volume of empirical research that accompanied it, the curvilinear relationship is most persuasive. On the one hand, a person who does not disclose at all is probably unable to form intimate relationships with others and remains socially isolated. On the other hand, the person who indiscriminantly reveals highly personal information about himself is likely to be maladjusted insomuch as he is self-absorbed to a degree which precludes sensitivity to others. A receiver of such excessive disclosure may also feel threatened if he assumes that he is expected to reciprocate. Cozby has thus advanced the following hypothesis. A person enjoying positive mental health is 'characterized by high disclosure to a few significant others and medium disclosure to others in the social environment', whereas a poorly adjusted person is 'characterized by either high or low disclosure to virtually everyone in the social environment'. Whatever the precise links between self-disclosure and mental health, the theoretical notion that self-disclosure is an inevitable forerunner of self-awareness remains of crucial importance.

Quality of self-disclosure

Jourard's theoretical work also suggests that self-disclosure is a prerequisite of intimacy between people. Relating openly to another person, or to several others as in group therapy, promotes reciprocal self-disclosure. The qualification however that the original self-disclosure is not indiscriminate or indiscreet applies. Initially, the disclosure is comparatively superficial, but once both persons have exposed themselves, a relationship is instituted and the scaffold exists for further exchanges of personal material, progressively deeper in quality. The relationship becomes reinforced and intimacy established. As Yalom[8] points out, self-disclosure is necessary for the evolution of a meaningful relationship, a relationship typified by mutual involvement, responsibility, and a sense of commitment.

In this context we need to emphasize that self-disclosure is intrinsically a social act. It needs one or more people to act as recipients. Divulging personal material into a tape recorder, for example, does not constitute self-disclosure. It could be argued that certain forms of autobiography, explicit or veiled in the form of a novel, are comparable to self-disclosure as we have defined it earlier in the chapter. A typical illustration is Phillip Roth's *Portnoy's complaint*. What is obviously distinctive about such literary revelation is the absence of a specific recipient and with it the opportunity for reciprocity and the development of an intimate relationship.

Lieberman[9] also highlights the social context as paramount. Self-disclosure involves the taking of a risk because one cannot anticipate the exact response of the recipient. What is disclosed seems less relevant than the sheer act of divulging personal information. To quote Lieberman: 'It is the sense of well-being and confidence in other human beings and the feeling of acceptance that seem to be the active ingredients in making self-disclosure an important mechanism of change.' Readily apparent here is the considerable overlap that may occur between two or more therapeutic factors. We pointed earlier to the crucial need for a recipient of the discloser's personal relevations. It is obvious that the recipient is not merely a passive receptacle; simply his listening attentively may constitute a crucial signal to the discloser that he is being accepted unconditionally, whatever the content of his revelations. Notwithstanding the overlap, we regard it as useful to tease out the effects of self-disclosure and acceptance since one or the other may predominate and they are qualitatively different in their therapeutic implications.

Empirical research

A substantial volume of research has been done on self-disclosure over the past twenty-five years, probably because it has seemed an easy factor both to define and to measure; obviously it is more accessible to the investigating observer than many other therapeutic factors. Furthermore, the development of the Jourard self-disclosure questionnaire (JSDQ) to measure the respondent's self-reported patterns of divulging personal information, appears to have influenced researchers to study self-disclosure as a therapeutic factor in itself or as a vehicle for setting other therapeutic factors into motion.[5] One might add that the advent of the JSDQ in the late 1950s and its subsequent immense popularity could also account for the relatively few theoretical advances in the field. As we have just seen, apart from Jourard's own contribution, theoretical discussion has been scanty.

The Jourard self-disclosure questionnaire (JSDQ)

Because of the widespread use of the JSDQ, we begin by describing it briefly. The respondent is instructed to indicate the extent to which he has talked about each of 60 items to his mother, father, male friend, female friend, and (if appropriate) his spouse—'that is, the extent to which you made yourself known to that person'. A zero score is given if the respondent has told the other person nothing about a particular aspect of himself; a rating of one if he has disclosed in general terms; and a rating of two if he has talked in full detail with the result that the recipient knows the discloser well in respect of the particular item and could describe him accurately. Scores are summed to yield totals for disclosure to a particular recipient, as well as an overall score.

The items cover six areas: (a) attitudes and opinions on a range of chiefly social issues, including religion, government, race, sexual morality and drinking; (b) tastes and interests concerning food, beverages, music, clothing, etc.; (c) work and/or studies, including ambitions, choice of career, and job qualifications; (d) money—salary, other income, total financial worth; (e) personality—good and bad points, sex life, capacity to be hurt deeply; and (f) body—appearance, health, sexual performance.

A number of variations of the instrument in terms of length, target persons, and instructions have been devised, with the generally unstated premiss that they reflect the same phenomenon. This assumption is probably unwarranted in view of the futile endeavour to confirm the validity of the primary questionnaire. Cozby[7] in reviewing these efforts concludes that 'there is little evidence for the predictive validity of the JSDQ. Researchers have been unable to find a relationship between the JSDQ and actual disclosure in a situation or ratings of actual disclosure made by peers. . . . It is clear that the JSDQ does not actively predict actual disclosure.' We need therefore to bear in mind this weakness of the most popular questionnaire in the empirical study of self-disclosure. We are obviously obliged to observe carefully the methodology of the particular investigation and to note its results cautiously.

Turning to the investigations themselves, for convenience we review the place of self-disclosure in group therapy by discussing:

(a) the relationship between self-disclosure and other therapeutic factors;
(b) the effect of the therapist on the patient's self-disclosure;
(c) the relationship between self-disclosure and various group processes such as the patient's need for social approval, and reciprocity;
(d) the relationship between self-disclosure and outcome.

The relationship between self-disclosure and other therapeutic factors

Self-disclosure and cohesiveness Several studies have explored the association between self-disclosure within a group and *cohesiveness* (see also Chapter 4). Query[10, 11] set out to test the linked hypotheses that (a) a group comprising high self-disclosing members would demonstrate more attraction between them than a group of low self-disclosing members, and (b) members higher on self-disclosure would be particularly attracted to one another. In a relatively well-controlled investigation, nurses met in one of six therapy groups for twenty-four sessions. They completed a specially devised questionnaire based on the Jourard scale and were then allocated on the basis of their scores to either high-, medium-, or low-disclosing groups. Participants' ratings of attraction for their group and for fellow members were obtained at the end of the programme. The first hypothesis was supported: nurses in high-disclosing groups were more attracted to their group than colleagues in medium- and low-disclosing groups. However, mutual attraction between members did not differ among the groups. Query provides a rather inadequate explanation for these discrepant findings, namely, that high self-disclosure may alienate members and a withholding member may be preferred to someone who reveals a great deal. One would assume, however, that attraction to the group and mutual liking would be closely associated. We return to the more specific question of the relationship between liking and self-disclosure later in the chapter.

Johnson and Ridener[12] obtained a similar result, although the groups they studied were of a different character, both in composition and duration. Twenty-three student volunteers were assigned to one of three groups according to their scores on a brief version of the JSDQ. Each group met on four occasions—a total of two hours only—for the purpose of discussing 'issues in higher education'. Participants completed a questionnaire mid-way and after the programme, which measured their perception of how cohesive their group had been in terms of such features as liking and co-operation between members. Repeated administration of the JSDQ during the course of the group revealed a consistency of response. As the authors had hypothesized, a significant association was found between perceived cohesiveness and self-disclosure. Like the Query study, however, there was no correlation between self-disclosure and perceived liking among group members. Again a surprise and, as Johnson and Ridener aptly point out, a contradiction of Jourard's[5] assertion that self-disclosure reflects interpersonal closeness.

One possible factor in explaining the positive relationship between self-disclosure and attraction to the group but the absence of such a link between self-disclosure and liking of group members, lies in the nature of the groups. Johnson and Ridener's groups, for example, met only very briefly, for four half-hourly sessions. Query's groups were admittedly longer, twenty-four sessions, but still considerably less than the typical long-term out-patient therapy group. Possibly there was insufficient time in both experiments for self-disclosure to leave a more personal mark; intimacy between members either did not develop or did so in embryonic form only. Obviously, the data in both studies are not sufficient to clarify this point.

Yet another study to examine links between self-disclosure and cohesiveness is by Kirshner.[13] Eight groups participated in eight sessions of encounter-type exercises 'led' by audiotape. Two experimental conditions were compared: the first was designed to promote high personal disclosure; the second to keep it at a minimum. The dependent variables were various measures of cohesiveness. As in the previous two investigations, a significant association was found between self-disclosure and all measures of cohesiveness.

In summary, three reasonably designed and executed studies all point to the same link. A group in which self-disclosure is a feature is also likely to evolve into a cohesive group. The exact nature of the relationship between the two factors does not emerge clearly but we surmise that self-disclosure is both facilitated by, and contributes to, members' attraction to their group. Since cohesiveness, in the sense implicit in the above studies, probably reflects total group cohesiveness rather than personal acceptance (see Chapter 4), we can infer that this is a case in which a therapeutic factor—self-disclosure—is inextricably bound up with a condition for change—cohesiveness. This illustrates neatly a point we made in Chapter 1—that therapeutic factors, conditions for change, and techniques are interdependent to a substantial degree.

Since none of the three studies cited involved clinical groups, the question of whether the association applies to patient samples is unsettled. However, assuming that an extrapolation can be made to the clinical setting, the implications for the group therapist are obvious. He should inculcate norms whereby cohesiveness is promoted early in the life of the group, as this is bound to increase the likelihood of the operation of several factors, including self-disclosure. Conversely, encouraging moderate self-disclosure during this phase is likely to influence the growth of cohesiveness.

Self-disclosure and other factors The relationship between self-disclosure and therapeutic factors other than cohesiveness has not been investigated empirically for reasons which are obscure. Yet it is likely that close links do exist. We mentioned at the outset of the chapter the common clinical occurrence of a patient disclosing something intimately personal and at the same time releasing intense emotion thereby bringing relief. It would be interesting to learn to what extent such linkage takes place and whether the effects are additive or otherwise. On first inspection, it would be reasonable to conjecture that there was advantage in a patient reaping the rewards of self-disclosure and gaining from associated emotional catharsis. But it also may be the case that each factor tends to blur the effects of the other so that the patient becomes bewildered by the experience he is undergoing. If Jourard's postulate—that self-disclosure is the forerunner of greater self-awareness—is correct, the concurrence of intense, emotional release might obfuscate rather than clarify. (This is not to negate the need for a modicum of emotional arousal in the learning process.) It could also be argued, conversely, that the potential benefit of catharsis—relief gained from emotional discharge—may be diminished if the associated self-disclosure predominates.

Another link, to which we have just alluded, is that between self-disclosure and insight. Jourard took pains to emphasize that self-disclosure was a *sine qua non* of self-awareness. Unfortunately, this theoretical notion has not been examined systematically. Do patients in group therapy who reveal personal information about themselves acquire more self-understanding than their non-disclosing peers? How does vicarious learning fit into the picture? Can a patient acquire insight about himself or a particular problem through close identification with the revelations of another member? We could speculate that other members' self-disclosures, if they mirror those of the vicarious learner, could enable him to achieve self-understanding without necessarily going through the process of self-disclosure himself.

There is undoubtedly an overlap between self-disclosure and universality (see Chapter 8). It is difficult to see how universality could operate effectively without group members sharing their problems and disclosing personal information about themselves. Patients obviously require such knowledge before they can come to the realization that they are not substantially different from their peers and that their problems are not unique.

Self-disclosure may have interesting relationships with other therapeutic factors too; there is ample scope for systematic research in this area.

The effect of the therapist on patients' self-disclosure

If we accept the desirability of self-disclosure by patients in group therapy, what role has the therapist in furthering the process? This is part of a broader issue concerning his general style. Should he act as a model of the behaviour he wishes to inculcate in his patients? Should he, for example, relate to them in an open, 'transparent' way in order to facilitate greater trust? Should he adopt an egalitarian model on the assumption that both therapist and patient share similar concerns, albeit to a differing degree? Alternatively, can the therapist promote forms of behaviour in his patient, including self-disclosure, by making explicit norms he regards as necessary, but without exemplifying these norms himself.

All these questions are complex and will be answered by therapists according to their theoretical school and personal temperament. The psychoanalytically orientated group therapist, for example, has traditionally retreated from the idea of self-disclosure. Instead, he adopts a relatively neutral status in order that he may serve as a screen for his patient's projections. Emphasis on transference requires that he act as an incognito, although this posture does not negate the possibility of his relating in a humane and understanding way. The psychoanalytic position has come under criticism from therapists belonging to the humanist-existential school and those influenced by the human potential movement. The work of Carl Rogers[4] is well known in this regard and his espousal of the centrality of attitudinal factors in the therapist does not need elaboration here. Suffice to say, a central plank in Rogers' thinking is that the therapist acts in a congruent fashion: he participates in a genuine encounter with his patients by being openly and freely himself. Jourard[5] is of the same opinion when he refers to the authentic therapist's spontaneity of response. Jourard's therapist acts as a model for his patients: '. . . I can come closest to eliciting and reinforcing authentic behaviour in my patient by manifesting it myself'. The therapist who relates in this way provides the patient with a model of interpersonal behaviour with which he can identify and which he can imitate.

The positions of the traditional psychoanalyst and the humanist-existentialist are at the extreme ends of a continuum of what has in recent years been termed 'transparency'. Although tempting, debate on the merits or otherwise of the 'transparent' therapist would be based on opinion only, however enlightening about the theoretical underpinnings of the two positions. The debate may also deflect us from the argument that there is no single correct therapist style to suit all patients, i.e. style needs to be modified according to individual needs. So, let us examine the effect of the therapist on self-disclosure by the patient.

The self-disclosing therapist A number of illuminating studies have been conducted on the group leader as an agent influencing self-disclosure. Subjects have included volunteer students, in-patients, and out-patients. There has also been considerable interest, applying an analogue research approach, in investigating the effect an interviewer can have on how much his interviewee discloses about himself.

Studies involving groups have shown conflicting results. For instance, Weigel and Warnath[4] looked at two groups, each comprising ten volunteer students who were offered 'the opportunity to learn more about themselves' in a programme of ten sessions. Another five students acted as controls. All subjects completed a variant of the JSDQ before commencement and immediately afterwards. One group was led by a therapist instructed to be as open and self-disclosing as possible, the other by a therapist given no special instructions of this kind; the difference was subsequently confirmed by group members' ratings. At the end of the programme, the two groups were similar in their levels of self-disclosure and no different from the control group. It is reasonable to conjecture that ten group sessions were too few to make an impact on the participants. Also possible is the need for modelled therapist behaviour to be accompanied by explicit instructions on how participants should be self-revealing. Another difficulty with this type of study involves individual differences in the therapists. Two therapists were used, one to lead each group, and although they could be differentiated in terms of self-disclosure, other personality factors no doubt exerted an influence on the students. This problem could have been diminished by using the same leader for both groups, in which case he would have acted as his own control, or by incorporating another pair of leaders, one self-disclosing, the other not. The limitations of the JSDQ also affect the findings. Direct measurement of self-disclosing behaviour in the group would have been far more preferable.

Many of these criticisms can be levelled at a similar study by Weiner and his colleagues.[15] They studied the same questions, but with clinical patients, hypothesizing that if the therapist exposed his own feelings in the context of the here-and-now, corresponding exposure by patients would occur. Two interrelated investigations were done, both using a variant of the ubiquitous JSDQ. Unlike Weigel and Warnath, however, segments of sessions were videotaped and rated for self-disclosure by therapists and patients. Overall, no significant relationship was found between therapist and patient disclosure of here-and-now feelings. Unfortunately, the shortcomings of the investigation reduce the credibility of the findings. A very small number of patients were involved only ten sessions were held, attendance was erratic, one of the groups folded after eight sessions, there were many uncontrolled variables (for example, no screening of patients), a discrepancy in self-disclosure between co-therapists was noted (which probably created some ambiguity about the value of self-disclosure), and there was a change in methodology mid-way through the experiment! Despite this catalogue of deficiencies, the authors' conclusions merit attention. They suggest that the simple absence or presence of self-disclosure in a therapist is not the critical factor. Instead, consideration should be given to the how, why, when, and where of such self-disclosure. It is indeed reasonable to assume that the mere summing of self-disclosures by the therapist and patients over a given segment of therapy may be less valuable than studying the nature and timing of self-disclosure by the therapist, and its impact on a particular patient. Of course studying such an array of questions would make research much more demanding but the findings would unquestionably be richer and more illuminating.

The 'transparent' therapist A contrast with the above two studies, both in terms of methodology and findings, is the investigation carried out by Truax and Carkhuff.[16] Much influenced by the Rogerian triad of attitudinal qualities in the therapist—warmth, empathy, and genuineness—this team regards the last as of the 'most basic significance'. Genuineness, or transparency, in the therapist serves as a model for the patient to imitate. Truax and Carkhuff aver that the patient cannot be expected to be transparent if the therapist himself is not open and real. The experimental hypothesis follows their line of thinking: the greater the transparency or congruence in the therapist, the greater the transparency (or self-exploration, to use their term) in the patient. Two scales were devised to test this hypothesis. The 'depth of intrapersonal exploration' scale is a measure of the degree of self-disclosure, self-exploration, and transparency by the patient during the course of therapy. Ratings are made on a ten-point scale: at one extreme, no personally relevant material is disclosed; at the other, the patient speaks about himself and his world, trying to discover new feelings and experiences. A parallel scale for the therapist is rated for the extent to which he is transparent and congruent in therapy sessions; at one extreme he exhibits a marked discrepancy between what he experiences and what he says, whereas at the other he is open to experience and feelings of all types without any trace of defensiveness.

Truax and Carkhuff examined the relationship between scores on these two scales in 40 psychiatric in-patients and in 40 institutionalized juvenile deliquents. All received intensive group therapy although the details of the treatment are not disclosed. A significant correlation was found between congruence in the therapist and intrapersonal exploration in the patient, thus confirming the hypothesis.

Focus on group process vs the individual patients Truax and Carkhuff obviously emphasize an attitude in the therapist and this is seen clearly in the criteria used in their rating scale—defensiveness, professionalism, openness to feelings, and so forth. A therapist, however, may possibly influence self-disclosure in his patients by adopting a certain type of group leadership. Pino and Cohen[17] conducted an investigation along these lines when they compared the effects of two types of group leadership. The first involves interventions that are chiefly about the group process; the second deals more directly with individual members. The researchers hypothesized that the leader focusing on group processes would be less effective in fostering self-disclosure than the second type of leader with his direct preoccupation with the members themselves.

Two leaders each led a couple of groups of students participating in a sensitivity-training programme, using one style of leadership with one group, and the other style with the second group. Differences in leadership pattern were confirmed *post hoc* by use of Bale's interaction process analysis, in which observers scored the therapists' activities. Ratings of students' self-references using taped segments served as an indicator of their level of self-disclosure. Interestingly, the results with both leaders contradicted the hypothesis. By way of explanation, the authors speculate that the group-process orientation was more effective because it entailed the clearer setting of group norms which enabled the subjects to know when and how much to disclose about themselves.

Self-disclosure by contract?

Of course, setting an explicit norm in order to achieve self-disclosure by patients can be specifically stressed by a group leader. It could be argued that the logical task for the therapist is to make it abundantly clear to the group what he believes it should seek to achieve. Ribner[18] has looked at this experimentally in a well-designed study of sixteen student groups. But it must be borne in mind that the investigation was analogue in nature, with the groups meeting on one occasion only. Ribner argues, in setting up his hypothesis, that a leader usually values self-disclosure by his members but rarely provides them with a series of rules, including a description of what he means by self-disclosure, at the outset. He proceeded to test the notion that an explicit contract regarding self-disclosure would enhance its occurrence. Based on responses to a modification of the JSDQ, students were selected to participate, half of them with high scores, the other half with low scores. Groups were composed in such a way as to yield eight high self-disclosure groups, eight low self-disclosure groups, and eight mixed groups. All participants were told that the purpose of the group meeting was to study how people became acquainted. Half the groups were then instructed to follow a contract—to engage in self-disclosing behaviour which was defined precisely. The other groups acted as controls. Ratings, with high inter-rater reliability, were made from audiotapes of self-disclosure during the session. Three dimensions were considered in this rating: the intimacy of topics, the frequency of self-disclosure, and the depth of self-disclosure in terms of a personal–impersonal continuum. The result was as predicted. The contract served to increase significantly the frequency and depth of self-disclosure (however, the level of intimacy of topics discussed was not affected, probably because of the small variation in the categories of topics covered) but the results were not influenced by group composition.

Ribner himself concludes that the group leader can influence his members to act in a specific way through the use of a contract. He also adds the important point that there was no evidence, at least in his study, that such a contract stifled individual initiative.

Support for Ribner's position comes from the work of Scheiderer.[19] Although his study was also confined to the rating of self-disclosure by group members during a single session, the subjects were self-referred students attending a counselling service and the session involved was the first encounter with the counsellor. They were randomly assigned to one of four conditions: control; modelling; specific instructions; and a combination of modelling and specific instructions. In the modelling condition, students saw a brief videotape of a 'patient' exhibiting 'optimal' self-disclosing behaviour. The students receiving specific instructions were told how important it was to be open and honest in describing their feelings and problems in the impending therapy. This last condition proved the most effective in fostering self-disclosure. The modelling and combined conditions were both superior to the control. There was also a trend for students receiving specific instructions to rate their session as more effective than their counterparts in the other conditions.

The interesting finding that modelling is less effective than instruction should be viewed with some caution. Although the opportunity was provided to observe self-disclosing behaviour, the tape was a brief one—nine minutes—and the viewers may have noted other aspects of the 'patient' behaviour. We should also bear in mind that this form of modelling is quite different to the situation in which the therapist, in a continuing therapeutic encounter, serves as a model for his patients to imitate.

The findings of Ribner[18] and Scheiderer[19] point to the utility of the therapist setting highly specific guidelines. The studies warrant replication with therapy groups since it is in the clinical setting that leaders appear to show reluctance to establish a contract with their patients to carry out a particular form of behaviour. A common concern among therapists is that they will act in an unduly directive or managerial manner. It should be possible however to offer unambiguous guidelines to the prospective patient constructively and without hint of authoritarianism.

Group size Ribner's attention to group composition is noteworthy and it is of interest that the different levels of self-disclosing tendency exerted no effect on the relationship between setting a contract and actual self-disclosure in the experimental sessions. Other compositional variables come to mind, including the most fundamental—group size. Does the leader have an equal effect on self-disclosure whatever the number of subjects in his group? In an analogue study, Drag[20] examined this issue. He noted the effect of the experimenter in discussion groups composed of either two, four, or eight subjects whose task was to reveal information about themselves. In groups where the experimenter himself disclosed, the effect on subjects' self-disclosure was not as marked in the eight person group as in the two or four person group, suggesting that disclosure by the experimenter was not sufficient to reduce the inhibitory effect of relatively 'large' groups.

The patients' view of the therapist Another important aspect of the association between therapist and patient self-disclosure relates to how patients view their disclosing therapist. Do they value his 'transparency'? Does it enhance therapy from their point of view? Is any particular form of therapist self-disclosure welcome? Is there an optimum timing for his self-disclosure? Robert Dies[21] has tackled this subject in an excellent series of investigations. His first step was to devise an instrument to measure attitudes of group members towards therapist self-disclosure. The 'group therapist orientation' scale, a twenty item questionnaire is the result. Illustrative items include: 'A good group therapist often expresses his feelings about group members openly and honestly'; 'The therapist should not be afraid to admit that he shares many of the conflicts that his client experiences in their lives'; 'Therapist self-disclosure is essential for optimal group development'; and 'It is at times helpful for a therapist to share his own past or current real-life problems so that group members can see that he too is human'. Data provided by Dies concerning the validity, reliability, and internal consistency of his scale bolsters confidence in its application.

With this task accomplished, Dies[22] proceeded to obtain opinions of patients receiving group treatment. Unfortunately only twenty-four patients covering ten therapists participated. The total possible sample is not mentioned but obviously there is a chance that the respondents constituted a biased group. The 'group therapist orientation' scale was completed under two sets of instructions— how would your therapist *actually* respond to the questionnaire and how would you *like* your therapist to respond to the questionnaire? The patients also rated their therapists on twenty bipolar adjectives, including likeability, helpfulness, and emotional stability. Therapists judged to be self-revealing were seen as more friendly, trusting, and intimate but also as less relaxed, strong, stable, and sensitive than their less self-disclosing counterparts. There was also an interesting finding related to the timing of self-disclosure. Patients who had been in therapy for ten or more sessions preferred their therapists to be more disclosing whereas those embarking on therapy preferred them to be less so.

The appraisal of self-revealing therapists as less stable echoes a finding by Weigel and Warnath,[14] whose subjects saw their disclosing leaders as more popular but also as less 'mentally healthy' than non-disclosing leaders. The researchers surmised that the participants had an initial image of their leaders as professional experts and that this image was then disturbed by their self-disclosing behaviour.

The opposite assessment of self-disclosing therapists was found in two analogue studies. Nilsson *et al.*[23] had 240 students view a simulated counselling session on videotape. They saw a non-disclosing counsellor, or one who shared his feelings about the client's problems, or a counsellor divulging information about his personal life with special reference to material brought up by the client. Viewers then completed a questionnaire on which they rated the counsellor's competence, trustworthiness, warmth, understanding, likeability, and emotional stability. Overall, the two disclosing counsellors were rated more favourably than the non-disclosing one—they were liked better, seen as warmer, more sensitive, more honest, and as having a better self-concept. Moreover, the discloser of personal material was rated more favourably than the counsellor who expressed feelings about the client's problems. The authors were quick to comment that theirs was an analogue study which could not answer such questions as whether a counsellor should or should not disclose, or what he should disclose, or when.

Another analogue study, by Bundza and Simonson,[24] portrayed various simulated psychotherapy sessions on paper, including a session with no therapist self-disclosure, one in which warm remarks were made, and one in which the therapist was self-revealing. The forty-five student judges involved in the study preferred the transparent therapist; he was seen as the most caring. This study is again analogue in form so that extrapolation to the clinical setting is questionable.

Timing If we return to the work of Dies,[22] we can better appreciate the complex nature of the effect of therapist self-disclosure. In the study by him described earlier, the timing of disclosure was found to be an important factor. Dies conjectures that therapist self-disclosure early on in group therapy may evoke anxiety in patients because it occurs when they particularly require support and structure. The therapist's task during this period is to set appropriate norms in order to establish that desired structure; while doing so, he probably has to transmit a sense of competence and confidence. A therapist's revelations of his own conflicts and personal experiences would clearly obtrude. With maturation of the group, however, his self-disclosure becomes more appropriate. But even at this stage, cautions Dies, disclosure should not be an end in itself but always a means to an end. We are also reminded by him of other factors involved in therapist self-disclosure, in particular characteristics of the group, such as its type, composition, and purpose; and the nature of the disclosure itself, such as here-and-now feelings or personal concerns and problems.

Content of the therapist's disclosures Having raised the question of self-disclosure as a multidimensional process, Dies, together with Cohen[25] focused on two obvious aspects—its content and related level of intimacy. Again he relied on the 'customer' although in this study volunteer students rather than patients were used. In fact 108 of them were asked to assess statements which might be made by a group therapist or encounter group leader. The sixty-five items in the questionnaire covered a wide range of potential items of self-disclosure, including comments about his professional goals, his own emotional stability, feelings of sexual attraction towards a group member, anger towards a member, past suicidal thoughts, fears that the group will fail, and past problems with his spouse. These examples reveal that the content of self-disclosure may be concerned with past and present information unconnected with the group, as well as current feelings and attitudes towards himself, his patients, or the group as a whole. Respondents were asked how helpful or harmful they found each statement, in the context of a therapy group and an encounter group. Responses were sought for three separate periods: during the first, eighth, and fifteenth sessions.

Subjects preferred a leader who shares his positive strivings, both personal and professional, and divulges normal emotional experiences, such as loneliness, anger and worries. There were reservations, however, about the therapist's confrontation—showing anger and disdain—of a member, especially early on in the group. Reservation also applied to the therapist being openly critical of the group by revealing frustration or boredom.

Dies's earlier point about the multidimensional character of self-disclosure is clearly seen in these results as well as in two other findings. The students were more positive about disclosure by encounter group leaders compared to group therapists. The temporal factor again emerged as relevant—respondents preferred therapists to reveal themselves gradually over the first eight weeks and then more so over the following seven weeks. As usual, we are stuck with interesting data but also with the qualification that the sample was a biased one—psychology students not involved in therapy and therefore replying hypothetically only. It would be a most revealing exercise to administer the same questionnaire to patients about to enter group therapy or to those who have been in therapy for some time and to consider the actual self-disclosure pattern of their therapist and how they preferred this pattern.

The research approach by Dies to the subject of therapist self-disclosure is based on a masterful appraisal of all its ramifications. His excellent review of the whole subject[26] includes a distillate of his own thinking as well as an assessment of the literature. A summary of his views warrants mention here. Firstly, the question of whether therapist self-disclosure is effective is comparable to the question of whether group therapy works—it is far too broad, almost meaningless. It can only be intelligently examined when broken down into specific parts—when, where, why, to whom. Secondly, and linked with the first point, 'sweeping generalizations regarding group leader transparency are patently inappropriate'—it must be tailored to the particular group being led. Thirdly, transparency should not be an end in itself. Self-disclosure by the therapist should only serve to promote certain group processes which in turn pave the way for patient change. Finally, self-disclosure should be seen by the therapist as only one of many potential behaviours on his part, and needs to be integrated into his overall model of group leadership.

The relationship between self-disclosure and specific group processes

As we have just seen, considerable attention has been paid to the effect of therapist self-disclosure on patient self-disclosure, to a large extent on the assumption that the latter will reciprocate. In group therapy, however, there are obviously other sources of influence on a particular member's self-disclosure—his fellow members. How therefore do forces within the group enhance or impede mutual self-disclosure?

Mutual liking and reciprocity Worthy and his colleagues[27] and Certner[28] have focused on two aspects of this topic—to what extent is self-disclosure between members influenced by reciprocity, and how is this process affected by their liking for one another? Beginning with the theories on social interaction of Homans[29] and Thibaut and Kelley,[30] who postulate that social interaction can be explained in terms of rewards for the participants, Worthy *et al.* argue as follows: the receipt of a self-disclosure is a social reward; greater rewards are associated with greater social attraction; therefore, one who provides rewards will be liked; at the same time the discloser will extend more social rewards to those he likes. So, liking and self-disclosure will be positively related.

Based on these premises, the researchers hypothesized that a person asked to disclose personal information selectively would initially reveal more to those he liked better and, after a period of mutual self-disclosure, a person would have greater liking for those from whom he had received intimate information. A second hypothesis concerned the process of reciprocity—a person would disclose intimate information to those who had given him similar information. The resultant experiment is ingenious. Students met in groups of four and were told to 'get acquainted'. Ten minutes later they rated their liking for one another. They then exchanged notes, on which they answered one of seven personal questions of varying intimacy (these questions, which covered a wide range of topics from food preferences to sex, had been rated previously for level of intimacy). Each student exchanged a note with her three co-members specifying the number of the question (hence a particular level of intimacy) the recipient should answer, and in turn answered the questions asked of her. This procedure was repeated on ten occasions with different sets of questions. Then, the quartet again rated their liking for one another. The results were as predicted—the students initially disclosed more to those to whom they felt attracted and at the end of the experiment they preferred peers from whom they had received more intimate disclosure. Also, students exchanged increasingly intimate details about themselves with other members if the latter acted similarly.

Certner[28] replicated this experiment exactly but also tested the notion that there might be a sex difference, with women revealing more than men (in view of the consistent finding that women disclose more than men.[7] No such sex differences emerged in his experiment but the basic hypotheses concerning reciprocity and the link between self-disclosure and liking were confirmed.

We face the dilemma of whether these laboratory-based findings extend to therapy groups. It would appear as if the threat involved in the small experimental group was low. A single meeting was held and no responsibilities or obligations to co-members in the future were sought; there was only a small chance of further liaison. There was probably too a sense in participants that this experiment was 'interesting'. The students were normal volunteers and we must assume that they were not psychologically vulnerable. In therapy groups, all these factors would be reversed and social exchange theories may well be less applicable. So, as Cozby[31] points out, rewards of self-disclosure are offset by its costs, especially anxiety over divulging material that one would prefer to keep private. In the above laboratory experiments, the rewards probably exceeded this source of anxiety. Yet we can assume, on the basis of clinical observation, that reciprocity does play a role in the self-disclosure process in therapy groups (unfortunately it would be difficult to replicate the experimental designs because of the marked intrusiveness of the procedure).

We would be inclined to agree with Allen[32] who draws out implications of experimental work for the group therapist. He argues that the reciprocity phenomenon suggests that a patient unable to respond to a fellow member's self-disclosure is likely to become alienated from the group. Conversely, the over-disclosing member is likely to meet the same fate, since the group may feel threatened by the intensity of his revelations and resist responding at that same level. The over-discloser may also be viewed as lacking discretion and therefore as untrustworthy.[33] Allen therefore concludes that a 'large inter-member discrepancy in self-disclosure could lead to a vicious cycle for some members' and that 'a more moderate degree of discrepancy would be ideal'. With the proper conditions, the likely pattern is that members who are able to risk self-disclosure will do so and others will then imitate them. A 'benign cycle' is set up with the level of disclosure progressively deepening. Allen aptly describes this process as 'mutuality with someone slightly in the lead'.

How does the therapist achieve this benign cycle? Allen suggests that much depends on the selection of patients: any large discrepancies in their self-disclosing tendencies should be avoided. But this is not as straightforward as it first appears. How does the therapist identify his prospective patients' propensity to reveal themselves? Clinicians know only too well that the assessment procedure is not always an accurate guide to a patient's later intra-group behaviour. A further complication is where to draw the boundary—what is a moderate self-disclosing tendency and at what levels does it become unreasonably high or low?

Self-disclosure and liking We commented earlier on the relationship between liking and self-disclosure. We can now take this further by considering some specific experimental work on the topic, while bearing in mind that the literature in general suggests that self-disclosure and liking are closely linked.

Kahn and Rudestam[34] conducted a small investigation of students participating in a ten-week encounter group. They predicted a significant correlation between liking a particular member and the level of his self-disclosure. A further hypothesis was that self-disclosure would become less important as members got to know one another. The methodology was straightforward. At the first, sixth, and tenth sessions, each student rank-ordered his peers in terms of their perceived levels of self-disclosure and his liking for them. High correlations, as predicted, were found at the beginning and middle of the programme but these diminished by the final session. We thus have confirmation of the frequent finding that a member is attracted to fellows he perceives as self-disclosers (bear in mind that there was no objective rating of self-disclosure). Kahn and Rudestam surmise that self-disclosure serves an important role in the early stages of a group but that inter-member attraction thereafter may be under the influence of other factors.

In a similar experiment, Weigel and his colleagues[35] studied a much bigger sample. Seventy-four students requesting therapy were assigned to either a sensitivity group, a therapy group, or a marathon group. Similar results were obtained as in the Kahn and Rudestam experiment with positive correlations between liking of other members and their perceived level of self-disclosure. Additional data included a positive correlation between perceived mental health of fellow members and their self-disclosure. The students also rated therapists for self-disclosure and mental health and here a negative correlation was found (cf. ref. 14).

What are the implications of these findings for group therapy?

Self-disclosure appears to be a desirable characteristic and is more pertinent early on in the group's development, although most researchers caution against extreme self-disclosure lest it is perceived as a threat by group members. We have also noted the widely held view that early self-disclosure by the therapist carries the risk that he will be regarded as 'unfit' to lead the group competently. Conversely, once the group has established a sense of maturity, therapist self-disclosure appears to be advantageous.

Self-disclosure and the need for social approval The final variable for consideration and which probably has a bearing on a patient's self-disclosure is his need for social approval. Patients entering therapy commonly lack self-esteem and hanker for the group's positive approval. Whether this will take place rests to a degree on how much they reveal of themselves to their peers. To our knowledge, only one study is available which examines this issue.

Anchor and his colleagues[36] dealt with the relationship between a patient's need for social approval, as measured on the Marlowe–Crowne social desirability scale, and the level of his self-disclosure. A sample of psychiatric in-patients met for a single videotaped discussion in one of four groups. The number of personal statements made by each participant was measured as an indicator of self-disclosure. As the researchers predicted, a curvilinear relationship emerged, with greater self-disclosure in patients who had an intermediate score on social desirability. Anchor *et al.* suggested that those with a high need for social approval might regard self-disclosure as a threat to potential acceptance by the group and thus become defensive. Their discussion is confined to the high scorers and no explanation is offered for the low self-disclosure of low social desirability scorers.

They float the interesting idea of using the Marlow–Crowne instrument as a screening device in selection for certain forms of group therapy. Identification of patients with a pronounced need for social approval would then allow 'special steps' to be taken, such as desensitization to therapy, relaxation training, or highly structured treatment, presumably as a prelude to subsequent insight-orientated group therapy. The recommendation deserves attention but requires a much more sturdy empirical foundation; the study reported on a small sample, consisting of male in-patients only, and was analogue in type. There is obviously a need for its replication with group therapy patients over an extended period. In the interim, clinical observation suggests it is conceivable that patients who crave approval become progressively more able to reveal themselves as group cohesiveness evolves; as they do, they probably experience a diminished need for that approval. In any event, the Marlowe–Crowne scale could be used as an aid for the therapist, rather than as a screening procedure, in order that he may be alert to the special needs of the high scorer.

Self-disclosure and outcome

Finally, in this section on empirical research, we turn to what is obviously a key issue: the relationship between patients' self-disclosure and outcome. Alas, the effort here seems inversely proportional to the importance of the topic and the literature is sparse. We have been able to track down only a handful of studies, with such special clinical samples as to allow only the most limited extrapolation to the field of group therapy generally.

Before considering these studies we need to remind ourselves of a theoretical issue mentioned earlier in the chapter. If Jourard's dictum that 'make thyself known, and thou shall then know thyself' is valid, and greater overall self-awareness together with insight about one's problems is a suitable goal for group therapy, then self-disclosure should be conducive to the therapeutic process and thus contribute to change. Allen[32] widens the perspective here when he holds that self-disclosure plays a significant role in group therapy in three interrelated ways—as a presenting problem (inability to be open about oneself), as a means of improving interpersonal adjustment, and as a goal of treatment.

Does empirical work, though slender in amount, buttress theory? When assessing the effect of therapist self-disclosure on patient self-disclosure, we considered the useful contribution of Truax and Carkhuff.[16] In their investigation they also put forward the hypothesis that the greater the degree of self-exploration by the patient, the greater the degree of 'constructive personality change'. Using their own 'depth of intrapersonal exploration' scale as a measure of self-disclosure, self-exploration, and transparency (rated by judges from audiotaped segments of treatment), the authors examined the relationship between scores on this scale and clinical change, based on a measure of adjustment completed by patients and by 'experienced counsellors and clinicians'.

One sample consisted of forty hospitalized psychiatric patients, the other of forty institutionalized juvenile delinquents. Both participated in a group therapy programme, described only as 'intensive'. The results for each sample differed. In the case of the psychiatric patients, self-disclosure was correlated positively with personality change, whereas in the delinquent group, the *less* the self-disclosure, the greater was the improvement. This contradictory set of findings show only too clearly the complexity of self-disclosure. To reiterate a point made earlier—it cannot be conceptualized as unitary, and circumstances, such as by whom, to whom, and where, are undoubtedly salient.

Truax and Carkhuff feel that their 'surprising and puzzling finding' needs further exploration. In the interim, they differentiate between the psychiatric patient, who perhaps is lacking in *self-understanding* and presumably, according to Jourard's theory, gains by self-disclosure, and the delinquent, whose central problem is that he has little understanding of the social world that surrounds him. Still, this differentiation does little to explain the negative association between self-disclosure and change in the latter group.

The crucial importance of specifying the nature of a clinical sample and also the outcome measure used is seen in the study by Strassberg and his colleagues.[37] Eighteen male patients, most of them chronic schizophrenics with an average period of ten years in hospital, were assigned to one of three therapy groups which met thrice weekly for ten weeks. From audiotapes of sessions, each patient was rated for the number of personal self-disclosure statements made. Outcome was evaluated on several dimensions—self-report (symptom check-list, self-concept, and the MMPI), behaviour (mainly hospital adjustment), and intellectual ability.

On most outcome measures, patients who disclosed less about themselves during the group benefited more from treatment than those who revealed a greater amount of personal information. Interestingly, the opposite relationship was found in the case of six indices of outcome based on behavioural ratings made by ward staff. Strassberg *et al.* surmise that high disclosers do less well because they might be more prepared to admit to personal problems in their post-therapy self-reports. In other words, the thirty sessions enabled those who were more self-disclosing to face the reality about themselves. Alternatively, they suggest that disclosure may have been made in a socially inappropriate way and thus evoked critical feedback. Moreover, the discloser may have misconstrued potentially helpful feedback as criticism. This point reinforces the theme permeating this chapter, namely, that self-disclosure is a process which always takes place in a social context and therefore has social consequences. In this context, could it be, as Strassberg *et al.* speculate, that the positive relationship between self-disclosure and ratings of ward behaviour made by the staff reflects their preference for compliant behaviour? In other words, do staff, regarding self-disclosure as desirable, give approving recognition to those engaging in it?

The only other study of the effects of self-disclosure on outcome we have come across involves, yet again, a very distinct sample—volunteer students in encounter groups. In the Stanford encounter group study,[38] students participated in one of seventeen encounter groups representing various schools and were followed up six months later. They were assessed comprehensively and assigned, for the purpose of examining the effects of various therapeutic factors, to one of three groups—learners, unchanged, and negative outcome.

Self-disclosure was examined chiefly through the most important event questionnaire, which students completed at the end of each group session. The questionnaire asked them to write a report on what event had proved the most important for them personally. Raters subsequently coded each report according to a classification of therapeutic factors, including self-disclosure. Self-disclosure in turn was categorized with regard to its consequences, positive or negative, and whether it had led to personal insight. Amounts of self-disclosure in early and later sessions were compared. The total amount of self-disclosure reported in the 'events' did not differ between the three groups, but learners reported significantly more events leading to insight, compared to those who were unchanged or had negative outcomes. A self-rating by the students of the level of self-disclosure made echoed this difference. The importance of timing is apparent from the finding that the three outcome groups reported similar levels of self-disclosure for early sessions; but for later sessions, learners reported a greater level than their non-learning counterparts.

These results lead the researchers to conclude that, firstly, 'self-disclosure plays an important role in learning if, and only if, certain other conditions are present. Self-disclosure *alone* [their italics] does not appear to be a mechanism that is associated with differences in the amount of learning.' The discloser must be able to apply self-disclosure for cognitive understanding to occur. Secondly, the timing of beneficial self-disclosure in later sessions points to the context in which it is made. The responses to the discloser must demonstrate support and understanding.

Whatever the explanations for these assorted findings, we are left with a number of questions which only an extended series of empirical studies will clarify. The attempt to answer the global question of whether self-disclosure by a patient contributes to his improvement is, as we pointed out earlier, rather futile. Instead, the question must be broken down into its component parts: what sort of patient with what type of problems benefits in what sort of way from what form of self-disclosure, to whom; and in what form of group therapy? We can illustrate this through brief mention of another study done by the Strassberg group,[39] even though it was done on patients in short-term individual therapy. Clients were seen by trainee therapists for an average of eleven sessions. Taped segments of the second session were rated by an independent judge for the client's level of intimacy of self-disclosure. At termination therapists rated their client's inclination to divulge personal material and, in collaboration with their supervisors, assessed outcome. No significant relationship was found between outcome and self-disclosure as rated by the independent judge. However, when therapists' ratings of their clients' self-disclosure was the measure used, there was greater improvement among high disclosers. Here, two measures of self-disclosure were used, different in source and method, and both different from the measure used by Strassberg in his earlier study.[37] If we compare the two studies further, we note several gross differences: the clinical samples (mildly disturbed vs. chronic schizophrenic); mixed sex vs. male only; the nature of the therapy (group vs. individual); duration of therapy (thirty group sessions vs. an average of eleven individual sessions); the setting (hospital vs. outpatient clinic); and timing of rating of intra-therapy self-disclosure (second individual therapy session only vs. every fifth group session). Indubitably, other differences in subjects and method exist between the two studies but the examples cited serve to demonstrate that detailed and precise specification is crucial in grappling with the issue of the association between self-disclosure and outcome.

The paucity of studies probably testifies to the exceedingly tough demands the question throws up, and yet little progress will be achieved until we recognize the multidimensional and complex nature of the question and conduct studies with the requisite rigour.

References

1. Freud, S. *Introductory lectures on psychoanalysis* (Standard edition) Vol. 15. Hogarth, London (1961).
2. Schilder, P. Results and problems of group psychotherapy in severe neuroses. In: *Group psychotherapy and group function* (eds. M. Rosenbaum and M. Berger). Basic Books, New York (1975).
3. Foulkes, S. H. *Therapeutic group analysis*. Allen and Unwin, London (1964).
4. Rogers, C. R. *On becoming a person*. Houghton Mifflin, Boston (1961).
5. Jourard, S. *The transparent self*. Van Nostrand, New York (1971).
6. See: Doster, J. A. and Nesbitt, J. G. Psychotherapy and self-disclosure. In: *Self-disclosure* (ed. G. Chelune). Jossey-Bass, San Francisco (1979). (A useful description of the place of self-disclosure in humanist-existential thinking.)
7. Cozby, P. C. Self-disclosure: a literature review. *Psychological Bulletin* **79**, 73–91 (1973).
8. Yalom, I. D. *The theory and practice of group psychotherapy*. Basic Books, New York (1975).
9. Lieberman, M. A. Group methods. In: *Helping people change* (eds. F. H. Kanfer and A. P. Goldstein). Pergamon, New York (1981).
10. Query, W. T. Self-disclosure as a variable in group psychotherapy. *International Journal of Group Psychotherapy* **14**, 107–15 (1964).
11. Query, W. T. An experimental investigation of self-disclosure and its effect upon some properties of psychotherapeutic groups. *Dissertation Abstracts International* **31**, 2263 (1970).
12. Johnson, D. and Ridener, L. Self-disclosure, participation, and perceived cohesiveness in small group interaction. *Psychological Reports* **35**, 361–3 (1974).
13. Kirshner, B. The effect of experimental manipulation of self-disclosure on group cohesiveness. *Dissertation Abstracts International* **37**, 3081–2 (1976).
14. Weigel, R. G. and Warnath, G. F. The effects of group therapy on reported self-disclosure. *International Journal of Group Psychotherapy* **18**, 31–41 (1968).
15. Weiner, M. S., Rosson, B., and Cody, B. S. Studies of therapeutic and patient affective self-disclosure. In: *Group psychotherapy from the southwest* (ed. M. Rosenbaum). Gordon and Breach, New York (1974).
16. Truax, C. and Carkhuff, R. Correlations between therapist and patient

self-disclosure: a predictor of outcome. *Journal of Counseling Psychology* **12**, 3–9 (1965).

17. Pino, C. J. and Cohen, H. Trainer style and trainee self-disclosure. *International Journal of Group Psychotherapy* **21**, 202–13 (1971).
18. Ribner, N. J. Effects of an explicit group contract on self-disclosure and group cohesiveness. *Journal of Counseling Psychology* **21**, 116–20 (1974).
19. Scheiderer, E. G. Effects of instructions and modeling in producing self-disclosure in the initial clinical interview. *Journal of Consulting and Clinical Psychology* **45**, 378–84 (1977).
20. Drag, R. M. Experimenter behaviour and group size as variables influencing self-disclosure. *Dissertation Abstracts* **30**, 2416 (1969).
21. Dies, R. R. Group therapist self-disclosure: development and validation of a scale. *Journal of Consulting and Clinical Psychology* **41**, 57–103 (1973).
22. Dies, R. R. Group therapist self-disclosure: an evaluation by clients. *Journal of Counseling Psychology* **20**, 344–8 (1973).
23. Nilsson, D. E., Strassberg, D. S., and Bannon, J. Perceptions of counselor self-disclosure: an analogue study. *Journal of Counseling Psychology* **26**, 399–404 (1979).
24. Bundza, K. A. and Simonson, N. R. Therapist self-disclosure: its effect on impressions of therapist and willingness to disclose. *Psychotherapy: Theory, Research and Practice* **10**, 215–17 (1973).
25. Dies, R. R. and Cohen, L. Content considerations in group therapist self-disclosure. *International Journal of Group Psychotherapy* **26**, 71–88 (1976).
26. Dies, R. R. Group therapist transparency: a critique of theory and research. *International Journal of Group Psychotherapy* **27**, 177–200 (1977).
27. Worthy, M., Gary, A., and Kahn, G. Self-disclosure as an exchange process. *Journal of Personality and Social Psychology* **13**, 59–63 (1969).
28. Certner, B. C. Exchange of self-disclosures in same-sexed groups of strangers. *Journal of Consulting and Clinical Psychology* **40**, 292–7 (1973).
29. Homans, G. C. *Social behaviour: its elementary forms*. Harcourt–Brace, New York (1961).
30. Thibaut, J. W. and Kelley, H. H. *The social psychology of groups*. Wiley, New York (1959).
31. Cozby, P. C. Self-disclosure, reciprocity and liking. *Sociometry* **35**, 151–60 (1972).
32. Allen, J. G. Implications of research in self-disclosure for group psychotherapy. *International Journal of Group Psychotherapy* **24**, 306–21 (1974).
33. See Levin and Gergen in reference, 7, p. 81.
34. Kahn, M. H. and Rudestam, K. E. The relationship between liking and perceived self-disclosure in small groups. *Journal of Psychology* **78**, 81–5 (1971).

35. Weigel, R. G., Dinges, N., Dyer, R., *et al.* Perceived self-disclosure, mental health, and who is liked in group treatment. *Journal of Counseling Psychology* **19**, 47–52 (1972).
36. Anchor, K. N., Vojtisek, J. E., and Berger, S. E. Social desirability as the predictor of self-disclosure in groups. *Psychotherapy: Theory, Research and Practice* **9**, 260–4 (1972).
37. Strassberg, D. S., Roback, H. B., Anchor, K. N., *et al.* Self-disclosure in group therapy with schizophrenics. *Archives of General Psychiatry* **32**, 1259–61 (1975).
38. Lieberman, M. A., Yalom, I. D., and Miles, M. B. *Encounter groups: first facts.* Basic Books, New York (1973).
39. Strassberg, D. S., Anchor, K. N., Gabel, H., *et al.* Client self-disclosure in short-term psychotherapy. *Psychotherapy: Theory, Research and Practice* **15**, 153–7 (1978).

6 Catharsis

Historical perspective

The arousal and discharge of intense emotions for therapeutic purposes has long been recognized. The phenomenon of catharsis, introduced into the clinical arena by Breuer and Freud[1] at the end of the last century, can be traced back to ancient Greece. An Aristotelian concept, catharsis referred then to the purifying and relieving of emotions by art, and was applied initially to the effects of tragic drama.

Breuer and Freud, in their classical investigation of hysteria, incorporated the arousal and release of strong emotions in their psychotherapy and were the first to reuse the term catharsis; they meant by it: '. . . bringing clearly to light the memory of the event by which [each individual hysterical symptom] was provoked and in arousing its accompanying effect'. The patient was required to describe the event in all the vivid detail she could muster and to put the associated affect into words. Language was a substitute for action and through it the affect could be equally well 'abreacted'. These two aspects were entirely interdependent: 'recollection without affect almost invariably produces no result'. The affect covered a wide range of feelings including anger, guilt, fear, and sexual passion.

Since those pioneering efforts, catharsis (abreaction, ventilation of feelings, emotional arousal, emotional expressivity are commonplace synonyms) has retained its place in the therapist's lexicon, including that of the group therapist. It figured prominently, for example, during the Second World War, when abreaction techniques were widely applied to deal with conversion symptoms. The soldier was encouraged to re-experience the frightening battle circumstances under which his neurosis had developed and to ventilate the associated feelings of fear or panic.[2]

Emphasis on catharsis has diminished, however. Nowadays, many schools of group therapy still invoke the value of catharsis but mostly as subsidiary to other therapeutic factors of a more cognitive nature. Slavson,[3] for example, claims that in his psychoanalytic approach, catharsis in itself is of limited value. He places its application in terms of the transference. If one assumes, as Slavson does, that the therapist is the symbolic centre of all therapeutic processes, then every cathartic event in the group can be regarded as relating to him. The value of catharsis therefore lies in the insight that follows it, especially concerning aspects of the transference involved. In Slavson's view, the therapist's function in linking catharsis with insight is central, whereas the catharsis itself is secondary.

Theorists holding other positions also bridge catharsis and insight. Yalom,[4] for instance, suggests that in the interpersonalist framework, it is crucial that open emotional expression becomes a group norm. If not, therapy becomes an academic affair. On the other hand catharsis must be complemented by other therapeutic factors, and the patient experiencing the arousal and release of intense feeling must make sense of that experience in order to profit.

There are exceptions to this trend of regarding catharsis as secondary to cognitive factors. Notable among them are Janov's primal scream therapy[5] and Gestalt therapy.[6] In the latter, the expression of intense emotions—sadness, affection, anger—both in words and in action is strongly encouraged. The direct experiencing of one's immediate feelings is viewed as a cardinal therapeutic mechanism. These forms of catharsis have something of a ritualistic quality and may paradoxically contradict the very process they purport to represent by robbing the emotional experience of its spontaneity. On the other hand ritualized hostility has been intentionally applied to train patients in using aggression more constructively. Bach[7] describes such a programme. A group made up of several couples meet weekly and are trained to 'fight', with the goal of learning how to manage aggression and conflict more effectively. 'Rage release rituals . . . to discharge and control hate and anger' have the effect, according to Bach, of clearing the decks for a more rational approach to the couple's relationship. Ingenious and inventive, but the follow-up study Bach conducted to test the effects of 'constructive aggression' is woefully inadequate.

Catharsis as a therapeutic factor

From the brief account thus far, it may be noted that the concept of catharsis can cover more than a single process: emotional arousal; the ventilation of feelings; directly experiencing one's immediate feelings; and the expression simultaneously of previously repressed memories and associated affect. Looking at the efforts to define catharsis as a therapeutic factor would therefore be instructive.

The ninth factor in the classification by Corsini and Rosenberg[8] is labelled 'ventilation' and defined as '. . . the release of feelings and expression of ideas usually repressed in other non-therapeutic situations'.Terms and phrases gleaned by the authors from their survey of the group therapy literature include: catharsis, abreaction, ventilation of hostility, emotional release, release of hostility in a socially acceptable way, relief of guilt through confession, ventilation of guilt, ventilation of anxiety, release of emotional tension, release of unconscious material, and verbalization of fantasy.

The most noteworthy aspect of the definition is the way it combines two processes: the 'release of feelings' (hostility, guilt, anxiety, and tension) and the 'expression of ideas' (the release of unconscious material). This seems to us an unfortunate coupling. The two processes involved are dissimilar, on both theoretical and clinical grounds. This is not to negate their possible concurrence and interrelationship. True, a patient may, for instance, release intense anger in reminiscing about his childhood and also describe at the same time how emotionally impoverished was the family atmosphere. He may go even further and through free association begin to discover the origins of his strong feelings. But, emotional ventilation and disclosure of personal information will have different therapeutic effects. Verbal and perhaps behavioural (including bodily movement, shouting, or crying) discharge of anger brings in its wake a sense of relief. Phrases like 'blowing off steam', 'getting it off my chest', and 'unbottling myself' reflect the resultant feeling of ease and comfort. But recollection of an early memory, in the above context, is potentially therapeutic for different reasons: it may constitute self-disclosure (see Chapter 5) of private, personal information previously kept secret; it may be echoed by one or more co-members, in which case the therapeutic factor of universality (see Chapter 8) applies, allowing the patient to realize that he is not alone in his experience of early emotional deprivation; and it may lead to insight (see Chapter 2) inasmuch as the patient learns that his strong feelings of resentment are linked to a grievance about the way he was reared. The third component—discovering the origins of his strong feelings, much or all of it hitherto repressed in the unconscious—harks back to a part of Freud's original thinking in *Studies on hysteria*[1] but subsequently divorced from the concept of catharsis and elaborated as free association and making the unconscious conscious.

A similar double-barrelled definition of catharsis is evident in Yalom's[4] work. His questionnaire on therapeutic factors (see Chapter 1) contains a category labelled catharsis, which is composed of five items: getting things off one's chest; expressing negative or positive feelings towards a co-member; expressing such feelings towards the therapist; learning how to express feelings; and being able to say what is bothering oneself instead of holding it in. We note the inclusion under the same rubric the discharge of feelings and disclosure of personal material previously kept to the self. 'Getting things off one's chest' is ambiguous and could entail emotional release or self-disclosure. To complicate matters, we are introduced to two other ingredients. The first concerns *how* to express feelings (reflected in 'being able to say . . .'), i.e. developing a particular skill. Yalom intimates briefly that we are here concerned with the attainment of a skill for future use, akin to the ethos of social skills training. The second additional ingredient relates to the here-and-now expression of feelings towards peers or therapists. Presumably, Yalom regards it as therapeutically beneficial for the patient to express such emotions as anger and affection in the group, when appropriate. This is quite different to the expression of similar emotions relating to key figures in the patient's life, past or current.

In our own efforts at classification[9] we have included a separate category to take care of the 'expression of ideas' and 'being able to reveal what is bothersome', namely self-disclosure. This factor is not included as a separate entity by either Corsini and Rosenberg or Yalom. We also regard the skill of being emotionally expressive as conceptually belonging to another therapeutic factor, namely, learning from interpersonal action. As we saw in Chapter 3, this covers the patient's attempts 'to relate constructively and adaptively within the group', and includes by implication, the expression of affection, anger, or other feelings to co-members.

A definition of catharsis

How do we then define catharsis? As *emotional release*, i.e. ventilation of feelings (either positive or negative and about either life events or other group members), which brings some measure of *relief*. The factor operates when a patient releases feelings, leading to relief, within the group, either of past or here-and-now material. These feelings include anger, affection, sorrow, and grief which have been previously difficult or impossible to discharge.

The specification in our definition of other group members covers situations similar to those mentioned above concerning interaction, but the emphasis is on release of emotions bringing relief. A clinical illustration will help to clarify the difference:

> Albert, tense throughout the meeting, was prodded by the co-therapists to talk about what was bothering him. He burst out in anger that he did not feel they were being supportive or helpful to anybody, particularly not to David, who had just had a fight with his wife and was asking for advice. After a while he calmed down. Albert had felt all 'bottled up' for quite a while and felt much better after 'letting off steam'.

Other examples of catharsis obtained by our use of the 'most important event' questionnaire are:

> I told the group about my early childhood and how sad a time it had been for me. This made me tearful and I cried for quite a while. Afterwards I felt relieved to have gotten some of the sadness out of me.

> Hilda broke down and cried at the end of the meeting, expressing anger against the therapists for not being directive and supportive. This enabled her to talk in the following session about her intense need for a wise, adult person on whom she could be dependent.

> Jock was overtly provocative to several group members, principally Pam, whom he 'baited' for most of the session. Eventually it became obvious to the rest of the group, and led to a discussion where he expressed impatience and frustration with the group. This was the first time that negative feelings had been aired so directly. It was important for Jock to express them to relieve his own tension and it opened up possibilities for both he and the

group to respond with aggression, which all felt was present and in need of release.

Andrew told us about a row at work. He had been bottling up his feelings about this and had become depressed and almost suicidal at home. He described this in vivid detail in the group. He commented that he felt much better because he had been able to share his feelings of resentment and depression and this was a great relief.

Empirical research

Expression of anger

Whatever limits are drawn around the concept of catharsis, the attention devoted to it by researchers has been paltry. Two investigators have looked at the expression of anger in therapy groups. The first, Haer,[10] noted its effect on the frequency and style of the group's aggressive responses; and the second, Liberman,[11] tested the hypothesis that group members would resolve their problems with authority and develop greater independence by expressing their feelings of hostility and disappointment towards the therapist.

In Haer's study,[10] he led two small psychoanalytic groups for twenty sessions, during which he encouraged the ventilation of feelings. Taped sessions were then coded for the occurrence of expression of anger by the patients and for the frequency of aggressive responses by co-members in the half-hour preceding and half-hour succeeding episodes of 'cathartic anger'. Aggressive responses declined following the anger, evidently supporting its beneficial cathartic effects. Whilst not indicating that catharsis (of anger) is therapeutic, Haer's study does at least show that emotional discharge can influence patterns of interaction. The findings are limited, however, by the small sample and by Haer's participation as both therapist and researcher.

Liberman,[11] in a better executed study, though still of a small sample, focused on the therapist's role in promoting expression of anger by his patients. His chief hypothesis—that patients would benefit clinically by overtly expressing anger towards the therapist for failing to gratify their wishes for dependency—was based on the following assumptions: (1) the therapist as the central and most valued figure in the group can effectively prompt and reinforce patients' behaviour of a particular kind (see Chapter 4 for a similar experiment based on this assumption regarding cohesiveness); (2) the therapist helps patients to resolve their problems with dependency by accepting and encouraging hostility and disappointment directed towards himself and by deflecting on to himself undue hostility between members; (3) a therapist who systematically prompts and reinforces patients' behaviour in this way induces more effective behavioural and personal change than a therapist using an intuitive, less planned approach.

Two matched groups of out-patients were formed which met weekly for nine months. The two therapists involved were matched for group therapy experience and on a personality inventory. One was trained to use methods to increase the expression of hostility and disappointment (about his non-directive role) directed towards himself—chiefly through verbal prompting and reinforcement. Expression included annoyance, irritation, frustration, anger, and sarcasm. The experimental therapist also redirected towards himself potentially destructive hostility manifested between members. The control therapist, by contrast, led his group intuitively, using an analytic approach. With the aid of tapes and non-participant observers, the therapists' interventions were coded as reinforcement and/or prompt and the patients' expressions of hostility to the therapist were rated. As thought, therapist prompting and reinforcement effectively promoted the expression of hostility, both in timing and amount. However, catharsis of this kind was not related to outcome, as measured by a range of behavioural and personality measures, including the obvious dimensions of dominance—submissiveness and independence–dependence.

Like Haer, Liberman has demonstrated that the therapist plays a prominent role in promoting specific patterns of emotional expression. The question, to what end, remains something of a puzzle. There was no therapeutic impact in Liberman's study and one does question the notion that prompting and reinforcing hostility as he engineered it could be expected to lead to a decrease in patients' dependency and submissiveness. In our view the process is too mechanistic. We conjecture that what is missing in the therapy is the opportunity for the patients to gain insight into their intra-group behaviour and to note the links between their 'transference' to the therapist and their capacity for independence. Despite these comments, we should note the care with which the experiment was conceived and carried out. It certainly shows that catharsis can be systematically studied, affording potential guidelines for the clinician.

Emotionality and duration of the therapy session

An alternative way to promote emotional expressiveness in groups, apart from specific interventions by the therapist, is to modify the format of the group itself. An obvious example in this context is the marathon group. The customary ninety minute session is extended into one lasting several hours, even an entire weekend. George Bach, F. Stoller, and others[12] devised the concept originally on the assumption that the conditions involved, e.g. members being together for long stretches, eating together, and becoming less inhibited because of fatigue, would lead to a more intense emotional experience.

This notion was examined by Myerhoff and colleagues[12] in their comparison of emotionality in marathon and traditional therapy groups. Psychiatric in-patients were assigned either to a group which met for three two-hourly sessions a week over three weeks, or for three six-hourly sessions over three days. Both groups thus received the same time in therapy. They were also led by the same therapist who, it was demonstrated with the aid of observers, acted consistently throughout his leadership. An adjective check-list designed to measure emotional responses was administered to patients after each two-hourly interval of treatment. Emotionality, the dependent variable, was defined as the sum of adjectives checked by the patient at each administration. Overall, there was not a higher degree of emotionality in the marathon compared to the traditional group except for the expression of negative feelings. The authors' own speculation is captured in the phrase: 'too tired to be polite'. Thus the myth is dispelled that time-extended sessions allow for a greater emotional experience. Moreover the heightened negative emotional expressiveness cannot be regarded automatically as intrinsically therapeutic.

Emotionality and outcome

Only one study has tackled substantially the relationship between emotional expressiveness and therapeutic outcome, but on volunteers. In the Stanford encounter group study,[13] students who underwent thirty hours of a group experience and were followed up six months later were categorized as learners, unchanged, or negative outcomes. The authors were able to conclude from their data that: 'though people may feel good about getting up feelings and may believe that it is instrumental in their learning, no evidence yet supports the belief that expressivity *per se* is specifically associated with differences in individual growth'. Although the sample as a whole ranked catharsis third out of fourteen therapeutic mechanisms in terms of helpfulness, and a third of the 'most important events' reported by participants covered emotional expressiveness, no significant differences emerged between the three outcome groups in respect of expression of those feelings leading to insight or positive effect.

But the picture was different in the case of the ventilation of aggressive feelings which produced a negative effect: students with a negative outcome had significantly more experience of this form of catharsis than unchanged and learner groups. The implication is that the former were unable to apply catharsis for constructive learning, because their form of expressiveness was inappropriate, or because they misconstrued the ensuing group feedback, or because of a combination of both factors.

Adverse effects of catharsis

That catharsis can have negative sequelae is an important clinical issue. The slogan 'let your feelings hang out' is too diffuse and non-specific to serve as a useful guideline to group leaders. At the least, ventilation of feelings must bring a sense of relief. If self-understanding follows later this is of course even more desirable. Contrariwise, catharsis that is too intense for the patient to bear and brings only an unresolved state of distressing arousal can only be anti-therapeutic and lead to deterioration. This was forcefully illustrated to one of the present authors (S.B.) when, in a study of the effects of an intense group experience on the process of a patient's individual therapy, a patient 'suffered some significant psychological harm and distress ("casualty" status) as a result of (her) weekend group experience'.[14]

The experimental design was briefly as follows: patients judged by their therapists to be somewhat 'stuck' in their long-term individual treatment were assigned to one of three matched groups, all of which met over a weekend. The two experimental groups, led by Gestalt therapists, were designed to arouse affect in their members, in contrast to the control group—an experience consisting of meditation and Tai Chi. The impact of the groups on individual therapy was reviewed six and twelve weeks later. At six weeks, patients in the experimental groups showed, on some measures, a significantly greater improvement in the quality of their individual therapy than control patients, but by twelve weeks these differences had evaporated. This may support the notion, previously commented upon in this chapter, that catharsis *per se* is of limited value and must be supplemented by some form of cognitive learning.

Returning to the subject of risk and the damaging effect of intense catharsis, we refer to the worst casualty in the 'weekend group experience' study. She was a middle-aged, divorced woman who participated actively in the group and expressed many powerful emotions. At one session she displayed a massive catharsis. As she reported: '. . . I started talking about my sexual experiences and then, with the leader's help, got in touch with sorrow that made me cry and cry. I was extremely distressed and felt physically numb, tingly, and finally sweaty. I didn't want to be let off the hook but worried about the unleashing of some horrible thing I couldn't contain or control.' She compared the experience to surgery: 'I was cut open [by choice] but nothing good came out of it. I have had to seal something over that I know hasn't been cleared out properly. Why all that hell with no reward?' At the three month follow-up, this patient was suicidal, required antidepressant medication, and was more defensive and distrustful in her individual therapy. Later, still shaken by the group experience, she quit her individual therapy.

Conclusions

Does the empirical research, in concert with the theoretical issues, lead to the formulation of guidelines for the group therapist? We conclude that catharsis—the ventilation of intense emotions which brings a sense of relief, and which may secondarily pave the way for greater self-understanding—has a distinct but circumscribed place in group therapy. Treatment will inevitably include the arousal of emotions in patients, probably a necessary basic ingredient of all the psychotherapies[15] and without which cognitive factors, such as self-understanding and vicarious learning, cannot operate effectively.

Moreover, it is a commonplace that patients have bottled up

feelings—shame, guilt, grief, depression, resentment, anger, jealousy, anxiety, worry, and despair are frequently encountered in clinical practice—whose discharge in the group is beneficial to them. The sheer act of letting go of such feelings affords relief. But two caveats are noteworthy. Firstly, the act in itself is unlikely to be sufficient in bringing about substantial clinical change.[16] Any practitioner who subscribes to the tenet—cure through catharsis—will probably rob his patients of any durable effects. Secondly, unlicensed and unbridled release of emotion is hazardous. The measure of efficacy of any act of catharsis lies not in how dramatic, profound, or intense it is but in what benefits come in its wake, be it confined to a sense of ease and comfort or be it more comprehensive, including new self-understanding, greater self-awareness, or budding reappraisal of some aspect of oneself. Weiner[17] sums up our own position when he concludes his review of the subject thus.

> If, as therapists, we can clearly see the complexity of catharsis, we may have greater capacity to prescribe it intelligently and to understand it when it occurs spontaneously in the therapeutic situation. Our principal validation for catharsis as an important element in treatment continues to be the observation by patients that they feel better by virtue of it, provided it has occurred in an appropriate way in an appropriate context.

References

1. Breuer, J. and Freud, S. *Studies on hysteria* (Standard edition) Vol. 2. Hogarth Press, London (1955).
2. Grinker, R. R. and Spiegel, J. P. *War neurosis*. Blakiston, New York (1945).
3. Slavson, S. L. The anatomy and clinical applications of group interaction. *International Journal of Group Psychotherapy* **19**, 3–15 (1969).
4. Yalom, I. D. *The theory and practice of group psychotherapy*. Basic Books, New York (1975).
5. Janov, A. *The primal scream*. Putnam, New York (1970).
6. See, for example: Perls, F., Hefferline, R. F., and Goodman, P. *Gestalt therapy*. Julian Press, New York (1958).
7. Bach, G. R. Constructive aggression in growth groups. In: *The group as agent of change* (eds. A. Jacobs and W. Spradlin). Behavioural Publications, New York (1974).
8. Corsini, R. and Rosenberg, B. Mechanisms of group psychotherapy: processes and dynamics. *Journal of Abnormal and Social Psychology* **51**, 406–11 (1955).
9. Bloch, S., Reibstein, J., Crouch, E. *et al.* A method for the study of

therapeutic factors in group psychotherapy. *British Journal of Psychiatry* **134**, 257–63 (1979).
10. Haer, J. L. Anger in relation to aggression in psychotherapy groups. *Journal of Social Psychology* **76**, 123–7 (1968).
11. Liberman, R. A behavioural approach to group dynamics: II. Reinforcing and prompting hostility to the therapist in group therapy. *Behaviour Therapy* **1**, 312–27 (1970).
12. Myerhoff, H. L., Jacobs, A., and Stoller, F. Emotionality in marathon and traditional psychotherapy groups. *Psychotherapy: Theory, Research and Practice* **7**, 33–6 (1970).
13. Lieberman, M. A., Yalom, I. D., and Miles, M. B. *Encounter groups: first facts*. Basic Books, New York (1973).
14. Yalom, I. D., Bond, G., Bloch, S., *et al.* The effect of a weekend group experience on the course of individual psychotherapy. *Archives of General Psychiatry* **34**, 399–415 (1977).
15. Frank, J. D. *Persuasion and healing: a comparative study of psychotherapy*. Johns Hopkins University Press, London (1973).
16. Marshall, J. R. The expression of feelings. *Archives of General Psychiatry* **27**, 786–90 (1972).
17. Weiner, M. F. Catharsis: a review. *Group process* **71**, 173–84 (1977).

7 Guidance

Historical perspectives

Guidance, the imparting of information and the giving of direct advice, has been only moderately emphasized as a therapeutic factor by group therapists, although self-help organizations in the mental health field, such as Alcoholics Anonymous and Recovery Inc., have made explicit use of didactic methods in their groups. It is noteworthy that physicians who pioneered group treatment applied guidance as a central element. As we saw in Chapter 1, the best known example is Joseph Pratt,[1] who gave instruction to groups of patients suffering from tuberculosis to help them learn how they might care for themselves more effectively. Other therapists, such as Lazell[2] and Marsh[3] adopted a similar model with psychiatric patients—creating highly structured groups whose members were perceived as 'students' and tutored on aspects of mental health.

The relatively low priority attached to guidance arose early in the history of group therapy. The model of Pratt and his immediate successors was short-lived and supplanted by the work of psychoanalysts who began to apply their theories and methods to groups of patients. The didactic element was strongly eschewed. It is no surprise therefore that Corsini and Rosenberg's[4] classic review fails to mention guidance as a specific therapeutic factor, and it appears only rarely in pre-1955 literature.

The picture has remained more or less the same since. In reviewing the slim volume of work dealing with guidance we discern a common theme. In long-term outpatient groups composed of patients who are psychologically minded, guidance by the therapist should be stringently avoided since it is seen as leading to undesirable dependence which may hamper clinical change and personal development. On the other hand, group therapy with more disabled patients, especially those treated in a ward setting, and specialized groups set up with a more specific educative purpose (for instance, a group consisting of patients' relatives) can be more didactic.

Definition

Before embarking on a detailed review of the literature on guidance, we need to define the term. As mentioned at the outset, we see it as the imparting of information and the giving of direct advice. The factor operates when the group member: receives useful information and instruction from the therapist about mental health, mental illness, and general (but *not* personal) psychodynamics; or obtains explicit advice, suggestions, or guidance about his problems from either the therapist or fellow-patients.[5] Examples of guidance as a therapeutic factor, elicited by us with the aid of the 'most important event' questionnaire, are:

Susan was told by the therapist that the tablets she takes each night often make people feel sluggish the next morning, even up to some hours after waking. Therefore she should not be so harsh on herself for having such a hard time 'getting going' each morning. This information decreased her sense of guilt about not helping with family chores.

I was advised by the group to join some student activities which would enable me to meet other people. Such participation would also help to take me out of constant contact with my old girlfriend, for I find such contact painful. I found this a most helpful suggestion and resolved to follow it.

Andrew asked: 'Are all effeminate men queer?' Tom immediately answered, 'No', and there was further discussion about an incident in which a man had made homosexual advances to Andrew. It became clear that he harboured a number of misconceptions about homosexuality and it was important that the rest of the group clarified these with him.

Basil was told by several members that he was potentially appealing physically. It was suggested that he could make himself more attractive by taking care of his body and that this would then make him feel better about himself. There was a useful discussion about how to lose weight and how to groom oneself more effectively.

Gail was advised by two of the women members that she should discuss her husband's illness with her children openly. The women thought the children would be mentally harmed if their father died unexpectedly. After exploring this theme, Gail came to understand that the advice offered was sensible and appropriate.

Theoretical contributions

In reviewing the literature on guidance we consider four aspects: specific didactic models of group therapy, systematic research, self-help groups and pre-therapy training.

Guidance and didactic models of group therapy

First, let us consider models of group therapy in which educational methods are central. Helpful in this respect is Slavson's[6] distinction between counselling, guidance, and therapy groups. The first two, in his view, deal especially with ego functioning and to a lesser extent with self-image, whereas therapy groups attempt to go much further and effect basic change in personality. Gilbert[7] elaborates on this differentiation, and provides as an example of a guidance group, a mothers' group which aims, by altering their attitudes, to lead mothers to be more content and better able to care for their children (the latter are not necessarily involved). Such a group has the specific purpose of guiding mothers in an understanding of the management of child behaviour, although members may readily stray on to other topics, especially complaints about husbands!

Tracy[8] has described a parents' guidance group in which both spouses participate. Groups were generally composed of five couples and two single parents and run in a structured fashion, covering selected topics, such as parent–child communication, how to praise and criticize children, their discipline, and how to handle rivalry within the family. A questionnaire-based follow-up demonstrated improvement in behaviour of the children and in the parent–child relationship, but no attempt was made to test whether this change was the result of the group or of concomitant treatment in a child guidance clinic.

Maxmen's educative model Perhaps the most notable contribution to the development of a didactic model in group therapy is that of

Maxmen.[9] His 'educative model' devised for the running of in-patient groups is refreshingly clear and rational. Emphasizing the need for a theoretical approach designed specifically for short-term psychiatric in-patients, he offers a specific framework coupled with a consideration of its practical implications. Because in-patients are usually more disturbed and dependent than their out-patient counterparts, and the group on a psychiatric ward is subject to a constantly changing membership, the goals of in-patient group therapy must necessarily be less ambitious than those set for an out-patient group. Moreover, the hospital setting, which facilitates patients' extra-group socialization and participation in other forms of treatment, suggests that typical methods used in an out-patient group must be substantially modified when applied to hospitalized patients. Maxmen backs up his ideas by citing several studies which demonstrate that in-patents regard a different range of factors as being helpful in their group therapy compared to members of out-patient groups.

He sets goals for an educative therapy group which are attainable in the short-term (weeks rather than months), merit the involvement of staff, and which complement the hospital's primary objective of reducing aberrant behaviour. Thus, an educative group should teach its members: (a) to accept help from others; (b) to recognize that their problems are not unique; (c) to realize that they can be of help to others; (d) to identify maladaptive behaviour in themselves; and (e) to avoid potentially demanding circumstances that might precipitate the recrudescence of symptoms. In summary, patients must be taught to think clinically and to respond effectively to the consequences of their illness.

To accomplish this overall goal, the therapist facilitates therapeutic behaviour by group members towards each other. The opportunity to act therapeutically promotes hope, enhances group cohesiveness, encourages altruistic behaviour, and demonstrates the universality of problems—underlining the therapeutic factors of instillation of hope, acceptance, altruism, and universality, all of which Maxmen has found to be most valued in his own study of a sample of 100 inpatients.[10] The therapist's responsibility includes the setting of group boundaries, establishing group norms, focusing on behaviour in the here-and-now, and redirecting the group's attention if necessary. Maxmen usefully discusses how these tasks and other technical operations may be realized. Because of the importance of this work, we return to it in Chapter 9.

The Soviet approach Ziferstein[11] has outlined an educative model of group treatment that he observed while working in the USSR. The emphasis on a collectivist rather than on an individualist ethic, he points out, underlies Soviet psychiatry's traditional approach to group therapy. Although he does not cite the pervasive influence of Pavlov, the examples quoted betray evidence of such an influence—for example, stress is placed on 're-education' of patients with neurotic disorders, and achieved through encouragement, praise, and other rewards.

The therapist plays an active role in this form of therapy since he guides the direction of the group, offers emotional support, and gives advice for the solution of day-to-day problems. In assisting the patient to reappraise his priorities and values, the therapist is conceptualized as a 'teacher of life'. In addition, he intervenes directly in helping to change life circumstances that may be causally related to his patient's problem, such as employment. In all this, no effort is made to elucidate the origin of symptoms. On the contrary, the emphasis is consistently on support, guidance, and re-education. To Western therapists, this approach would probably be regarded as unduly paternalistic, and limited because of its failure to appreciate the variation of individual human needs. None the less, it is likely to have much in common with the early Western didactic models of Pratt,[1] Lazell,[2] and Marsh[3] (see Chapter 1).

Empirical research

There has been little systematic research on the role of guidance in groups, a fact perhaps reflecting the low opinion of it held by clinicians. Two studies of specialized groups with a prominent educational core are disappointingly weak. In the first, Shrader *et al.*[12] examined a group approach for new mothers experiencing difficulty in coping with their children. Guidance took the form of conveying to group members the results of research in areas related to their problems. Preliminary outcome data were described as promising but the projected definitive report does not seem to have materialized. In another use of a specialized group, Loranger[13] compared the effects of educational, conventional, and a combined form of group therapy, in the treatment of problem drinkers. Since the project was reported in abstract form only, it is impossible to assess the stated conclusion that education was an effective therapeutic tool.

One study of the use of guidance in group therapy which stands out as an example of careful research is that by Flowers.[14] In a preamble, he reviews the work on guidance in individual therapy, concluding that the case against its utility has not been adequately made, and adding that the studies have tended to demonstrate that therapists trained not to proffer advice seldom do so. His own experiment was well planned and executed, though it used as subjects a highly atypical sample—compulsorily detained sex-offenders. Small groups were led by psychiatric nurses trained to give advice of various types—simple direct advice, the offering of alternatives, the provision of detailed instructions, and the giving of advice about the group process itself. Patients in groups led by trained therapists achieved greater improvement on specified goals than did controls. Providing alternatives and detailed instructions were equally potent in promoting this change, and both were more beneficial than giving simple advice. There was no testing of the efficacy of offering advice about the process of therapy but this form of guidance probably falls outside the definition we have used. In noting these results we should realize that the outcome criteria were derived from the items of advice actually given, and were thus closely linked to the goals set by the therapists, rather than the patients' own goals. None the less, we can conclude from Flowers' study that specific ways of giving advice directly affect patients' behaviour.

Self-help groups

As we mentioned earlier, there are long established self-help groups that make use of didactic methods. More recently, since the 1960s, there has been a rapid expansion in the self-help movement; the variety and scope of self-help groups has correspondingly grown. The question of whether these constitute a form of psychotherapy is of interest but beyond the remit of this chapter; certainly, therapy and self-help groups appear to overlap in terms of their goals and methods. Two interesting studies, which incorporate a discussion of guidance, comment on this association. In the first, Hurvitz[15] sampled the work of several different sorts of self-help groups. He concluded that their manifest popularity was in part attributable to their inherent component of guidance. This led him to suggest that the giving of advice could be used constructively and profitably in conventional therapy; moreover, such therapy should concern itself with the patient's 'real-life circumstances'.

Lieberman[16] has contributed a thoughtful and well-argued chapter on the change mechanisms involved in the self-help group. He looked carefully at groups run by several different organizations and concluded that there were major distinguishing features between various types of self-help groups, according to the therapeutic factors they appeared to stress. Unlike Hurvitz, Lieberman suggests that guidance is not a core feature of all self-help groups. For example, in women's consciousness-raising groups, it seems to be undervalued. This approach by Lieberman and his associates, emerging a decade after that of Hurvitz, reflects a growing sophistication in the study of the self-help phenomenon. At this point, we could probably assume that although guidance is not uniformly central to all forms of self-help groups, it remains an important element.

Killilea,[17] in a splendidly comprehensive and illuminating review of the literature on the subject, includes guidance as one of the seven characteristics common to self-help groups. She particularly specifies the use of the group as a forum for the exchange of information. Members are able to obtain more understanding of the nature of their condition or problem through the provision of specific information. A bereaved person, for example, can gather information from more experienced group members about funeral arrangements, business matters, and the nature of grief on anniversaries and how to cope with it.

These observations about self-help groups together with the theoretical contributions on models of group therapy and the one reasonable experiment by Flowers,[14] tend to point in the same direction, namely that didactic methods can play an important role in certain forms of groups. That guidance is, by and large, not highly regarded by clinicians probably stems from their experience of working in traditional insight-orientated group therapy. There, the provision and exchange of information is probably best avoided as it tends to promote dependency in the patient and robs him of the opportunity to make important discoveries for himself. We would concur but hastily add that in group therapy, which is more behavioural in approach and applied to patients in whom the acquisition of insight is not a primary goal, therapist prejudice against an educational component deprives those patients of the potential benefits that may follow its judicious use.

Pre-therapy training

Our account of guidance would be incomplete were we to omit the phenomenon of pre-therapy training. By this we mean the explicit instruction of patients about the nature of group therapy *before* they embark on it. Since it does not occur within the context of therapy itself, preparation is not strictly a form of guidance, but it may have an indirect role in promoting the efficacy of group therapy.

Rabin[18] has contributed a useful review of the orientating of patients for group therapy. He categorizes preparatory methods as: factual—in which administrative information and basic group rules only are given, in order to give a minimum structure to the experience; recorded material—written, audiotaped, or videotaped, designed to inform the prospective member about group therapy and to specify the type of behaviour expected of him; lecture or explanatory interview—in which the therapist spends time with his prospective patients, either individually or as a group, discussing the nature of group treatment and the patient's role therein; a group experience—a brief 'intake' group in which the therapist is more active than in the typical therapy group; and an individual experience—prior individual therapy aimed at educating the patient for entry into group therapy.

Pioneering work in this context was done by Malamud and Machover.[19] They devised a 'workshop in self-understanding' as a prelude to group therapy *per se*. It consisted of fifteen sessions and was aimed at clarifying reasons for psychological dysfunction and methods for self-exploration. The workshop not only proved helpful in preparing patients for treatment but also left some feeling sufficiently improved not to need the definitive treatment. These observations, however, were made on a small sample and were not based on a controlled study.

The 'intake' group, listed by Rabin,[18] is discussed comprehensively by Gauron and his colleagues.[20] Their twice-weekly 'orientation group' which meets for four sessions of ninety minutes each and is led by trainee therapists, emphasizes a here-and-now approach. Interestingly, they also use written material which deals explicitly with forms of behaviour expected, to introduce the orientation group itself. The group incorporates rehearsal of the interpersonal skills described in the material, supplemented by videotape feedback. Benefits are claimed for patients, for the out-patient groups which they eventually form, and for trainee therapists. For example, the authors suggest that patients achieve an understanding of the nature of group therapy, begin to see it as a learning process, become less anxious about entering definitive therapy, gain hope about its benefits, and realize that improvement will depend on the contribution they themselves make. The approach is described in fine detail, derived no doubt from a great deal of thought and planning. An evaluative study would be a logical next step.

Martin and Shewmaker[21] discuss the effect of written instructions on a group led by one of the authors. The material was prepared specifically for non-psychotic patients of above average intelligence who comprised the group, and contained details about the purpose and methods of group treatment. Interesting observations are presented about the way in which the document seemed to affect group process. In particular, it assumed the status of a yardstick against which actual group events could be measured.*

Several studies have been done on the effects of preparing members in both laboratory and therapy groups. Virtually all these address themselves to the question of the influence of a pre-group experience on the pattern of interaction within the definitive group.

*The preparation of a patient is not restricted to the period before the group begins. Conceivably, he may be guided through the initial phase of treatment itself in terms of desirable norms, patient's role, therapist's role, and so forth. Yalom *et al.*[22] have described the use of a written summary of each group meeting which is mailed out to participants for their perusal and study before the next meeting. Among the several purposes which this technique serves is the promotion and reinforcement of specific group norms. For example, the therapist as author can make explicit to his patients that communication in the group proceeds on several levels simultaneously, thus enhancing their appreciation and understanding of group process. He can also identify particularly productive sessions or segments of sessions, explaining the basis of this productivity.

Pre-group instruction in the laboratory setting

D'Augelli and Chinski[23] set out to demonstrate the effect of pre-training on the level of personal discussion and interpersonal feedback in groups of student volunteers. Twelve small groups consisted of members rated high in psychological-mindedness and twelve other groups were rated low on this quality. All groups were given audiotaped instructions at the start of a two hour, leaderless group session. In one-third of the groups, instructions gave a detailed description of the desired intra-group behaviour (self-disclosure, feedback, and focus on the here-and-now). These students were then encouraged to practise this behaviour before the group proceeded. For another third of the groups, the instructions were similar to the 'practice' instructions except that the members did not do any practising. The final third of the groups acted as controls—they received a lecture on the history of 'sensitivity training' and were merely told to 'act appropriately'. Ratings of the sessions revealed that the more psychologically minded students engaged in more personal discussion and offered more personal rather than impersonal feedback than their less psychologically minded counterparts. Both modes of pre-training led to higher levels of personal discussion and feedback than the control groups. Against the expectations of the researchers, however, the non-practise condition emerged as more effective than the practise one. These differences were more pronounced in the groups containing the psychologically minded students.

In another laboratory experiment. Bednar and Battersby[24] randomly assigned volunteer students to one of eight different two-hour experiential workshops on interpersonal relations. The groups were all run identically except for the initial instructions given. These were all written but contained general *or* specific statements about group goals and behaviour expected. For example, general goals read: 'The goal of today's group meeting is to start learning about interpersonal relationships'; whereas specific goals read: 'The goal of today's group meeting is to start learning about interpersonal relationships. This will include attempts on your part to talk about yourself openly and non-defensively so that you can see how it affects forming new interpersonal relationships'. Each of the eight groups received different combinations of general and specific instructions. The dependent variables used in assessment of the quality of early group development included measures of personal discomfort, group cohesiveness, attitudes towards the group experience (all rated by the participants), and interpersonal behaviour (rated by both participants and independent judges).

The investigators sought to examine the influence of instructions—'cognitive structure'—on the way in which a group evolves. As in many such laboratory-based experiments the design is impressive. However, expecting a group to last for only one session might in itself have affected a participant's behaviour. The caveat about generalizing findings from the laboratory to therapy applies, since the form of the session differed radically from a first meeting of a therapy group. None the less, the results are interesting in that they showed that specific instructions were associated with greater levels of cohesiveness, self-disclosure, and interpersonal feedback, less stilted social behaviour, and more favourable attitudes towards the group experience. Personal discomfort did not vary significantly. The specific behavioural instructions that proved so didactically effective were: 'There are a number of ways to start new interpersonal relationships that you can explore and try out during this workshop. One way is to work towards letting others know a great deal about yourself. This is called self-disclosure. This can be accomplished by talking about your own life concerns and identifying primary sources of happiness and sadness in your life. Your feelings about yourself and important life events are what we are encouraging you to share with each other.'

An earlier experiment with similar aims and results was reported by Whalen.[25] She used a larger sample of students, but men only. They met in quartets for one session and were observed through a one-way screen. In one condition, groups were shown a brief film in which students modelled self-disclosure as a way of becoming acquainted. Both the film and the no-film groups received taped instructions at the outset, either detailed or minimal in amount. Groups viewing the film and receiving detailed instructions consistently resembled the group in the film, in demonstrating interaction in which personal exchange and feedback were emphasized at the expense of impersonal discussion. In the other conditions the resultant interaction was not as marked. Whalen's results obviously raise the interesting possibility of a synergistic effect between instructions and a clearly demonstrated model of the desired behaviour.

Pre-group instruction in the clinical setting

A series of studies on the effectiveness of a didactic orientation procedure in the clinical setting has been done, which complements the above laboratory-based work. In general, this research shows the benefits of such a procedure, both for patients embarking on individual[26] or group therapy. Yalom and his colleagues[27] conducted a controlled study in which patients were prepared for outpatient group treatment. Patients were randomly assigned to either an experimental or control group. Those in the former received a systematic talk designed to explain the rationale of therapy, enhance faith in its effectiveness, emphasize the attractiveness of the particular group involved, and encourage interaction. The groups, led by therapists naïve to the experimental design, were studied for the first twelve meetings using measures of cohesiveness, faith in therapy, and interaction, plus records of attendance. The preparatory session proved effective in fostering faith in treatment and promoting interaction within the group.

Role induction An interesting study by Strupp and Bloxom[28] deals with the preparation for group therapy of patients of low socio-economic status. On the premiss that these patients are more likely to misconceive the nature of therapy, exhibit poor motivation out of a feeling of helplessness about their condition, and sense self-examination as a threat, the investigators developed a 'role-induction' film dealing dramatically with a man whose volatile temper brings him into conflict with authority, leads him to lose both job and family, and to contemplate suicide. He joins a therapy group. The film then illustrates how the process of the group helps him to develop insight into his behaviour, and the translation of new knowledge into practice.

Strupp and Bloxom selected over 100 patients referred for counselling, on the basis of their low income, poor motivation and limited educational attainment. They were assigned to groups on clinical grounds. Therapy was preceded by either the role-induction film, a role-induction interview, or a control film not specifically relevant to therapy. Experienced therapists led the groups for twelve weeks while research staff administered tests prior to the first session and then throughout the twelve weeks. The results remind us of the difference between satisfaction felt by a patient and his actual outcome. Patients who were prepared for therapy, by whichever method, were more satisfied with the experience; the film was more effective than the interview in this respect. Patients' self-ratings of improvement were also greatest in groups viewing the film. However, there were no consistent trends in therapists' ratings of outcome. Interestingly, attendance was unusually good in all groups no matter whether induction took place or not, reflecting perhaps the patients' perception that they were receiving considerable attention. The results point particularly to the notion that preparation for therapy may lead patients to feel more satisfied with their experience of treatment though the question of whether their outcome is influenced remains open.

Another study designed to test the value of a role-induction film also yielded inconsistent findings.[29] Ninety prison inmates, assigned to either an experimental or control condition, were treated in short-term group therapy and assessed pre- and post-treatment on their expectations, self evaluation of progress, attendance, and quality of interaction during the sessions. Peer and therapist ratings of outcome completed the battery of measures. In the experimental condition, subjects viewed a tape in which desirable 'therapeutic behaviours' were prominent; they were then guided to imitate these through role-play.

As a result, they seemed to enter treatment with clearer expectations and showed superior interaction in the first session than their control counterparts. The outcome of experimental subjects was also superior in terms of therapist and peer ratings. However, self-report measures of outcome, attendance and interactional patterns after the first session did not differ between the two conditions. In view of these inconsistent results, the authors limit their claim of the value of pre-training to the initial phase of treatment only. They also comment on a potential therapist effect, namely that the uniformly high skills of the therapists involved in their experiment may have 'compensated for the lack of pre-training of controls'.

An interesting study by Wogan *et al.*[30] also demonstrates the difficulties in carrying out research in this field, even when attempts are made to achieve controlled conditions. Their sample consisted of students with long-standing psychological problems seen at a university clinic. Of the nine groups studied, two served as controls and received no instructions; the other seven were prepared for therapy in one of the following ways: listening to a tape which stressed self-disclosure, feedback, and getting in touch with here-and-now feelings; participation in a one-hour structured sensitivity-training group in which exercises were devised to facilitate disclosure of feelings; or attending a one-hour leaderless group (the last served as a placebo condition). Ratings by the patient of his own target symptoms and a measure of interaction based on audiotapes of the sessions were used to note the effects of the four treatment conditions. Members of the 'tape induction' groups showed most improvement, the placebo group the least, but the effect was weak. The form of preparation did not influence the nature of the group's interaction. The results, however, were confounded by potent therapist effects: it was noticeable that the high outcome groups were led by particularly active therapists.

Experimental problems The final study on preparation for group therapy illustrates experimental difficulty rather than the credibility of results. Dick and her colleagues[31] studied 105 patients referred for treatment to a psychotherapy unit. Here they received daily therapy in the form of one large group and three small group sessions over a period of twelve weeks. Other activities, such as psychodrama and art therapy, were also part of the programme. Patients in the experimental condition had a period of individual therapy preparatory to the group work. All patients were interviewed in the first and twelfth weeks of their definitive therapy, covering such topics as attitudes to themselves and their satisfaction with life. No significant differences were found between experimental and control conditions either in the proportion of dropouts or on the outcome criteria derived from the interview. Unfortunately, the use of retrospective controls means that the effects of changes in the unit's organization and staff during the interim period were untested. Furthermore, it is questionable whether the individual therapy was designed as specific preparation for the group programme or was merely an additional, small component of an overall package of treatments.

Conclusions

Our impression of the above research work on pre-therapy training is that a form of orientation which enables the patient to obtain an idea of what therapy is about and what his role and that of the therapist will be in the process warrants a routine place in clinical practice. Even if the effects of the preparatory procedure are inconsistent with regard to outcome, the fact that patients' satisfaction is enhanced (surely an important variable in its own right) and the group process influenced advantageously is sufficient reason for its application. But it remains unclear from the studies described whether the beneficial effects endure. In any event, preparation would seem less crucial in long-term insight-orientated groups in which there is ample opportunity to unravel any initial misconceptions and to reduce confusion about the nature of the treatment.

With regard to guidance in general, it would be reasonable to conclude that its apparent unpopularity among therapists can be ascribed more to a form of prejudice than to informed judgement. Clinical lore, which suggests that it has only a limited role in insight-orientated group therapy, is probably correct, although this does not negate the relevance of pre-therapy training. On the other hand, as Maxmen has demonstrated, guidance can have a pre-eminent role in group treatment where insight (in the classical psychodynamic sense) is not the primary objective. For example, a central place for guidance in short term in-patient group therapy and for groups composed of patients' relative seems justified. We make these comments tentatively since the volume of knowledge on guidance (pre-therapy training aside) is minimal. The whole subject very much awaits the attention of the research investigator.

References

1. Pratt, J. H. The tuberculosis class: an experiment in home treatment. In: *Group psychotherapy and group function* (eds. M. Rosenbaum and M. Berger). Basic Books, New York (1975).
2. Lazell, E. The group treatment of dementia praecox. *Psychoanalytic Review* **8**, 168–79 (1921).
3. Marsh, L. C. Group therapy and the psychiatric clinic. *Journal of Nervous and Mental Disease* **82**, 381–92 (1935).
4. Corsini, R. and Rosenberg, B. Mechanisms of group psychotherapy: processes and dynamics. *Journal of Abnormal and Social Psychology* **51**, 406–11 (1955).
5. Bloch, S., Reibstein, J., Crouch, E., *et al.* A method for the study of therapeutic factors in group psychotherapy. *British Journal of Psychiatry* **134**, 257–63 (1979).
6. Slavson, S. R. *A textbook in analytic group psychotherapy*. International Universities Press, New York (1964).
7. Gilbert, J. G. Group guidance, counselling and psychotherapy. *National Catholic Guidance Conference Journal* **14**, 162–5 (1970).
8. Tracy, J. T. Analysis of parent guidance groups. *Journal of Psychiatric Nursing and Mental Health Services* **9**, 18–23 (1971).

9. Maxmen, J. S. An educative model for in-patient group therapy. *International Journal of Group Psychotherapy* **28**, 321–38 (1978).
10. Maxmen, J. S. Group therapy as viewed by hospitalized patients. *Archives of General Psychiatry* **28**, 404–8 (1973).
11. Ziferstein, I. Group psychotherapy in the Soviet Union. *American Journal of Psychiatry* **129**, 107–12 (1972).
12. Shrader, W., Altman, S., and Leventhal, T. A didactic approach to structure in short-term group therapy. *American Journal of Orthopsychiatry* **39**, 493–7 (1969).
13. Loranger, P. An analysis of problem drinkers undergoing treatment through educational therapy, group therapy and family orientation. *Dissertation Abstracts International* **33**, 4350 (1973).
14. Flowers, J. V. The differential outcome effects of simple advice, alternatives and instructions in group psychotherapy. *International Journal of Group Psychotherapy* **29**, 305–16 (1979).
15. Hurvitz, N. Peer self-help psychotherapy groups and their implication for psychotherapy. *Psychotherapy: Theory, Research and Practice* **7**, 41–9 (1970).
16. Lieberman, M. A. Analysing change mechanisms in groups. In: *Self-help groups for coping with crisis* (eds. M. A. Lieberman and L. D. Borman). Jossey–Bass, San Francisco (1980).
17. Killilea, M. Mutual help organizations: interpretations in the literature. In: *Support systems and mutual help* (eds. G. Caplan and M. Killilea). Grune and Stratton, New York (1976).
18. Rabin, H. M. Preparing patients for group psychotherapy. *International Journal of Group Psychotherapy* **20**, 135–45 (1970).
19. Malamud, D. I. and Machover, S. *Towards self-understanding: group techniques in self-confrontation.* Charles C. Thomas, Springfield, Ill. (1965).
20. Gauron, E. F., Steinmark, S. W., and Gersh, F. S. The orientation group in pre-therapy training. *Perspectives in Psychiatric Care* **15**, 32–7 (1977).
21. Martin, H. and Shewmaker, K. Written instructions in group psychotherapy. *Group Psychotherapy* **15**, 24–9 (1962).
22. Yalom, I. D., Brown, S., and Bloch, S. The written summary as a group psychotherapy technique. *Archives of General Psychiatry* **32**, 605–13 (1975).
23. D'Augelli, A. R. and Chinsky, J. M. Interpersonal skills and pretraining. *Journal of Consulting and Clinical Psychology* **42**, 65–72 (1974).
24. Bednar, R. L. and Battersby, C. P. The effects of specific cognitive structure on early group development. *Journal of Applied Behavioural Science* **12**, 513–22 (1976).
25. Whalen, C. Effects of a model and written instructions on group verbal behaviours. *Journal of Consulting and Clinical Psychology* **33**, 509–21 (1969).
26. See, e.g.: Sloane, R. B., Cristol, A. H., Pepernik, M. C., *et al.* Role

preparation and expectation of improvement in psychotherapy. *Journal of Nervous and Mental Disease* **150**, 18–26 (1970).

27. Yalom, I. D., Houts, P. S., Newell, G., *et al.* Preparation of patients for group therapy: a controlled study. *Archives of General Psychiatry* **17**, 416–27 (1967).
28. Strupp, H. H. and Bloxom, A. L. Preparing lower-class patients for group psychotherapy. *Journal of Consulting and Clinical Psychology* **41**, 373–84 (1973).
29. Hilkey, J. H., Wilhelm, C. L., and Horne, A. M. Comparative effectiveness of videotape pre-training versus no pre-training on selected process and outcome variables in group therapy. *Psychological Reports* **50**, 1151–9 (1982).
30. Wogan, M., Getter, H., Amdur, M. J., *et al.* Influencing interaction and outcomes in group psychotherapy. *Small Group Behaviour* **8**, 25–46 (1977).
31. Dick, B. M., Pawlick, J. S., Woods, D., *et al.* A controlled evaluation of initial brief psychotherapy in subsequent group therapy. *British Journal of Clinical and Social Psychiatry* **1**, 47–9 (1982).

8 Universality, altruism, vicarious learning, and instillation of hope

This chapter deals with a variegated group of therapeutic factors—universality, altruism, vicarious learning, and instillation of hope. We have assembled them here not because they share any intrinsic properties but solely because they resemble one another in their relative neglect by clinicians, theorists, and research investigators. We speculate on the possible reasons for this in the course of the chapter.

Universality

The paltry attention devoted to universality—the realization by the patient that 'we are all in the same boat'—is probably attributable to two interrelated features that typify its occurrence: firstly, it is apt to be experienced only at the outset of group therapy, when the initial sharing of problems, thoughts, feelings, and fantasies dispels members' sense of uniqueness and aloneness; secondly, it is an experience felt implicitly and not commonly articulated, so that its potency is not perhaps fully appreciated by the therapist or any external observer. Indeed, this second reason may equally apply to the other three factors covered in this chapter; they are characteristically subtle, covert therapeutic processes which rarely make the 'headlines' in the life of a therapy group.

Historical perspectives

Despite these observations, universality has enjoyed a long history. Over half a century ago, Trigant Burrow, the pioneering group analyst, attached the 'greatest significance' to the group's provision of a forum that enabled each patient to recognize the 'common nature of his conflict'.[1] This process of mutual recognition, he noted, was especially valuable in reducing patients' resistance, whose essence was 'undoubtedly one's sense of isolation in one's own conflicts'. The psychoanalytic basis of Burrow's approach is apparent from his stress on the commonality of inner conflicts, but such a focus, though limited in scope, still constitutes the first attempt at identifying the clinical cogency of universality.

Another group analyst, Louis Wender,[2] later widened the concept when he referred to the group's property of facilitating a patient to learn that his problems are not peculiar to himself and that many co-members have similar underlying difficulties. Both Burrow and Wender also added another dimension to universality—the mutual recognition of problems shared enabled the patient to adopt a more 'disinterested' or 'detached' view—essentially to perceive himself and his problems more objectively.

By the time Corsini and Rosenberg[3] reviewed the group therapy literature for their classificatory endeavour, a number of other clinicians, chiefly during the 1940s, had mentioned universality, though in various terms Foulkes,[4] for example, referred to the patient's realization that others have 'similar morbid ideas, anxieties, or impulses'; this discovery brought relief in at least two ways: a diminution of anxiety and guilt, and a welcome feeling of not being the only sufferer. Corsini and Rosenberg themselves highlighted the realization by the patient that he is not unique and that others share identical or very similar problems, a formulation which has remained by and large the gist of subsequent definitions.

Definition

In our own classification, we have stipulated that universality operates when the patient: perceives that other group members have similar problems and feelings, this perception reducing his sense of uniqueness; or he experiences a sense that he is not alone with his problems and feelings. Five examples derived from our work with the 'most important event' questionnaire serve to illustrate the factor:

I told the group how I sometimes feel unbearably insecure in large groups. I find that I am thinking that anything I say will be stupid so I clam up and say nothing at all. This makes me feel even more inadequate. Both Martin and Anne told me that precisely the same thing happens to them. It was a relief for me to know that others suffer from the same problem.

Lynn complained about difficulty she had been having in the first stage of a relationship. She felt that she is the one who makes everything 'go wrong' since she feels desperately insecure. Georgina and Helen both agreed that her feelings were very familiar to them. Lynn felt comforted that her insecurity did not signify that she was a hopeless freak.

I found the extended session (a marathon) very useful as we managed to cover a lot of ground and I felt I knew everyone a little better afterwards. I was particularly interested when we talked about 'inner selves' and how afraid we are of showing them. Jack and Ken seemed to have this in common with me while Nancy had said the same thing previously. I enjoyed and welcomed this sharing experience.

The most important event for me was the discovery that Lesley has an almost identical problem to my own. By listening to her describe her problem I found it easier to accept that it is not me only who has such an embarrassing thing to conceal [aggressive feelings towards her mother which sometimes are felt as murderous impulses].

I cannot recall any one event which was most important to me. However, I have been made aware that people have more unhappy feelings than I had previously thought. It is that which I find very reassuring. I have always thought no one could be as miserable as I have felt.

Universality as a therapeutic factor

In recent years, with the advent of the systematic study of processes that typify the self-help or mutual-help group, the relevance of universality as a therapeutic factor has again attracted attention, although still limited in scope. Lieberman,[5] for example, suggests that the self-help group is organized around the aim of maximizing universality to exert a supportive effect. This is probably a correct view. The emphasis in the self-help movement on the homogeneity of suffering, disability, or plight is most striking. Members are universally undergoing some common, clearly identifiable experience, whether it be the 'battle to remain dry' of Alcoholics Anonymous, the process of mourning for a dead child as in Compassionate Friends, the shame and guilt of having abused one's own child as in

Parents Anonymous, and so forth. Other less clinical and more political groups, such as the Gay Movement, probably also maximize universality in the sense of dispelling the idea that the 'problem' is peculiar to the individual person. Indeed, it is argued that homosexuality is a normal variant of sexual expression and it is social attitudes to it that are irrational and abnormal.

In this regard, the effects of universality are closely related to another feature of some self-help groups—their destigmatizing potential. As Robinson[6] points out, a sense of stigma may diminish through a change in a person's self-perception that follows his participation in a group composed of people similar to himself. He feels less 'odd', that his problem is not at all unusual.

Robinson's comments on destigmatization may explain the benefits of universality more generally in group therapy. So may Lieberman's notion that the factor brings relief from a previously held pervasive negative self-image. Equally plausible is the aforementioned concept of Foulkes that suffering is more tolerable if experienced communally. The reports quoted from our patients suggest that a multi-dimensional view of universality is tenable. But, in the present state of knowledge, identification of the specific therapeutic contributions of universality remain within the realm of conjecture.

Altruism

At first sight it would seem strange to encounter the phenomenon of altruism—placing other people's interests before one's own—in group therapy. After all, a patient commonly enters a group in a distressed and bewildered state; uppermost is his need for help that will bring relief. That fellow patients are similarly afflicted is remote from his thoughts, and that he may be able to contribute to their welfare unimaginable. Indeed, many neurotic or personality disordered patients have been so long absorbed with their own handicaps that any sensitivity to the plight of others has altogether evaporated. When their own condition is one of perplexity and demoralization, what hope, they reckon, is there of acting helpfully towards fellow group members?

The broader context

There appears to be an inherent impulse in man to feel that he is of value to others, that he is wanted. If we consider the phenomenon of altruism more broadly, this impulse (we enter disputable territory if we refer to the urge to be helpful as instinctive) has at least two aspects, behavioural and cognitive. Ethologists have observed altruistic behaviour not only in man but also in lower animals, especially those that live in groups.[7] Plainly, there is biological advantage to a species in one animal protecting another in the face of predators. In considering altruism as a therapeutic factor, however, we are more concerned with its cognitive dimension, namely the self-evaluative quality inherent in the act of placing another person's interests and needs ahead of one's own.[8]

From the late 1940s, a handful of group therapists began to focus on this self-evaluative process. They pointed out the benefit a patient could derive from extending a hand to his peers, whether it was by offering a concrete suggestion, some advice, an interpretation, expressing a feeling of reassurance or encouragement, or by placing aside his own needs in favour of those of his fellows.[3] We may note, with interest, that neither the didactic nor the psychoanalytic models of group therapy found a place for altruism.

Since these early observations, little attention has been paid to this factor by either clinicians, theorists, or research investigators. Lieberman, for example, devotes a mere seven lines to it in an account of therapeutic factors.[5] Notwithstanding, we are persuaded by our own clinical observations that altruistic behaviour is a constant feature of group therapy, and that it yields benefits to its exponents. The mechanism whereby the latter occurs is likely to revolve around the patient's realization, probably subtle and gradual, that: 'I can be of help to others and sensitive to their needs; I have something to offer them; I am important in the eyes of another person'. This discovery in turn probably serves to boost self-esteem, and paves the way for further altruistic acts and an associated diminution in morbid self-preoccupation.

Definition

With these points in mind, we have suggested that altruism is based in the patient feeling better about himself, or learning something positive about himself, through the help he extends to his fellow group members. In the effort to be helpful he discovers his potential to be of value to others, and this in turn improves his self-image.

Altruism operates when the patient: offers support, reassurance, suggestions, or comments to help other group members; shares similar problems with the purpose of helping other members; feels a sense of being needed and helpful; can forget about himself in favour of another member; and recognizes that he wants to do something for a fellow member.

The following examples of altruism as a therapeutic factor were obtained using the 'most important event' questionnaire:

Nancy was talking of her guilt in criticizing her parents. I found I could reassure her, saying that occasionally I also felt unreasonably angry towards my parents, and suggesting that it was important to explore the whole range of one's feelings about them. I felt good that Nancy seemed to appreciate my helping her in this way.

Karen found she was becoming involved in Arthur's discussion of his problems at work. She began offering comments about his boss, and advice about how to deal with him, which Arthur seemed to accept. This was the first occasion on which Karen was not concentrating solely on her own problems, and she was pleased to discover that she wanted to be helpful to others.

Colin discovered that his girlfriend had been seeing his best friend and divulged this to the group. James felt angry on his behalf, and expressed this. James then realized with much relief that he did feel that he wanted to help someone else and was able to do so.

Yvonne was feeling very depressed and upset. I desperately wanted to help her. After she had said that nobody seemed to find her or what she said interesting, I was able to say to her quite genuinely: 'You're interesting *to me*.' It was very difficult for me to do this. Since then Yvonne has spent more time over her appearance and seems to be in high spirits. This pleases me very much.

In the sympathetic embrace which Kate gave Jill during the latter's revelation of the termination of her pregnancy, Kate was able to offer something that Jill found most valuable, and Kate appeared awfully pleased to have done so.

Altruism and the self-help group

Like universality, altruism has achieved a measure of prominence in the context of the self-help group. Its common alternative title—the mutual-help group—suggests as much. Marie Killilea,[9] in a review of the literature in this field, includes altruism as one of seven shared properties that typify such groups. Her account of the factor is similar to the one we have provided in that she highlights the helper taking pleasure from the sense of giving of himself, and through this experience becoming less self-absorbed and more sensitive to others. Altruism probably plays a more central role in self-help groups than in conventional therapy groups. Because members of the former can so readily identify with the experience of their peers (see universality), and because professional leadership and help is absent, an unambiguous norm of giving of one's self to one's fellows prevails. Alcoholics Anonymous illustrates this well. Mutual help is a pivotal feature, with any member who feels vulnerable to losing his sobriety able to seek unhesitatingly the support of his peers, which they give freely and energetically in such circumstances, even if personally inconvenient or dislocating.[10] The rewards stemming from the altruistic effort obviously outweigh the personal cost; indeed, the level of sacrifice experienced by the donor may conceivably contribute to the satisfaction he derives from placing the interests of others before his own. More concretely, the concept of sponsorship—veteran AA members assuming specific responsibility for shepherding a newcomer into the ways of the organization—testifies to the importance attached to altruism.[11]

More has probably been learned about altruism through the study of the self-help movement than in any other way. The translation of the results and knowledge to conventional therapy groups would be a welcome development and would, hopefully, spur the theoretical and empirical study of altruism in group therapy generally.

Vicarious learning

Common clinical observation strongly suggests that learning through the observation of others is an omnipresent feature of psychotherapy. Group therapy of course provides even more opportunities for such learning to take place, since a group member has not only the therapist (or co-therapists) but also several peers to identify with or to imitate. Notwithstanding, vicarious learning has received little attention from theorists and virtually none from research investigators. We would have anticipated that the group therapies were ideally suited for the study of this therapeutic factor and its relative neglect is therefore puzzling.

Recognition and development of the concept

Nevertheless, the salience of a member's observations of the rest of his group was recognized early on in the development of group therapy. In 1927, Burrow, for example, referred to it thus: 'A significant aspect of these group sessions lies in the circumstance that the patient is from the outset observer as well as observed. He becomes at once a responsible student of our common human problems, personal and social.'[1] More specifically, Burrow pointed out the intrinsic property of group therapy that enables each member to note features of his own neurosis in the neuroses of his co-members. Despite Burrow's contribution, only a minority of therapists made mention of the relevance of observation in subsequent years. Thus, when Corsini and Rosenberg[3] produced their classification of therapeutic factors, they could locate only six statements in the literature on group therapy referable to what they labelled 'spectator therapy'—a term borrowed from Moreno. These statements covered such processes as imitation and learning from the observation of co-members' experiences. A classification by Berzon *et al.*[12] a few years later retained this factor under the same title, but they appeared to restrict the concept to the imitation of fellow members' qualities of honesty, courage, openness, or expression of emotions. Yalom's questionnaire on therapeutic factors[13] includes the category of identification. A perusal of the five constituent items indicates that their essence is also imitation—of features in the therapist or in fellow-members.

Definition

In our own taxonomy, we have widened the concept to include two chief forms of learning: (a) imitation of qualities in others deemed desirable by the observer; and (b) learning that stems from the observer's identification with a fellow-patient's specific experience in therapy.

The term vicarious learning seems more apt to us than spectator therapy since it emphasizes both the cognitive basis of the factor and its quality as an active process, although obviously dependent on the presence of co-members. Identification is best conceptualized as a condition for change rather than as a therapeutic factor, in that it serves as a vehicle for this learning process. We thus regard the basis of vicarious learning as the patient experiencing something of value for himself through the observation of other group members, including the therapist. It operates when a patient benefits by observing the therapy experience of another patient; identifies with a co-member to the extent that he himself gains from the co-member's therapy experience; recognizes some positive aspect of the behaviour of the therapist, or of other patients, to imitate; or finds models in the positive behaviour of other group members, including the therapist, towards which he can strive.

To illustrate, here are examples derived from our use of the 'most important event' questionnaire:

Albert complained that he had not yet learned how to be properly assertive. Sometimes he is too assertive, sometimes too passive. Others reminded him of occasions in the group when he had been both appropriately and inappropriately assertive. Joan identified with Albert's problems and felt the group's work with him was also helping her to understand her own difficulties in 'speaking her mind'.

Mike had been bullying Charles for the past few weeks. Then for the first time, Charles told Mike off. Vic had been silently and angrily siding with Charles. When Vic saw that Charles could stand up to Mike, he felt that from this, he himself had learned how to face up to bullying types.

Fred showed in the last meeting that during the course of his participation in group therapy he had become much more patient and responsive to others. Because I can identify with Fred, I feel that I also have begun to learn how to be more sensitive.

I learnt much last week from the openness of Cathie in her stating and describing her basic problems. Her frankness made me feel like a hypocrite because being honest with people is my biggest hang-up.

Corinne revealed more about herself than ever before. I made an effort to understand her since we seem to be on the same wavelength. I came away with more knowledge than ever before. I realized that her talking at cross purposes with her husband was very similar to my own marital problem. I learned quite a bit from her revelations about the basis for my own troubles with Bob.

Identification

The central process involved in the operation of vicarious learning is identification. A believes that an experience of B is similar to his own, or B behaves in a way that strikes a particular chord with A. A process of learning then follows this initial identification. A may model his behaviour either consciously or unconsciously on that of B, or he may come to appreciate how B has developed some specific self-understanding and then apply the same cognitive lessons to himself.

Identification in the context of group therapy has not attracted much attention. Kissen[14] is one of the few contributors to the subject. He regards identification, particularly a patient's identification with his therapist, as a salient component of treatment. Operating from the assumption that the patient tends to assume personal qualities of the therapist, Kissen considers the efforts that have been made to conceptualize this process in terms of psychoanalytic theory and various forms of learning theory. Despite his criticism of the psychoanalytic position, Kissen concludes that an integration of various aspects of a variety of models is a prerequisite to a proper understanding of the concept and to its further study through generating testable hypotheses. For example, he speculates that the degree of identification with the therapist by his patients should be influenced by such therapist characteristics as his style of expression, the social status with which he is perceived, and how his competence is regarded.

We have found only one study in which identification has been examined empirically in the context of group therapy. Jeske[15] set out to test the hypothesis that a patient's identification with his co-members would be associated with clinical improvement. Defining identification as a 'process by which a person considers himself to be like another person in some respects and models his own behaviour after him', Jeske argues that not only mere imitation is involved but also that the observer becomes emotionally caught up with the model, experiencing the latter's 'successes and defeats as his own'.

An ingenious method was employed to record identification. Each patient, participating in a brief therapy programme, was instructed to press a button held in the palm of his hand, each time he identified with a fellow patient. Clinical improvement as measured on a self-report personality inventory was found to correlate positively with identification; patients who improved recorded twice the number of identifications of those who did not change. Identification was mostly related to problems that patients had raised during the assessment interview or during the course of treatment. As a result of these findings, Jeske suggested that therapists should encourage identification and provide opportunities for its occurrence. But his study is too limited to offer any firm guidelines to the clinician. A replication of his work with a larger sample, a control condition, and superior outcome measures would be a welcome contribution to the study of vicarious learning.

Modelling

As our own definition reveals, another central aspect of vicarious learning is modelling. Albert Bandura is undoubtedly the most important theorist and systematic researcher of this process. He and Rosenthal define a model as 'any stimulus array so organized that an observer can extract and act on the main information conveyed by environmental events without needing to first perform overtly'.[16] Two stages of modelling—acquisition and performance—are distinguished. In the first stage, observation enables the subject to learn a response to the model's behaviour. The sensory events are registered, and then coded for memory. Reinforcement is unnecessary during acquisition but can contribute. In the second stage, performance, the subject is now in a position, subject to adequate motivation, to initiate activity by relying on his memory stores, and here reinforcement may play a role.

A chief function of modelling is either to reinforce the inhibition of a particular response or to exert a disinhibitory effect. In the former, which is uncommonly used in clinical work, the observer learns by perceiving the negative repercussions of some behaviour to curb its performance. Disinhibition is far more useful clinically, and especially pertinent in the case of irrational fears. For instance, a patient's behaviour may be inhibited by anxiety. He observes a model engaging in the anxiety-provoking behaviour without coming to harm. The patient's expectation of becoming more effective himself is enhanced, his optimism increases, and he is more willing to risk coping with the frightening situation. The actual performance of the previously fearful behaviour serves to strengthen the patient's sense of 'self-efficacy', and thus to boost his confidence further.

Bandura and Rosenthal refer to the widespread clinical application of modelling and to its future potential. It would seem that this potential has barely been touched in conventional group therapy. This is somewhat surprising. We would support Bednar and his colleagues[17] in their claim that modelling techniques have a specific application to group therapy and provide a source of interpersonal learning. In their view, Bandura's work is sufficiently advanced to serve as a basis for group therapy application.

Despite this claim, the empirical work on modelling in the group context is scanty. A well-planned and well-executed study by Falloon and his associates[18,19] demonstrates the value of conducting research in this area. Psychiatric out-patients diagnosed as mainly neurotic and personality-disordered and presenting with difficulties in interpersonal behaviour, were randomly assigned to either a discussion group or to a group in which modelling and role-playing predominated. In each case, sessions were held weekly for ten weeks. Assessment on target problems, social adjustment, and several self-report questionnaires was made after therapy and at two follow-up points. Modelling and role-playing took the following form: before a session, patients studied a hand-out in which information was provided on the topic selected for examination—essentially a didactic component closely akin to the therapeutic factor of guidance. Much of the session was then devoted to modelling by the two co-leaders of social interactions regarded as problem areas for the group members. Following this demonstration, the therapists trained the group to perform the same patterns of behaviour. Specific homework assignments were given in relation to the social skills taught and practised.

The modelling/role-playing condition exerted a more beneficial effect than the guided discussion condition, although this superiority diminished somewhat at follow-up. An additional finding of interest was the enhancement through modelling and role-playing of interpersonal variables within the group, such as attraction to the group and to the therapists. Moreover, this latter attraction seemed to aid, as one might expect, the process of modelling.

Falloon's work raises the obvious question of whether explicit modelling by therapists is advantageous in group therapy generally. We should recall that the treatment in the experiment was of a special kind—short-term, highly structured, and designed to produce improvement in a particular area, i.e. social skills. In such focused therapy, explicit modelling would appear to fit well, and we would agree with Falloon's conclusion: '. . . the vicarious learning that occurs from watching a therapist perform a difficult social interaction is undoubtedly helpful'. In more conventional group therapy—long-term, relatively unstructured, and unfocused—therapist modelling of this type is likely to be incongruous and jar with other aspects of the group process. Here, what would seem more apt is *implicit* modelling by the therapist whereby certain desirable attitudes and behavioural patterns are manifest but without recourse to didactic procedures.

Psychodrama

The paucity of systematic work on vicarious learning is obvious. Yet, it is a factor used in one widely practised form of group psychotherapy, namely psychodrama.[20] Typically, a group member, the 'protagonist', is taken through a re-creation of past events or a creation of future events by the therapist. Co-members are encouraged to 'double' by standing behind the protagonist and relating feelings or memories which his 'drama' conjures up in them. In this case, vicarious learning is potentially bi-directional: the protagonist may identify with the elements of the experience which are 'doubled' and learn something new about himself from them; at the same time, all members observing the unfolding drama may note an aspect relevant to their own lives and come to share this later in the session.

The limited attention given to vicarious learning may reflect the difficulty of knowing quite how to study it. However, the example of psychodrama immediately suggests a form of investigation which is likely to be illuminating. A comparison of matched patients, some participating in psychodrama and others in conventional group therapy but otherwise treated under similar conditions, would enable the researcher to test whether the former precipitates vicarious learning, and whether such learning is valued by patients and contributes to outcome.

Instillation of hope

Lastly in this chapter we focus on instillation of hope (henceforth referred to as hope)—a therapeutic factor whereby the patient gains a sense of optimism about his progress or potential for progress through his actual experience in the therapy group. Immediately, we need to distinguish between hope as a factor that exerts its benefits in a group context specifically, from hope as a placebo effect in psychotherapy generally. Let us consider the latter first.

Hope as a placebo

The outstanding and ingenious experiments of Jerome Frank and his colleagues[21] at Johns Hopkins University have highlighted the salience in all forms of psychotherapy of the patient's hope that the treatment will make things better. The patient opts to obtain help from a professional therapist in the hope that his condition may thereby improve. Seeking out a professional therapist is not fortuitous. The patient has ascertained, directly or indirectly, that he is a potential beneficiary of treatment; the therapist has undergone a professional training and must presumably be expert in helping people like himself. This image may be reinforced upon the patient learning that a particular therapist has written professional articles or books or is a teacher of the subject or has had many years of clinical experience. The patient's hopes may be further promoted by the therapist's professional setting. If the latter works in a respected institution, he is likely to be identified by the patient with that institution. The other key dimension of this placebo effect in psychotherapy is the therapist's personal qualities, in particular his sense of confidence in what he does and his optimism in facilitating positive change in those he treats. These qualities will invariably be transmitted to the patient, generating further his hope for effective help.

Hope in the group context

While the general placebo effect applies as much to group therapy as it does to other forms of psychotherapy, the value of hope in the group context has a distinct, additional quality—the fact that the sources of that hope include not only the therapist but also other group members. For reasons difficult to explain, this particular aspect has been much neglected by therapists and theorists alike. True, Pratt[22] did note its potency and, as a result, arranged for 'star' patients to tell their peers how they had profited. This, he reported, they tended to do eagerly and encouragingly. However, Pratt's successors, with only one or two exceptions (Wender,[2] for example, included in his list of therapeutic factors, a patient obtaining a sense of hope that his problems are soluble), simply ignored the topic. Thus, by the time Corsini and Rosenberg[3] produced their classification of therapeutic factors, hope managed to obtain only minor mention amidst a lengthy list of miscellaneous items.

A further decade and a half elapsed before hope was properly recognized. Obviously stimulated by the work of Frank—done mainly in the 1950s and 1960s—Yalom[13] included the factor in his classification. He sees its contribution chiefly in group-specific terms. For example, since a group is heterogeneous with respect to the degree of improvement its members attain, the opportunity is provided for a patient to observe that one or more of his peers with similar problems have gained from treatment. Moreover, the therapist, Yalom advocates, should exploit this process by explicitly pointing out any improvement achieved in the group.

The difference between hope as a general placebo effect and its specific application in a group now becomes evident. The therapist by virtue of his status and qualities constitutes a form of placebo (the group therapist of course is no exception here) but it is the patient's peers who are essential in order to demonstrate that problems can be tackled effectively and that the group is a helpful forum. Mobilization of hope through this process therefore increases optimism as well as stimulating action. In this context, we should note that hope differs intrinsically from vicarious learning, in which a patient notes *how* his co-members tackle their problems, and learns indirectly from their therapy experience (see earlier in this chapter).

Definition

We are now in a position to define hope as a process which operates when the patient: sees that other group members have improved or are improving and that the group can be helpful to its members in accomplishing their goals; he is thus optimistic about the group's potential to help him too. Examples of hope using the 'most important event' questionnaire are:

In the past few meetings, Fiona has noted how the group has become more open. She herself has become much less defensive in her reactions to the criticism of others. This was a problem she had wanted to overcome. Consequently, she has realized that she has more faith in the group to actually help her.

I got angry with the therapist and I see now that I am able to confront people in authority. I am optimistic that I am improving. I see I can now get angry without the world collapsing and I know that I am getting somewhere and going somewhere. Getting angry in the group is a start. I can see now that the group can help.

On several occasions I have had to really think what I say in relation to others and how I feel about them. I feel optimistic because maybe soon we will all open up fully and then each benefit from that.

The discussion between Carol and Maureen concerning Maureen's worry about having an adverse effect on the group and wishing to leave was the most important event for me. I felt I had some understanding of Maureen's feelings and began to feel that she and indeed all of us were getting somewhere in tackling our problems.

Lorraine had a sense of relief that after talking openly last week the group was able to deal with her by being supportive and helpful. It symbolized her commitment, particularly to the idea of group therapy. She gained confidence that she could use the group profitably for herself.

In contrast to the study of hope as placebo, the neglect by researchers of hope as a therapeutic factor in a group-specific sense is striking. We have been unable to track down any studies on it, other than those in which patients in group therapy are asked to rate the value of hope as part of a broader enquiry into their perceptions of the relative helpfulness of various therapeutic factors (see Chapter 9).

One obvious future investigation is a controlled study in which the effects on process and outcome of explicitly mobilizing patients' hopes are compared with the effects of keeping hope to a minimum, within limits that are ethically permissible. In the experimental condition, the therapist would be trained to highlight gains made by members and to stress, with concrete examples, the healing power of the group. The goal would be to ensure that patients' hopes were repeatedly and consistently aroused. The experimental design would in many respects simulate the studies of the effects of preparing patients for therapy that we described in the chapter on guidance (see p. 179). Indeed, some of those investigations overlap with the study we are proposing here. But they differ in the one crucial respect that the experimental manipulation of patients' expectations is limited to a pre-therapy orientation phase.

In the meanwhile, until systematic knowledge becomes available, we can assume from both clinical lore and via extrapolation from the literature on 'preparation for therapy' that the instillation of hope, especially when based on concrete evidence of clinical progress within the group, is a reasonable factor to promote, and probably contributory to outcome. At the least, it is likely to enhance a patient's commitment to the therapeutic task. One caveat becomes obvious though. The therapist should not attempt to mobilize the patient's hopes unless it is warranted; ill-founded optimism can only be a retreat from reality and a prelude to disillusionment. Fortunately, clinical progress among some patients is a sufficiently prominent feature of the mature, working group to allow the therapist to deploy the arousal of hope to useful effect.

References

1. Burrow, T. The group method of analysis. *Psychoanalytic Review* **14**, 268–80 (1927).
2. Wender, L. The dynamics of group psychotherapy and its application. *Journal of Nervous and Mental Disease* **84**, 54–60 (1936).
3. Corsini, R. and Rosenberg, B. Mechanisms of group psychotherapy: processes and dynamics. *Journal of Abnormal and Social Psychology* **51**, 406–11 (1955).
4. Foulkes, S. H. *Therapeutic group analysis*. Allen and Unwin, London (1964).
5. Lieberman, M. A. Group methods. In: *Helping people change* (eds. F. H. Kanfer and A. P. Goldstein). Pergamon, New York (1980).
6. Robinson, D. Self-help health groups. In: *Small groups and personal change* (ed. P. B. Smith). Methuen, London (1980).
7. Dawkins, R. *The selfish gene*. Oxford University Press, Oxford (1978).
8. See, e.g.: Piaget, J. *The moral judgement of the child*. Kegan Paul, London (1932).
9. Killilea, M. Mutual help organizations: interpretations in the literature. In: *Support systems and mutual help: multidisciplinary explorations* (eds. G. Caplan and M. Killilea). Grune and Stratton, New York (1976).
10. Antze, P. The role of ideologies in peer psychotherapy organizations: some theoretical considerations and three case studies. *Journal of Applied Behavioural Science* **12**, 323–46 (1976).
11. Robinson, D. *Talking out of alcoholism: the self-help process of Alcoholics Anonymous*. Croom Helm, London (1979).

12. Berzon B., Pious, C., and Farson, R. The therapeutic event in group psychotherapy: A study of subjective reports by group members. *Journal of Individual Psychology* **19**, 204–12 (1963).
13. Yalom, I. D. *The theory and practice of group psychotherapy*. Basic Books, New York (1975).
14. Kissen, M. The concept of identification: an evaluation of its current status and its significance for group psychotherapy. In: *Group psychotherapy from the south-west* (ed. M. Rosenbaum). Gordon and Breach, New York (1974).
15. Jeske, J. O. Identification and therapeutic effectiveness in group therapy. *Journal of Counselling Psychology* **20**, 528–30 (1973).
16. Rosenthal, T. L. and Bandura, A. Psychological modeling: theory and practice. In: *Handbook of psychotherapy and behaviour changes* (eds. S. L. Garfield and A. E. Bergin). Wiley, New York (1978).
17. Bednar, R. L., Weet, C., Evensen, P., *et al.* Empirical guidelines for group therapy: pretraining, cohesion and modelling. *Journal of Applied and Behavioural Science* **10**, 149–65 (1974).
18. Falloon, I. Interpersonal variables in behavioural group therapy. *British Journal of Medical Psychology* **54,** 133–41 (1981).
19. Falloon, I., Lindley, P., McDonald, R., *et al.* Social skills training of out-patient groups. *British Journal of Psychiatry* **131**, 599–609 (1977).
20. Blatner, H. A. *Acting-in: practical applications of psychodramatic methods.* Springer, New York (1973).
21. Frank, J. D., Hoehn-Saric, R., Imber, S. D., *et al. Effective ingredients of successful psychotherapy*. Brunner–Mazel, New York (1978).
22. Pratt, J. H. The tuberculosis class: an experiment in home treatment. In: *Group psychotherapy and group function* (eds. M. Rosenbaum and M. Berger). Basic Books, New York (1975).

9 Therapeutic factors overall

In this chapter we turn to a consideration of the literature in group therapy devoted to 'therapeutic factors overall'. We use this phrase in covering contributions—either theoretical or empirical—in which an attempt is made to study a group of therapeutic factors at the same time. This approach differs from that adopted in the preceding seven chapters where factors were examined individually. Since most of the therapeutic factors that enter into this chapter have been dealt with earlier in the book, we shall be spared the task of redefining them; those we meet afresh will be examined briefly.

Theoretical aspects

It would be tempting to discuss the major theoretical schools in group therapy in terms of the therapeutic factors each of them incorporates; the snag is that this would require a book on its own. In any event, most of these theories do not apply explicitly the concepts behind therapeutic factors; the focus tends to be on more global phenomena, rather than on highlighting therapeutic mechanisms. Our look therefore is confined to those theoretical formulations which do emphasize therapeutic factors.

The psychoanalytic approach

A convenient starting point is the group psychoanalytic approach. The most representative theorist in this context has been Samuel Slavson. He argued in a seminal paper entitled 'A Systematic Theory', published in 1954,[1] that the same therapeutic mechanisms, with some minor variations, typify both individual and group analytic treatments, namely: transference, catharsis, insight, reality testing, and sublimation. Transference, for Slavson, is the bedrock on which the other factors rest. He suggests that repressed feelings and memories from childhood, concerning siblings as well as parents, are activated through their transference to either the therapist or to fellow group members. He coined the term 'libidinal transference' to refer to the process related to parents, and 'sibling transference' to that involving relations with siblings. A third form, 'identification transference', covers that aspect of transference in which other group members, including the therapist, serve as ideal models to be imitated. A further differentiation is made between positive and negative types of transference. Both are necessary for effective therapy—the first to keep the patient in the group (this amounts to his confidence and faith in the therapist and in therapy) and therefore always in the foreground; the second as temporary but enabling the patient to recognize and subsequently to understand such feelings as anger and aggression.

Catharsis, Slavson's second factor, is conceptualized broadly, but essentially consists of the patient disclosing, without censorship or inhibition, private thoughts, memories, and feelings. This free association is distinguished from associative thinking—the sharing of material concerned with current reality. Through the more important process of free association the patient comes to remember events from the past causally related to his present neurotic state. It would appear that free association is the vehicle whereby repressed material is uncovered, and that the recognition of links between this material and the neurosis is the more specific therapeutic factor. Learning in this way does not necessarily call for personal self-disclosure. Through strong identification with a fellow member's free associations, a patient may discover that his problems are identical or closely allied, and insight may ensue vicariously. This aspect of catharsis is obviously akin to the therapeutic factor of 'vicarious learning', which we discussed in Chapter 8.

Slavson includes an additional therapeutic factor under the rubric of catharsis, namely universalization (see Chapter 8). This he regards as an aid to catharsis. As members realize that they share similar problems and impulses, their defensiveness diminishes, with resultant enhancement of self-esteem and reduction in guilt, anxiety, and other burdensome feelings. These benefits in turn pave the way for even greater self-disclosure, and self-confrontation.

It comes as no surprise to note that Slavson regards his third factor, insight, as inextricably bound to the aforementioned factors of transference and catharsis; there is an 'organic unity' between them. Insight is that intellectual process whereby the patient learns about what motivates his behaviour and how repressed feelings and memories have influenced these motivations. To achieve insight, ego defences must be dealt with and understood in order that resistances to learning and change may diminish. Interpretation by the therapist and by fellow group members, especially concerning the transference, is the chief technique in the attainment of 'direct insight'. 'Derivative insight' is an additional form of learning; here the patient realizes important things about himself 'automatically', through the process of emotional growth inherent in his participation in the group experience. The concept of emotional growth is not well established but may be linked to Slavson's fourth factor, reality testing, of which more in a moment.

Insight is, in Slavson's view, less potent in group therapy than in individual treatment. The reason is simple: there is less opportunity 'to plumb the depths of the unconscious and the past'. The premiss on which this comparison is made is that optimal clinical change depends on gaining knowledge about one's past history and about what was previously beyond conscious awareness. As we noted in Chapter 2, this premiss derives from speculation, and the evidence for an association between depth of insight and depth of change is presently unavailable. Moreover, the subsidiary place accorded to insight derived from the patient's here-and-now experience, with the implication that this form of learning is less valuable than direct insight, seems more to reflect Slavson's adherence to classical psychoanalytic theory than appreciation of the group process as a specific context for self-learning.

Reality testing, the fourth factor in Slavson's classification, seems in part to embrace features of interpersonal learning in the context of the here-and-now. Here, he highlights the group's function as a little world: 'The therapy group constitutes a tangible and pressing reality to each of its members. It makes demands upon the individual which he must meet if he wishes to remain a part of it. He has to deal with the ego functioning of a number of people, react to them or withhold such reactions, restrain and compromise, attend to other contributors to the discussion and expose himself to their scrutiny.'

Although the patient undergoes this type of interpersonal experience in his day to day living and can learn the truth of things from it, the group carries the distinct advantage of providing a forum in which his reactions 'can be analysed, interpreted, and understood'; also this *in situ* testing of reality, with its penetrating sense of immediacy, provides less opportunity to retreat into defensive measures. Again, we must return to the distinction we drew in Chapter 2 between psychogenetic insight and interpersonal insight, because Slavson argues in the context of his account of here-and-now learning that this is all well and good but not *sufficient* for change. The additional ingredient required for fully fledged insight is an understanding of unconscious drives and conflicts that underlie interpersonal behaviour, and this must be coupled with the process of working through 'in the light of memories and earlier relationships'. We considered the debate in Chapter 2 so there is no need to pursue these issues now. But before completing this account of reality testing, we should point out that embedded in it is a therapeutic factor which we ourselves have preferred to treat separately—vicarious learning (see Chapter 8). Slavson refers in the main to the therapist as a positive model for his patient to imitate, in particular his 'calm mien and self-confident manner', and associated ability to cope effectively in the face of stress—an inevitable condition in the life of the group. Imitation is succeeded by incorporation of the therapist's desirable attributes. The whole process is likened to a child's identification with his parents. Fellow members as models receive cursory mention only, suggesting that the group leader is the crucial figure in this aspect of reality testing.

Slavson's final factor, sublimation, like reality testing, is something of a hybrid. It involves not only the conventional psychoanalytic concept of developing socially acceptable ways of dealing with primitive instinctual drives but also the therapeutic import derived from a sense of belonging and being accepted (see Chapter 4). The link between the two is obvious from the following quote: 'The group as such and the very fact of being a part of it sublimate and redirect many negative urges and habitual responses.'

How do we appraise Slavson's schema? As a pioneer of the method of group therapy, and more specifically of the transfer of psychoanalytic theory from the individual to the group context, he has few rivals. His predecessors—Trigant Burrow, Paul Schilder, and Louis Wender, among them (see Chapter 1)—experimented with this translocation but Slavson was one of the first to elaborate those theoretical concepts that underlie the functioning of psychoanalytic group therapy (Alexander Wolf[2] worked in parallel and deserves mention as another able pioneering theorist). In so doing, Slavson successfully teased out distinctive therapeutic components and thus fashioned a classification of factors.

In the light of subsequent theoretical and empirical advances, we would suggest that there are difficulties with this classification, the most prominent of which is the tendency to implant within a particular therapeutic factor, others which do not properly belong under its umbrella. Thus, for example, catharsis (more accurately self-disclosure) also encapsulates vicarious learning and universality, while modelling, a facet of vicarious learning, is included in the factor of reality testing; sublimation incorporates acceptance. The second issue concerns the nature of insight in group treatment and the validity of Slavson's heavy emphasis on psychogenetic insight. Finally, to regard the therapist as the chief model for imitation, with fellow members relegated to a subsidiary position, seems unduly discriminatory and not in keeping with the common clinical observation that, for a particular patient, any other group member—peer or therapist—may fulfil the role of model. Furthermore, Slavson's selection of such a quality as calmness in the face of stress constitutes a most limited view of the modelling process.

Like Slavson, Farrell[3] highlights the importance of transference in group therapy, regarding it as no less central here than in individual analytic therapy. We commented on his contribution in Chapter 3. We return to his ideas here in order to consider how they encompass a constellation of therapeutic factors. On the grounds that the group personifies and dramatizes the unconscious conflicts of its membership, he views insight as the key therapeutic ingredient in that it enables the patient to be liberated from the 'crippling maladaptive ties to his infantile perception of his relationship with his parents'. So far nothing new. Farrell's contribution lies in his elaboration of how the dynamics of transference operate to effect therapeutic change along a series of developmental steps. Firstly, members respond positively to the leader. Fear of their peers, however, paves the way for an attack on the leader, one which is fused with unconsciously motivated anger towards key family members. With the development of universality and cohesiveness comes recognition of the therapist as the agent responsible for these features in the group, and he now comes to be regarded as a 'mutually feared object'. Efforts are now made to obtain the therapist's help and when this is not forthcoming, members turn towards one another. This is fraught with complication and intermember hostility results. At this point 'collective resistance' intervenes, the therapist is set apart with hostility directed towards him, and positive bonds between members return. The therapist tolerates his position without need for reprisal. Instead, through interpretations, insight is offered which reduces the anger and allows positive feelings to emerge. Further interpretations can then be made which link feelings experienced in the group to key relationships from the past.

By considering transference in terms of a developmental sequence, we note how several therapeutic factors are operational, including universality, cohesiveness, catharsis, interaction, and self-understanding. The plausibility of the schema is open to debate and it could be argued that the pattern is unduly intricate and speculative.

Is psychoanalytic theory valid for group therapy?

The criticism that the application of psychoanalytic theory by such theorists as Slavson and Farrell is faulty, warrants our attention at this point. In their attachment to a theoretical model designed and elaborated in the highly specific context of insight-orientated, individually based treatment, have they tended to manipulate the model to fit the entirely different setting of a group of patients? Coupled with this potential source of error, have they through their concentration on what is fundamentally an 'intrapsychic' theory, tended to neglect those therapeutic forces which stem from specifically group processes?

Samuel Tawadros,[4] in a little known paper, has contributed usefully to these questions by distinguishing between factors exclusive to the group method and factors common to both individual and group therapy. In the latter category are included, for example, transference, the acquisition of insight, identification (actually vicarious learning), and free association. As we saw from the work of Slavson and Farrell, it is clear that these factors originated in the classic psychoanalytic approach and were applied, though in modified form, to the group setting. The classification by Tawadros of factors unique to group therapy illuminates nicely the group's inherent therapeutic power. Under the rubric of the 'socialization process', he covers two aspects: the patient's conformism to the group's values (a topic we look at shortly), and the opportunity to lessen self-absorption by developing an interest in fellow members and deriving satisfaction from the resultant altruism. Co-membership also enables the participant to re-evaluate his own problems and experience them in a new light—against those of his peers. This comparison is an advantageous step on the pathway to insight.

Two other forms of comparison are cited by Tawadros as exclusive to group therapy. The first he labels 'the homogeneity of suffering'—the realization by a patient that his fellows share many of his problems, that he is not unique in his suffering, and that he is not substantially different to others. We discussed this factor, universality, in Chapter 8. The second beneficial comparison involves the provision of hope, that improvement and change are possible. Reassurance results from the patient's observation that he is better off than some co-members while others have gained from the group experience (see Chapter 8 for our discussion of instillation of hope).

Tawadros then turns to a special quality of the group—its representation of the social world within which it exists. His misleading label for the therapeutic component that stems from the group as a social microcosm is 'activity of the patient'. That the group member must participate actively in order to gain from the experience and, indeed, that the group itself will only operate effectively with such active participation, is all too obvious. But this constitutes a condition for change and not a therapeutic factor in itself. A more apt label might be 'immediate experience of reality and opportunity for reality testing'. The group embodies a wide range of feelings, ideas, attitudes, and fantasies, normally met in everyday life—grief, despair, humour, rivalry, envy, jealousy, submissiveness, excitement, mutual comparison, self-doubt, to name but a few. Here is an opportunity for the patient to have direct experience of these aspects of reality and to gain a more accurate perception overall of what constitutes reality in himself and in his environment. Tawadros also links activity in the group to the therapeutic factor of acceptance, when he points to the group's potential to provide a patient with a sense of personal worth by enabling him to take initiatives and carry responsibilities, patterns of behaviour previously absent or rarely practised. Acceptance, this time in the form of unconditional positive regard, is introduced elsewhere in Tawadros's classification and is linked by him to altruism. This additional factor entitled 'meeting basic personality needs' seems merely replication. The same can be said of 'intellectualization in group discussion', which overlaps considerably with reality testing as described above.

Finally, we note the inclusion of family re-enactment as a distinctive group-based factor; this is misleadingly labelled as 'communal catharsis'. The presence in a group of the therapist as authority or parental figure, and fellow patients as sibling figures, facilitates the replay of key early family experiences which contribute to the ultimate acquisition of insight. In addition the group is experienced as a surrogate family which has the capacity to function effectively and harmoniously and thus may demonstrate the contrast with the original maladaptive and conflicted family. Whilst including this category in his list of factors, Tawadros is unimpressed by its therapeutic potential, preferring to view relationships in the group in a much wider context, namely in terms of the group as a social microcosm. As we shall see in the section on empirical research, his doubt has indeed been confirmed.

We offer no apology for our rather detailed account of the contribution by Tawadros. Although its flaws are obvious—overlap between factors, confusing categorization, and misleading labelling of the factors—he has shown the value of teasing out those therapeutic ingredients which are unique to the group approach. Moreover, we are reminded that it is unsatisfactory, conceptually, to extrapolate from one mode of therapy to another (in this case individual to group but it applies equally to other common extrapolations such as individual to marital, and individual to family). In the act of transposing a theoretical model that was devised for individual therapy, the theorist is obliged to take careful note of a number of interrelated questions: can the model be transposed in the first place; if it can, which of its elements cannot make the migration; of those that can, are any alterations required to make them fit more snugly into the group mode; what additional factors, not covered by the original model, but stemming from the uniqueness of the group process, must be incorporated; and, finally, what are the potential effects of the interaction of the two sets of factors—are they synergistic, complementary, or possibly disruptive?

As we stated at the outset of this section, it is not our purpose here to traverse the entire field of group treatment in order to ascertain the therapeutic factors each theoretical model embodies. Instead, we focus on models which explicitly highlight therapeutic factors. We omit one that unquestionably falls into this category, the dynamic-interactional (or interpersonalist) model (see Chapter 3); it would be unduly repetitious to consider this after our detailed account of its essential components in the chapters on interaction (see p. 76) and on insight (see p. 33). Moreover the model of Kelman[5] that we will consider overlaps substantially with it. We shall return to the interpersonalist model in the section on empirical research.

Specific models for group therapy

Three innovatory models of group therapy—those devised by Papanek,[6] Kelman,[5] and Maxmen[7]—incorporating specific sets of therapeutic factors, are noteworthy.

The Papanek model Papanek's approach begins with the interesting premiss that the therapist influences the group to form a culture based on humanistic values; this applies to all group therapists whatever their school of thought. Three values—the rough equivalent of therapeutic factors—underlie the goals of treatment: egalitarianism, honesty, and altruism. *Egalitarianism* is almost identical with the factor of acceptance (see Chapter 4): the patient is accepted with his admitted deficiencies and thus feels an equal. The experience goes beyond this insofar as he then comes to appreciate 'the advantages and pleasures of democratic and egalitarian values'. As he foregoes the need for an 'absolute benevolent power' and loses the fear of an 'absolute evil power', so he is able to assimilate the new egalitarian value and develop a 'democratic' personality. The emphasis placed by the group culture on *honesty*—embracing such qualities as candour and genuineness—facilitates the sort of atmosphere that enables the patient to cultivate this value in himself and to relinquish traits like insincerity, secretiveness, and evasiveness. The third value, *altruism*, is concerned with the promotion of social behaviour that leads to the experience of mutual identification and mutual helpfulness. The pleasure from understanding and communicating with others and the bolstering of self-esteem through the act of altruism ensue. The patient shifts from a previously immobilized position of self-absorption to one of social awareness. According to this model, overall change follows as the patient reappraises his values and succeeds in integrating egalitarianism, honesty, and altruism into his personality.

Papanek's approach is no doubt most appealing to therapists who espouse the tenets of humanistic psychology and align themselves with the associated human-potential movement. The values cherished by them are identical to those favoured by Papanek. However, his assertion that his model is applicable to all therapists, whatever their theoretical allegiance, is not likely to be met with universal acclaim. Moreover, the argument could be advanced that psychotherapy should, ideally, be value-free. No one, we suppose, would quibble with the idea of inculcating meritorious qualities like honesty and altruism in patients (we remain dubious about the concept of egalitarianism in this context), but is this the function of the therapist? Those clinicians within a more traditional mould would probably contend that the patient entering therapy has specific problems with which he needs to grapple, and that the way to improvement is principally through insight. Following the dispersal of disabling forces through the attainment of greater self-awareness, the patient should in theory be better equipped to make choices and decisions about the way he conducts his life, including the set of values he will pursue.

We ourselves are inclined to attend seriously to Papanek's thought-provoking model. We cannot easily retreat from reflecting deeply over whether values of the kind she stresses do have a place in psychotherapy. Since the publication of her paper, there has been a trend in group therapy towards a humanistic approach, exemplified by the development of the encounter group, the increasing popularity of such schools as the Gestalt and existential, and the rapid expansion of the human-potential movement in psychology and psychotherapy. Humanistic values permeate all these developments. Perhaps, we must face the reality that, nowadays, a substantial proportion of patients—dogged by a sense of malaise and lack of purpose—enter therapy to seek clarification of where they are going in their lives and hoping to achieve greater self-fulfilment.

Kelman's model Like Papanek, Herbert Kelman's theoretical model[5] of how groups facilitate change holds that the therapist is the principal figure involved. His basic assumption contains two related elements: psychotherapy is a process involving social influence, and the group therapist is the primary agent of this influence. Unlike Papanek, Kelman hastens to point out that his 'use of the term "social influence" does not carry any value connotations whatsoever'.

One of the many attractive features of Kelman's model is the way he has demarcated a specific, developmental sequence, and differentiated between changes taking place within and outside of the therapy group. Three processes whereby social influence can exert its effects are distinguished: compliance, identification, and internalization. All three are necessary for improvement, operate in conjunction with each other, and are concerned with clinical change occurring both within and outside the group. Kelman, in lucid and comprehensive fashion, takes his reader through the various steps of his model.

Within the therapy group, *compliance* is the first type of influence: the patient accepts the influence from the therapist and to a lesser extent from his fellow patients in order to obtain some reward (or to avoid punishment), or to win approval (or to avoid disapproval). The therapist's role is conceived of as a 'trainer'. Even if the therapist disavows such a directive stance, Kelman avers, he implicitly acts as a powerful agent who has the capability to offer or withhold approval. Much of the power emanates from the fact that the patient invariably feels anxious and insecure in the initial phase of treatment. The therapist is buttressed by the group members who 'can serve as additional sanctioning agents' by pressing a peer to conform to the norms of the group. These norms are set by the therapist and concern a commitment to productive therapeutic work. Motivation is what we are discussing, but motivation originating in the patient's need for the therapist's approval rather than the motivation brought by the patient to his therapy. It will be readily apparent that compliance in itself does not constitute a therapeutic factor. Yet, it is for Kelman an essential preliminary for therapeutic change. He refers to this form of influence as 'strictly a mediating step'. Following the terminology we outlined in the introductory chapter, we prefer to employ the term 'condition for change', i.e. compliance enables therapeutic factors to operate.

The second form of influence, *identification*, follows the patient's commitment to the group's work via compliance. He must now build up this commitment in order to continue in treatment and to withstand the strange, bewildering, and uncertain qualities of the experience, as yet unaccompanied by any sizeable benefit. But it is essential that he appreciates that benefit is likely to occur in the long term and that the interim experience is not hazardous. These developments ensue primarily through a process of identification with the therapist. Through his relationship with the therapist—one of conscious positive transference—the patient comes to enjoy trust in the clinical situation and his self-esteem is bolstered with the recognition that he is a 'person who is worthy of attention and acceptance'. Kelman elaborates on this latter aspect and clearly regards as paramount the therapist's role as an 'accepting' permissive, expert listener. The therapist is also a promoter of a patient's faith in his ability to be helpful. This is associated with the enhancement of hopefulness that change is likely. As with compliance, the therapist is aided by the group members in the process of identification. They act too in facilitating a patient's hopeful continuation in the group. This occurs in a variety of ways. For example, his sense of isolation wanes as he comes to feel that he has a place in the group and can obtain support from it. This acceptance takes place notwithstanding his deficiencies and flaws (see Chapter 4). He is also reassured by the realization that he is not unique and that many of his difficulties are shared with others (see Chapter 8). A further source of encouragement lies in the patient's use of peers as a reference group: he perceives that he is not as badly off as he had imagined; others appear to make progress, which provides hope that personal improvement can be accomplished (see Chapter 8).

Kelman suggests that identification, like compliance, is a means to an end rather than an end in itself. We shall see that this is reasonable in the context of his schema. Also, in view of the potential dangers of excessive identification, especially dependence on the therapist and/or the group at the expense of the therapeutic task, we need to be wary that the group does not evolve into a cosy, warm retreat where the participant feels secure and safe, even achieves greater self-regard, but where nothing further happens. In such a group there is no sense of challenge, no experience of intensely uncomfortable feelings from which he may learn, no constructive confrontation, no basic change of attitude, no fresh perspective. Despite this cautionary comment, we would interpose our own view that several of the elements contributing to identification are inherently therapeutic in themselves. In particular, as is obvious from our comments in earlier chapters, we would highlight the role of acceptance, universality, and instillation of hope. These factors may obviously pave the way for the effective operation of other therapeutic forces, but are too significant to be relegated merely to 'means'.

Kelman labels his third form of influence variously as '*internalization*' and (somewhat inaccurately) 'occurrence of corrective emotional experiences', the latter term clearly derived from the work of Alexander and French.[8] Internalization is defined, in rather clumsy jargon, as a person accepting 'influence in order to maintain the congruence of his actions and beliefs with his value system'. Its elaboration in the context of group therapy is much clearer. Internalization, as we have commented earlier, is regarded as the most therapeutic of these three forms of influence. The patient examines his attitudes and behaviour as they manifest themselves in the group, and particularly while he is undergoing associated, intense feelings. The examination is thus not limited to an intellectual pursuit. The effect is a change in the patient's conception of himself and his social relationships: 'He gains new insight, new understanding of the attitudes that he characteristically brings to his interpersonal relationships, of the behaviour patterns that result from them, and of the expectations of others' reactions that generally guide him.' With such insight come more realistic attitudes and expectations.

A central element in this process of learning is the therapist as an object of transference, although Kelman conceptualizes this more broadly than in conventional psychoanalytic therapy. However, if his allocation of space is any criterion, it appears as if fellow members are more important contributors than the therapist to internalization. Here, we enter territory covered in some detail in our account of interpersonal insight and learning from interpersonal action (see Chapters 2 and 3). Kelman's approach points to the acquisition of this form of insight much more so than psychogenetic insight and this is particularly obvious when he describes the role of peers in the process of learning. The presence of several collaborators, who serve as 'interaction objects' to the patient, provides a spectrum of interpersonal stimuli, and increases the chances of his characteristically pathological behaviour and attitudes emerging in therapy. This is especially likely if the group tends to be heterogeneous in terms of sex, social status, and personality style. The manifestation of the undesirable attitude or behaviour is followed by the group's here-and-now reactions to it. Both elements are then directly accessible as sources of learning.

Kelman cites two other theoretical advantages over individual therapy. The group as a social microcosm bears a similarity to the patient's everyday experience. Thus the learning taking place in therapy can be readily extrapolated to 'real life', and note taken of how undesired patterns of behaviour intrude there, as well as how various efforts to overcome them succeed or not. The second advantage over individual therapy is the opportunity for vicarious learning (see Chapter 8): the patient identifies with certain of his peers and can, through observation of their behaviour and efforts to change, acquire insight about himself and thus benefit indirectly. Vicarious learning is embedded in internalization, and this tends to underemphasize the value of the former. We would contend that vicarious learning warrants a distinct category in any schema of therapeutic factors; our own clinical observations strongly suggest that much learning about the self, either explicit or implicit, stems from observation and/or imitation of others.

As we mentioned earlier, Kelman distinguishes between the three forms of influence occurring *within* the group and *outside* of it. This is a most welcome and highly rational feature of his model. He is one of the few theorists in the field of psychotherapy to give emphasis rather than lip-service to what really is an obvious fact: changes in attitude and behaviour must extend to daily life if treatment is to be effective. The therapeutic endeavour is futile if learning and its effects remain confined to the setting of therapy. Kelman demonstrates how his three therapeutic forces operate in the patient's daily life in a manner complementary to their functioning in the therapeutic group. A particularly noteworthy point is the two-way traffic involved. We commonly refer to the generalizability of the effects of therapy to real life but, as Kelman shows in his model, the process also works in the opposite direction. For example, experimentation with some new form of behaviour outside may be brought to the group for appraisal. Such a behavioural change need not necessarily be based on clear insight. Rather, its subsequent examination in the group may yield definitive self-knowledge.

We could elaborate at much greater length on Kelman's model since it covers such wide ground and is so full of useful clinical detail. His contribution certainly merits close study. In terms of the linkage between therapeutic factors and group therapy theory, the model is masterful. We are not simply provided with a list of factors with tenuous links between them. On the contrary, the model takes into account a logical sequence of therapeutic steps, the distinctive role of the therapist amongst the group members, and the interplay between the sources of influence on the patient within and outside the group. Another feature that we alluded to earlier is the attention given to anti-therapeutic aspects. Kelman considers, at several points in his exposition, how a therapeutic factor can operate detrimentally. We cited earlier, for example, how over-identification with the therapist or with the group may occur.

An additional strength of the model lies in its potential for clinical and research application. Clinically, Kelman himself points out a number of implications concerning, *inter alia*, the selection of patients, composition of the group, the therapist as the setter of group norms, the inclusion of extra-therapy events for clinical inspection, and the potential misapplication of therapeutic factors. Much of it is grounded in common clinical observation and many points are readily convertible into testable hypotheses. This facility is unusual in group therapy theory, where much is, alas, too inferential or incoherent to permit of testing.

The Maxmen model Maxmen,[7] to whose model we now turn, is quite blunt when he declares: 'Pragmatic, not theoretical, considerations should dictate our therapeutic models, and it is hoped that patients can survive our theories. Groups should help and that objective should not be drowned by unrelenting waves of theory.' Strong words indeed! (We are confident that Maxmen would be happy with Kelman's model.)

Maxmen practises what he preaches. In 1973 he published the report of a study in which patients' views were sought about factors they had found helpful in their experience of group therapy.[9] Five years later his model of group therapy appeared, revealing to what a great extent he had been influenced by his patients. The most prominent quality of this model however is specificity, namely, its formulation for a particular form of group treatment—short-term, in-patient, group therapy. As Maxmen correctly points out, theories of therapy devised for long-term, out-patient groups have been applied to the in-patient setting without due thought to their appropriateness or relevance. Thus, for example, we have not uncommonly encountered insight-orientated groups—based on psychoanalytic principles—composed of relatively disturbed in-patients and participating for only a handful of sessions because their hospitalization is short-term. (Maxmen is of course referring here to a typical acute admission unit. We are not concerned here with long-stay wards for chronically ill patients or with specialized psychotherapeutic units such as therapeutic communities.) To make matters worse, the therapist is often a junior staff member with little theoretical knowledge and limited group experience.

Maxmen's first step in presenting his model is to highlight the particular characteristics of psychiatric in-patients: they are commonly more disturbed and disorganized than out-patients; their dependency is often intense; and they tend to feel hopeless, helpless, and ineffective. The unique features of institutional life are also relevant. Obviously, the patients are in contact with one another throughout the day, allowing for considerable extra-group socialization; they also share certain experiences, both therapeutic and counter-therapeutic, on the wards; the ties with their natural environment are broken thereby precluding the application of what they gain therapeutically to 'real-life'; they are frequently compelled to participate in the group because it is a component of the ward's programme; and many of them are involved in other treatments, some very different, e.g. medication.

These points are of course well known to those who treat in-patients but somehow have become neglected when the function of group therapy is considered. Maxmen argues that theoretical ideas appear to be more seductive than pragmatic ones in the in-patient group therapist's priorities. The other obvious pragmatic issue is efficacy: there are sparse data on this question but the available evidence indicates very limited success for previously applied models, mostly of a psychoanalytic kind.[10]

In the light of the above, Maxmen has formulated a model—he labels it 'educative'—which is eminently coherent, uncomplicated, and neatly tailored to the psychiatric in-patient. A key phrase reflecting the primary goal of the educative group is that it seeks 'to help in-patients think clinically and respond effectively to the consequences of their illnesses'. Behind this goal rests the assumption that in short-term hospitalization the need is to modify efficiently the disturbed behaviour of the patient in order that he can resume his place in the community promptly. But, and this is a crucial but, Maxmen does not see group therapy as the *primary* treatment in changing this disturbed behaviour. Other modes of treatment, such as medication, are more relevant. In so limiting the group's aim, the model is recognizing the brief period available for in-patient treatment.

Which therapeutic factors has Maxmen built into his model? They may be conveniently labelled as universality, altruism, and 'clinical understanding'. Through the operation of universality, patients become aware that their problems are not unique. Altruism—the realization that members act helpfully towards one another and the satisfaction derived therefrom—is associated with a fundamental assumption, namely 'that the group's value derives from patients having the experience of perceiving themselves, rather than the leader, as the principal therapeutic agents'. One of the therapist's chief tasks is to train his group to think and act therapeutically by inculcating a norm which explicitly declares that mutual help is central to the group's style of work. The patient's adoption of this helper's role, Maxmen hypothesizes, contributes to a reduction in his sense of incompetence and dependency, and to an increase in his self-esteem. Obviously, the converse also applies with the patient learning to accept help from his peers.

The third factor in Maxmen's model—'clinical understanding'—has a quality very much linked to the group's aim of encouraging patients to think in a clinical way: they learn to identify their own maladaptive behavioural pattern and to recognize and avoid those circumstances likely to precipitate recurrence of that pattern. To achieve this, attention is given predominantly to the behaviour and related feelings that have made admission to hospital necessary; and correspondingly to the here-and-now events in the group. Psychodynamic understanding through examination of a patient's early personal history is intentionally not striven for.

The educative model, particularly because of the features of insight just described, has been labelled 'superficial' and 'simple-minded'. Maxmen is refreshingly flexible in this regard, preferring to leave the overall question of efficacy to the empirical test. But he is not slow to counterattack, as we noted earlier—a theory may be highly refined, 'look good', but will be of little or no value unless it passes the tests of suitable applicability and reasonable effectiveness. Maxmen stresses that until the relative impact of different models is established, his own—for in-patients exclusively—in which the aim is limited to learning how to give and receive help, 'should never be underestimated'. We feel he can afford to be less defensive. His formulations are persuasively sensible when one reflects on the needs of the usual in-patient. Furthermore, he has opted for therapeutic factors which, at least from the point of view of a large cohort of his patients, are helpful.[9]

One final word on theoretical contributions for the sake of completeness. A number of descriptive articles have appeared over the years, for example, by Tenebaum,[11] Opler,[12] and Becker[13] which echo the work of Corsini and Rosenberg[14] but do not break new ground.

Empirical research

The most common research strategy in studying therapeutic factors overall relies on the group member as 'consumer'. His views are sought on what he has found helpful in his therapy experience. Of the two procedures to obtain this information, one is a direct inquiry, the other more oblique.

In the direct form, the patient is asked to rank in order of helpfulness to himself a number of statements which cover the various therapeutic factors. Yalom[15] constructed the original questionnaire by obtaining sixty items, covering twelve therapeutic factors, from a variety of sources. A definitive version was adopted following the recommendations of several group therapists. The respondent examines the sixty statements and assigns them to one of seven categories, from most to least helpful. The resultant Q-sort,[16] which resembles a normal distribution curve, allows for the analysis of the respondent's rank-ordering.

The second approach[17] has the advantage of being more indirect in that the group member is not provided with statements reflecting therapeutic factors but responds to an open-ended question. Although subject to variation, the basic enquiry revolves around the event, occurring during a group session (or over a series of sessions, or over an entire course of treatment), which the patient regards as most important or significant for himself. The written response is then categorized in terms of a classification of therapeutic factors. One may assume reasonably confidently that, provided assignment can be made reliably, the 'most important event' method is less biasing than the 'direct' questionnaire.

The method of enquiry is not the only feature of the empirical work that varies. Because of substantial differences in the samples studied, in the type of therapy given, and in the timing of questionnaire administration, the studies are not directly comparable. Matters are complicated by the absence of any good replications. The general result is a reasonable volume of research, but its cumulative quality is relatively poor. Despite this state of affairs, the work has yielded some interesting findings that warrant attention.

The questions that have been looked at within the framework of therapeutic factors overall are: (a) their comparative effectiveness—do some have a greater association with clinical change than others? (b) their comparative evaluation—regardless of outcome are some factors seen by patients as more helpful than others? (c) their relationship to group differences—do different types of groups have different associations with therapeutic factors? and (d) their relationship to individual differences—are differences among patients related in a particular way to therapeutic factors? Of these four questions, the second has been investigated most frequently, probably because it is the least complicated procedurally. But let us begin with the issue of comparative effectiveness. Questions (c) and (d) are in the main examined when relevant to the studies on questions (a) and (b).

Therapeutic factors and outcome

We have found only three studies which have explored the relationship between a constellation of therapeutic factors and outcome. One concerns long-term out-patient group therapy, another short-term encounter groups, and the third long-term institutional therapy of addicts. In the first, a retrospective study, Yalom and his colleagues[15] administered their therapeutic factor questionnaire on a single occasion to twenty out-patients who had recently terminated or were still in treatment. The average duration of therapy was sixteen months. The sample was obtained through the somewhat unconventional route of asking group therapists to refer their successful patients. This judgement was checked by a team of independent assessors, who interviewed the sample and made ratings of variables, such as symptoms and self-concept. No details, however, are provided about inter-rater reliability or about correlations between ratings from the different sources of therapist, patient, and independent assessor.

The rank-ordering of 12 therapeutic factors by the 20 patients indicated the following as the three most helpful factors: interpersonal-learning-input (in essence, feedback about one's behaviour), catharsis (a hybrid of self-disclosure and learning to express feelings), and acceptance (a sense of belonging to and being valued by the group). Family re-enactment (learning from parallels between the group as a symbolic family and one's family of origin), guidance (explicit and didactic advice and instruction), and identification (in essence, vicarious learning) were judged least helpful. The other six factors were valued in this order: insight, interaction, an existential factor, universality, instillation of hope, and altruism.

Although the work is limited by its retrospective nature and the other deficiencies already mentioned, the results show clearly the emphasis given to the interpersonal dimension—a patient learns from his peers how he comes across, he divulges personal material about himself, and he values the experience of being accepted by his fellows. There are at least three interpretations of the findings: the questionnaire is biased towards the 'interpersonal', as argued by Wiener[18] (see Chapter 2 for his criticism of Yalom); the patients have been 'trained' by therapists partial to an interpersonalist model and to factors central to this approach; or patients who profit from long-term group therapy do so by virtue of interpersonal-type factors. We are left to speculate about these alternatives.

In the second study, the investigation of encounter groups by Lieberman and his associates,[19] a therapeutic factor questionnaire was also administered—on a single occasion at the end of thirty hours of participation in one of various forms of encounter group, including Gestalt, transactional analysis, psychoanalytically orientated, and psychodrama. The student participants also wrote up their most important events following each group session. Unlike the first study this was prospective and outcome was assessed most comprehensively and thoroughly. 'High learners', about one-third of the sample, were distinguished from 'non-changers' and 'negative outcomes' chiefly on cognitive-type factors; the first rated insight, acceptance, advice and family re-enactment significantly more often than their non-profiting colleagues. The most important event questionnaire confirmed the emphasis placed on cognitive mechanisms by high learners compared to the other outcome groups. The former reported more episodes in which insight was prominent. Moreover, they were able to use the experience of fellow members in furthering their own self-knowledge.

Unusually, the study also succeeded in identifying the perception of therapeutic factors by the participants who had negative outcome or remained unchanged. Although they participated as actively as those who benefited, they seemed unable to make use of potentially therapeutic situations. For example, they did not record any benefit from events in the group in which they were not directly involved; thus, vicarious learning was not a strong feature of their experience.

Although the link between cognitive-type factors and positive change emerged as a reasonably consistent finding, the associations between other therapeutic factors and outcome were not as clear cut. One paradoxical problem facing the researchers was the sheer volume of data that emerged from the double-barrelled line of enquiry—direct questionnaire and the most important event questionnaire; the task of interpreting the myriad findings was obviously complicated.

The fifty male prison inmates—all former drug-addicts—making up the sample in the study by Steinfield and Mabli[20] are a rather special population but we make brief mention of their appraisal of therapeutic factors. Following the familiar research design, therapists were asked to identify their most successful group members who were about to terminate or had recently terminated. Unlike Yalom's study, no checks were made on the validity of this sampling procedure. These inmates had participated in twelve to fifteen hours per week of group therapy for an average of sixteen months. Just prior to release, they completed Yalom's therapeutic factor questionnaire. Insight emerged as the category most strongly emphasized, followed by an existential factor, catharsis (which also covers self-disclosure), and feedback. Least important were altruism, guidance, universality, and identification. Perhaps not surprising, in the light of the several hundreds of hours of group work in what was actually a therapeutic community setting, is the emphasis given to insight. The high ranking obtained by the existential category is of particular interest; this priority is not found anywhere else in the empirical work under review. A close look at the three items contributing to this ranking sheds some light on the unique result. The item ranked top of the 60 in the questionnaire reads: 'Learning that I must take ultimate responsibility for the way I live my life no matter how much guidance and support I get from others.' The two other items are concerned with the finiteness of life and having to face it alone. When we realize that the respondents were mostly poor, black heroin addicts, their preoccupation with existential issues becomes more understandable. They had, one assumes, seen premature death and wasted lives as a result of addiction among their peers. The threat of a similar fate was supposedly a constant bed-fellow. The minimal attention given to universality and altruism perhaps supports the hypothesis of an overwhelming engagement with personal life-and-death concerns.

The comparative evaluation of therapeutic factors by group members

We have traced several studies that focus on the comparative evaluation of therapeutic factors by group members, irrespective of their outcome. The non-cumulative character of research in this field, to which we alluded earlier, now becomes glaringly obvious. Consider, for example, some of the clinical samples and their respective therapies: out-patients in short-term groups, out-patients in long-term groups, in-patients in short-term therapy, participants in human relations groups, and prison inmates. Indeed, a very heterogeneous range of samples. We can but try to make some sense of the findings by grouping the various samples into clinical versus non-clinical and institutional versus non-institutional.

Out-patient studies Three studies have examined the views of out-patients. In the first, by Corder *et al.*,[21] 16 adolescents in various groups met weekly for nine to 12 months and completed Yalom's therapeutic factor questionnaire after at least half a year's membership. The results are difficult to interpret since they are presented only as a ranking of the 60 individual items in the questionnaire and not in terms of therapeutic factor categories. In any event, items selected as most helpful came from catharsis (more accurately a combination of self-disclosure and interaction) and interaction; items regarded as least helpful came from insight (in fact, learning about transference and about remote causes of current behaviour) and vicarious learning (specifically modelling). The study reveals strikingly that Yalom's categories are not internally consistent. Thus, for example, the item most prized was from catharsis ('Being able to say what was bothering me instead of holding it in'); at the same time the item regarded as second-least helpful was also from catharsis but obviously covered a quite different aspect of the group process ('Expressing negative and/or positive feelings towards the group leader'). (See Chapter 6 for a fuller account of the weakness of this category of catharsis, and Chapter 10 for attempts to improve Yalom's questionnaire.)

To obviate the methodological snags inherent in Yalom's questionnaire approach, Bloch and Reibstein[22] used the 'most important event' questionnaire. Thirty-three adult patients with neurosis or personality disorder, members of long-term groups, completed the questionnaire at regular intervals over the first six months of treatment. A team of three independent judges then assigned the events, with satisfactory reliability, to one of ten factors by following explicit instructions set out in a specially prepared manual.[17] Self-understanding emerged clearly as the most important factor in the patients' experience, reflected in over one-third of reported events. Other factors rated relatively frequently were self-disclosure (18 per cent) and interaction (13 per cent). Four factors were, by contrast, under-emphasized—guidance, catharsis, altruism, and universality. Acceptance, vicarious learning, and instillation of hope were of intermediate importance. The emphasis on a cognitive factor is not surprising considering the insight-orientated nature of the groups studied; and this probably accounts too for the complete neglect of guidance, which played almost no role in therapy. The differential appraisal of self-disclosure and catharsis suggests that their separation in our own classification of factors is justified.

As in the encounter group study,[19] the questionnaire was administered on several occasions throughout treatment. Repeated administration probably contributes more valid information than that obtained on a single occasion only. The respondent thinks about a circumscribed, relatively brief period—three sessions, for example—which enables him to recall more easily and, hopefully, more accurately the important event that took place during those sessions. By contrast, the selection of one event from a course lasting several weeks or months may suffer from the vagaries of clouded memories. Moreover, it is reasonable to assume that completion of the questionnaire at the end of therapy is apt to be biased by what a patient feels about his experience of group therapy overall and about his therapist. Repeated administration, at least in our own experience, is soon viewed by most patients as part of the routine of treatment and not as anything remarkable.

Raising the topic of potential bias should remind us that patients' views are naturally entirely subjective. Still, there is no question in our minds that consumer-orientated research is inherently worthwhile. The patients' views are obviously important in their own right. After all they are the recipients of all therapeutic efforts and without their co-operation treatment is futile. Furthermore, patients can be exceedingly percipient and astute about the therapeutic process overall. Foolhardy, even arrogant, is the therapist or investigator who avers that he exclusively is expert and knowledgeable.

Conversely, the therapist is well placed to contribute his views about therapeutic factors that are relevant to his own group members. It therefore puzzles us to discover that this cogent source has been tapped in only two studies. (See p. 232 for an account of Schaffer & Dreyer's work.) Bloch and Reibstein[22] also sought the views of their therapists using exactly the same procedure, i.e. asked therapists to select the most important event for each of their group members at three-weekly intervals over the first half year of their groups. Their accounts were assigned by independent judges to the classification of factors used for patients' responses. As with their patients, self-understanding was stressed most often, reflected in 38 per cent of the reported events. Other factors emerging as relatively important were interaction (25 per cent of events) and self-disclosure (19 per cent). Apart from acceptance, the remaining six factors in the classification were virtually ignored, amounting to a total of only seven per cent of reported events.

The importance placed by the therapists on self-understanding, while also stressing interaction and self-disclosure, is probably attributable to their orientation: they were all trained to use an interactional model[15] in which the patient is encouraged to be open and honest, to take risks, and to make intellectual sense of his emotional experience.

A simultaneous enquiry of both patients and their therapists covering the same therapy obviously has the advantage of enabling a comparison in perspective to be made. Two interesting differences between these perspectives are noteworthy. Although both patients and therapists value self-understanding, interaction, and self-disclosure, therapists consider interaction more important and in general tend to emphasize behavioural-type factors; patients on the other hand tend to stress cognitive-type factors. The possible bias of the method against the outside observer could account for this divergence; therapists may be more inclined to focus on observed behaviour than to hazard guesses about their patients' inner experiences, while patients can report subjective phenomena, such as new insights, learning from fellow group members, and feeling hopeful about improvement. There is some evidence for this explanation.

Self-understanding is a broadly defined factor that covers both public feedback about how the patient comes across to others and private, internal analyses of his own psychodynamics. An examination of the most important events coded as 'self-understanding' revealed that therapists emphasized the first type whereas patients focused on both.

The third study in which out-patients were the subjects, that by Dickoff and Lakin,[23] differs from Bloch and Reibstein's work in that therapy was relatively brief, averaging eleven sessions (in fact the sample received widely differing amounts of treatment). There were several other important differences: 28 patients were interviewed on aspects of their group experience, the enquiry took place between one and two-and-a-half years after the end of treatment, and their responses were transcribed and assigned to a rather idiosyncratic classification of therapeutic factors. How the questions asked led to the assignment to categories remains vague. In any event, the three resultant factors were: (a) suppression—'one forgets worries and gets rid of problems by "talking them off" . . .'; (b) support—mainly a combination of acceptance and universality; and (c) tools for action—insight, both interpersonal and intrapsychic, which may lead to changes in behaviour. Support was valued by nearly 60 per cent of the sample; suppression by about 30 per cent; and tools for action by a mere four patients. These findings differ substantially from those in the Bloch and Reibstein study, especially in the relative emphasis given to cognitive factors. Could it be that the patients studied by Dickoff and Lakin, attending an average of only eleven sessions, did not have sufficient time to learn how to use 'tools for action'? Also plausible is that these groups were more supportive and less insight-orientated in nature. A clue pointing in this direction is the brief description given of the therapist as a facilitator who showed 'interest, understanding, and acceptance', but who seems to have not made psychodynamic interpretations.

Dickoff and Lakin are unusual in looking at the question of the relationship between therapeutic factors and individual differences. Their most interesting finding in this regard is the significantly higher scores on the vocabulary scale of the Wechsler adult intelligence scale obtained by the quartet whose focus was on 'tools for action', compared to the other two groups. Thus verbal intelligence seems to be associated with an emphasis on cognitive learning. The authors surmise that 'limited intelligence may preclude the possibility of experiencing psychotherapy with emphasis on self-understanding', and draw implications for patient selection. It is widely agreed, though with a large measure of vagueness, that psychological-mindedness or conceptual ability is a requisite for insight-orientated group therapy. The Dickoff and Lakin study is a pointer to a more precise form of matching of patients in group therapy along dimensions of specific therapeutic factors.

The comparative evaluation of therapeutic factors by in-patients

The notion of specific factors for certain patients is compelling in the research by Maxmen.[9] We discussed his educative model in the section on theory and now confine ourselves to his empirical research, which is concerned with the comparative evaluation of therapeutic factors by in-patients. Bearing in mind the widespread use of group methods for patients briefly treated in psychiatric units, Maxmen's work warrants close attention. In-patients requiring short-term hospitalization were given, on a single occasion, a variant of Yalom's therapeutic factor questionnaire (as the timing of administration was not mentioned we must assume this was not standardized). One hundred consecutive participants in a group therapy programme constituted the research sample. Most were young or middle-aged adults, nearly two-thirds of them married, a quarter with previous experience of group therapy, and nearly half diagnosed as affective disorder; other diagnoses included personality disorder, schizophrenia (not severely disorganized schizophrenics), and alcoholism.

Group sessions were held each weekday and lasted one hour. Six patients and two co-therapists constituted the average membership. The approach used was interactional with a predominant here-and-now focus. Because of their brief period in hospital (on average, 18 days), patients attended an average of nine sessions. These details highlight the point, not sufficiently considered by clinicians, that in-patient group therapy is of necessity substantially different to its counterpart in the out-patient clinic and that the perception of factors helpful to in-patients is bound to differ correspondingly. The findings in the Maxmen study bear this out. Instillation of hope, cohesiveness (acceptance), altruism, and universality were judged most helpful of the twelve factors in the classification. Least emphasized factors were insight, guidance, family re-enactment, and identification (vicarious learning). Interaction and self-disclosure were of intermediate importance. Compare this picture with the findings in the out-patient-based studies already mentioned. It will be readily observed that factors of a cognitive and interactional type are given low priority by in-patients.

Maxmen's discussion of his results is intelligent and widely encompassing. He makes the following noteworthy points: (a) hope may be crucial in a patient for whom admission to a hospital reflects dismal failure and whose awareness of improvement in his fellow patients is highly encouraging; (b) although admission and group therapy were both limited in duration, acceptance probably prospered because the group met daily and its cohesiveness was reinforced by 'informal group contacts' between 'formal' sessions; (c) universality and altruism were to the fore because the group provided an opportunity for demoralized patients to begin to realize that co-members were in the same plight as themselves and that they were, through shared experiences of problems, able to aid one another; (d) self-disclosure is not prominent perhaps because the patients' brief group career does not permit sufficient trust to develop; (e) the short-term nature also precludes the proper utilization of cognitive learning, thus lessening the impact of insight as a therapeutic factor. More generally, Maxmen makes the salient comment that other variables, like length of sessions and the group's emotional atmosphere, and not the therapeutic factors studied, may be relevant in evaluating group therapy; and that although certain factors are emphasized by patients as helpful, it does not follow that they affect outcome (this latter point applies to all studies on comparative evaluation in which outcome is not focused on).

Three other studies also look at in-patient groups, but the settings, samples, and methods vary considerably. Macaskill[24] administered a brief version of Yalom's therapeutic factor questionnaire to nine women patients, diagnosed as borderline personality disorder and undergoing twice-weekly group therapy for an average of eleven months. Insight and altruism were rated as most helpful; interaction, vicarious learning, guidance, acceptance, and universality as least helpful. Macaskill surmises that the experience of the patients was chiefly one of individual therapy in groups. Given that the author played a central role as interpreter of his patients' narcissistic defences and transferences, it is not surprising that they attached high value to insight but saw interaction as least helpful.

Marcovitz and Smith[25] studied a population similar to Maxmen's—thirty in-patients, mostly depressives, in a short-term psychiatric unit. But the psychodynamic model they used differed radically from Maxmen's educative approach. Patients, who participated, on average, in eight sessions, completed Yalom's therapeutic factor questionnaire immediately prior to their discharge from the unit. Although they were also assessed on self-report scales of depression and showed improvement on these measures, no examination was made of the relationship between outcome and therapeutic factors. Presumably, this was regarded as futile in the light of the many other therapies the patients received concurrently. Ranked as most helpful were catharsis (in fact, self-disclosure), cohesiveness, and altruism (the latter two were, it will be recalled, also stressed by Maxmen's sample). Least helpful were vicarious learning, family re-enactment, and guidance. Intermediate were interaction, insight, instillation of hope, and universality. Among the implications the authors draw from their findings is 'the need to encourage patients to help each other by asking questions, showing concern, giving feedback, listening actively, and making constructive suggestions'.

The study of in-patients by Schaffer and Dreyer[26] is not readily comparable with the preceding trio because of the instrument used to measure patients' valuations of therapeutic factors ('How encounter groups work'—used to ascertain what a respondent regards as important in the way that encounter groups operate.)[19] An impressive sample of 100 in-patients in a crisis unit completed the questionnaire on two occasions one week apart. They selected the two items most relevant to their group therapy experience, which amounted to three sessions a day over an average ten-day period of hospitalization. Their choices remained similar over the week, suggesting stability in perception. Being responsible for oneself and insight were regarded as most helpful. Least helpful were vicarious learning (actually modelling), experimenting with new forms of behaviour, self-disclosure, and family re-enactment.

This is the only other study besides Bloch and Reibstein's[22] to enquire about therapists' perceptions of the value of therapeutic factors, although the methods differ markedly. Schaffer and Dreyer sought the general views of the thirty therapists working on the unit by having them complete the 'How encounter groups work' questionnaire for patients overall (not for specific patients as did Bloch and Reibstein). Again, the two most important therapeutic factors were requested. The responses, which bore little resemblance to those of the patients, revealed an emphasis on only three of the fourteen factors on the questionnaire—the expression of feelings, vicarious learning (modelling), and experimenting with behaviour. As in the Bloch and Reibstein study, therapists focused more on factors involving the interpersonal sphere, whereas their patients valued factors of an intrapersonal character. Our speculations to explain this difference (see p. 228) may well apply here too.

The comparative evaluation of therapeutic factors by non-patient subjects

Having covered the clinical field we consider now, more briefly, two studies on comparative evaluation of therapeutic factors by non-patient subjects. Berzon *et al.*,[27] were the first to use the 'most important event' approach, though we should note that their method was distinctly more biasing than later versions in that reference was made to the event which 'contributed most to you personally' rather than 'was the most important for you personally' (see reference 5, Chapter 2). Twenty-two volunteers—members of one of two groups which met weekly for fifteen sessions—satisfied the inclusion criteria of being able to function socially and occupationally and to communicate their subjective experience (presumably *not* the typical features of many patient samples). As they completed the questionnaire after each session, nearly 300 reports were available for assignment to a classification derived from Corsini and Rosenberg.[14] Of the nine factors, the three chosen as most helpful were insight ('increased awareness of own emotional dynamics'), universality, and altruism ('feeling positive regard, acceptance, sympathy for others'). Least important factors were acceptance and catharsis ('ventilating emotions').

As one would expect from such a sample—highly-educated, professional, volunteers—a cognitive factor stands out. This could be interpreted as 'personal growth', since insight here refers to new self-knowledge about matters like strengths and weaknesses, patterns of relating, and motivations. Less clear is the emphasis on universality. Could this be attributed to the mode of recruitment, that is, did those who volunteer have a need to overcome a sense of their being different in some way? It must remain speculation.

Two further findings are of interest in the work by the Berzon team. The first concerns the source of therapeutic influence. Interestingly, only 15 per cent of all events involved therapists, suggesting that co-members are the chief vehicle whereby therapeutic factors operate. The second finding highlights the probability, as common clinical observation suggests, that the unique personal traits, problems, and needs of a patient strongly influence the factors in the group that he perceives as helpful to himself. As Yalom[15] states, there are 'many therapeutic pathways through the group therapy experience'. Berzon *et al.* present in some detail a sample episode from one of the group sessions and the various perceptions of it by the nine members who opted to describe it. From their accounts it emerged that universality was the therapeutic ingredient for three respondents, insight for two, altruism for a further two, and interaction ('expressing self congruently, articulately, or assertively') for the final two. We reiterate the obvious point that perception of what is therapeutic in group therapy is inevitably an exceedingly subjective matter.

The sample in the other study using volunteers, by Sherry and Hurley,[28] is similar to Berzon's in at least two key respects—they were well educated (college students) and reasonably well adjusted (three of the twenty volunteers were excluded on the grounds of being emotionally unstable). The students participated in one of three 'growth groups' lasting ten sessions. Yalom's therapeutic factor questionnaire[15] was completed after the final session. The top pair of items were both from the category 'interpersonal learning-input', chiefly concerned with receiving feedback about how one comes across. An item about the expression of feelings was also ranked highly. The different emphasis here, compared to the focus on cognitive factors by Berzon's subjects, is probably attributable to the group leader's promotion of interaction as a dominant feature. The different modes of enquiry and frequency of administration could also be contributory. Although the description of what was done in the groups is sketchy, the authors do cite the prominence given to unstructured, here-and-now interaction. One possible hypothesis is that group members' perceptions of what is helpful to them are, at least in part, influenced by the perceptions of their therapists. One way to try to answer this question is through a parallel enquiry of both patients and their therapists.

But as we saw in the studies by Bloch and Reibstein[22] and Schaffer and Dreyer,[26] who adopted this approach, the matter is complicated by possible differences in reference points, i.e. the therapist focuses more on readily observable overt behaviour than the patient, who also considers more subjective cognitive experiences.

Therapeutic factors and differences between individuals and groups

In covering the systematic research on therapeutic factors collectively, we have pointed out the association between therapeutic factors and individual and group differences. Most of the studies discussed have not however set out with this issue principally in mind (the one by Dickoff and Lakin[24] may be an exception with their look at the effect of verbal intelligence). Only two teams have tackled this subject directly.

Butler and Fuhriman[29] focused on individual differences by comparing the evaluation of therapeutic factors by two contrasting clinical samples: patients attending a day treatment programme and patients participating in out-patient therapy groups. The former were obviously more impaired: they had been, on average, four years in treatment, and two-thirds of them had some form of psychosis. The out-patients had been in treatment, on average, for just under two years, and 84 per cent of them were diagnosed as either neurotic or personality-disordered. These differences were echoed in their respective ratings by therapists on an operational 'level of functioning' scale. The out-patients' average rating fell into the category of 'moderate difficulty in functioning'; the day-patients' average rating was in the category of 'major impairment in functioning'.

Both samples completed, on one occasion only and during the course of their treatment, a variant of the therapeutic factor instrument used by Lieberman *et al.*[19] in their study of encounter groups. The analysis of the perceptions of the two samples showed several, substantial differences. The out-patients discriminated more subtly between the therapeutic factors, with most stress placed on self-understanding, universality, feedback, and catharsis; least importance was attached to recapitulation of the family group and identification. The day-patients failed to discriminate in this way with most factors being apportioned the same value. The one exception was cohesiveness, which stood out from the rest as the only highly valued factor. The authors' attempts to explain these differences are compelling. The importance of cohesiveness for the day-patients is attributed to the group serving as a caring forum in the face of their social isolation—a forum in which they are not judged and do not feel under threat. In contrast, the out-patients emphasize self-understanding—they have adequate ego strength (as reflected in their 'level of functioning' ratings) to introspect and to benefit from this process. Their ego strength also enables them to cope with, and value, feedback from their peers, and thus to appreciate the relevance of interpersonal learning.

Level of functioning has been further examined by the same pair of researchers.[30] A sample of 91 out-patients completed a modified version of Yalom's therapeutic factor questionnaire (that is, not the same instrument as used in the foregoing study) on a single occasion, during treatment. Patients were also rated by their therapists for level of functioning on the same operational scale. Those scoring above the sample's median level were labelled as relatively high in functioning with their mean score falling into the category of 'some difficulty in functioning . . . due to normal responses to developmental crisis . . . but . . . symptoms do not seriously impair functioning'. Patients scoring below the median had a mean score which fell into the category of 'moderate difficulty in functioning . . . due to moderate symptoms . . . functioning may be constricted but still appropriate'.

Patients' level of functioning was significantly related to four therapeutic factors: catharsis, self-understanding, feedback, and interaction, with better functioning patients apportioning greater value to them than their disadvantaged counterparts. Again, the authors posit that patients rated as 'higher functioning' have the required ego strength to manage and to profit from inherently risky processes in treatment, particularly the honest and open expression of feelings, the close examination of one's behaviour, the toleration and appreciation of feedback especially criticism, and the effort to achieve intimacy with co-members.

Butler and Fuhriman then logically pose the interrelated questions: must patients have a certain minimal level of ego strength to benefit from group therapy or is such low ego strength amenable to change (here they are referring mainly to a patient's capacity to cope with the anxiety entailed in facing close interpersonal relationships in the group)? The question is a tantalizing one, which has exercised the minds of many a therapist in the past but with little tangible result (see Bloch[31] for a summary of some of this work). How to utilize such a vague construct as 'level of functioning' in a clinically meaningful way is a complex, unanswered question. The effort by Butler and Fuhriman reveals the difficulties involved. By dividing their sample at the median into two groups in terms of level of functioning, they conceded that the designation of 'lower functioning' was only relative. But the resultant sub-sample turns out to have almost the same average level of functioning (52 with a range of 35–59) as their out-patient sample in their previous study described earlier (55, with a range 38–72), and the latter they described as 'a higher functioning out-patient population'. An inevitable scepticism creeps in about the validity of the instrument purporting to measure level of functioning. The picture is further complicated by the timing of the measurement. Patients had been in group treatment for a substantial period (average 20 months for high functioning and average 23 months for low functioning patients) when the rating was made. No data are provided about base line measurements. It would therefore be reasonable to assume that therapists were influenced in their ratings by actual clinical changes they observed in their patients and/or by how effectively their patients succeeded in making use of the group.

Study of the relationship between patients' evaluations of therapeutic factors and their levels of functioning is worthwhile and deserves replication, providing the latter are measured before or close to the onset of treatment and that their validity is checked. Also patients' perceptions should be obtained at a standardized point, such as at termination of therapy.

Interestingly, Butler and Fuhriman did look at the relationship between length of time in the group and patient perceptions, and found that those who had been group members for longer periods stressed cohesiveness, self-understanding, and interaction significantly more than patients who had been treated for shorter periods.

The other team which has directly tackled the influence of individual and group differences on the evaluation of therapeutic factors is Rohrbaugh and Bartels.[32] They investigated the relationship between the age, sex, education, and previous group experience of individuals in the group and their perceptions of therapeutic factors. The influence of group variables, such as size and duration, on the perception of these factors was also examined.

The sample comprised of 72 subjects in 13 therapy or human relations groups. They completed Yalom's questionnaire on one occasion, although timing of its administration appears to have varied (an obvious flaw) and was carried out by the therapists themselves (another weakness). Demographic data and a measure of cohesiveness were obtained from group members at the same time. Therapists provided data about their groups on a number of variables. Correlations were then computed between the 14 'item clusters' from a factor analysis of Yalom's questionnaire (similar to the questionnaire's twelve original categories) and individual and group differences enumerated above. Several correlations were significant indicating that 'characteristics of groups and/or their members *do* account for at least some variation in perceptions of the various change mechanisms'. They found that therapy groups value insight more, and 'relatedness' (a cluster comprising cohesiveness and interaction) less, compared to human relations groups; the more educated group member emphasizes relatedness and devalues an existential factor and guidance. Generally, group variables appear more important than individual differences in respondents' evaluations of therapeutic factors. Thus, for example, age, sex, previous group experience, attraction to the group, and verbal participation were unrelated. (Yalom[15] similarly found no effect of age and sex in his study of 20 improved patients.)

Any interpretation of the above study is confounded by its two major defects: the varied timing of the questionnaire's administration and the suspect sampling—in some of the 13 groups, a sizeable proportion of subjects did not complete the questionnaire at all. As the authors themselves put it, this work 'indicates that participants' perceptions of [therapeutic] factors in therapy and growth groups are complex and not easily dimensionalized'.

Implications for future research

Throughout the section on empirical work we have emphasized how the uniqueness of the individual coupled with the particular features of the group in which he participates are bound to lead to a highly personal appraisal of the factors he regards as helpful. Notwithstanding, the study of the comparative effectiveness and evaluation of therapeutic factors is worthwhile, although there is considerable room for improvement in research design and methods. We have already referred to the need for replication of studies, using similar samples and measures. Failing that, research in this field can have no cumulative effect.

One question shouts out for attention—what is the relationship between therapeutic factors and group development? The clinician would be better able to promote therapeutic forces if he were more certain about timing. One testable hypothesis, for instance, is that certain factors are especially relevant in the early phase of the group—universality, acceptance, and instillation of hope are the obvious examples—whereas other factors—e.g. insight and interaction—become operational following the establishment of a trusting, mature atmosphere in the group.

Also, what about therapeutic factors from the perspective of the group member who does not change or who deteriorates? The encounter group study of Lieberman *et al.*[19] tackled this topic to some extent. How do failed patients perceive therapeutic factors? What has prevented them from using the factors constructively? Related to this topic is the question of how the factors we assume to be therapeutic can also, under certain circumstances, be anti-therapeutic. Kelman[5] is one of the few theorists to keep this in mind in the course of formulating his model. The empirical researcher has a role in erecting suitable hypotheses to investigate this most important matter.

References

1. Slavson, S. R. A systematic theory. In: *Dynamics of group psychotherapy* (ed. M. Schiffer). Jason Aronson, New York (1979).
2. Wolf, A. Psychoanalysis in groups. In: *Group psychotherapy and group function* (eds. M. Rosenbaum and M. Berger). Basic Books, New York (1975).
3. Farrell, M. P. Transference dynamics of group psychotherapy. *Archives of General Psychiatry* **6**, 66–76 (1962).
4. Tawadros, S. Factors in group psychotherapy. *International Journal of Social Psychiatry* **2**, 44–50 (1956).
5. Kelman, H. C. The role of the group in the induction of therapeutic change. *International Journal of Group Psychotherapy* **13**, 399–432 (1963).
6. Papanek, H. Ethical change of values in group psychotherapy. *International Journal of Group Psychotherapy* **8**, 435–44 (1958).
7. Maxmen, J. S. An educative model for in-patient group therapy. *International Journal of Group Psychotherapy* **29**, 321–38 (1978).
8. Alexander, F. and French, T. M. *Psychoanalytic therapy*. Ronald Press, New York (1946).

9. Maxmen, J. S. Group therapy as viewed by hospitalized patients. *Archives of General Psychiatry* **28**, 404–8 (1973).
10. See e.g.: Pattison E. M., Brissenden A., and Wohl, T. Assessing specific effects of in-patient group psychotherapy. *International Journal of Group Psychotherapy* **17,** 283–97 (1967).
11. Tenebaum, S. A discussion of the therapy that resides in a group. *Psychotherapy: Theory, Research and Practice* **1**, 253–5 (1970).
12. Opler, M. K. Group psychotherapy: individual and cultural dynamics in group process. *American Journal of Psychiatry* **114**, 433–8 (1957).
13. Becker, B. J. The psychodynamics of analytic group psychotherapy. *American Journal of Psychoanalysis* **32**, 177–85 (1972).
14. Corsini, R. and Rosenberg, B. Mechanisms of group psychotherapy: processes and dynamics. *Journal of Abnormal and Social Psychology* **51**, 406–11 (1955).
15. Yalom, I. D. *The theory and practice of group psychotherapy*. Basic Books, New York (1975).
16. Block, J. *The Q-sort method in personality assessment and psychiatric research*. Charles C. Thomas, Springfield, Ill. (1961).
17. Bloch, S., Reibstein, J., Crouch, E., *et al.* A method for the study of therapeutic factors in group psychotherapy. *British Journal of Psychiatry* **134**, 257–63 (1979).
18. Weiner, M. F. Genetic vs. interpersonal insight. *International Journal of Group Psychotherapy* **24**, 230–7 (1974).
19. Lieberman, M. A., Yalom, I. D., and Miles, M. B. *Encounter groups: first facts*. Basic Books, New York (1973).
20. Steinfeld, G. and Mabli, J. Perceived curative factors in group therapy by residents of a therapeutic community. *Criminal Justice Behaviour* **1**, 278–88 (1974).
21. Corder, B. F., Whiteside, M. S., and Haizlip, T. M. A study of curative factors in group psychotherapy with adolescents. *International Journal of Group Psychotherapy* **31**, 345–54 (1981).
22. Bloch, S. and Reibstein, J. Perceptions by patients and therapists of therapeutic factors in group psychotherapy. *British Journal of Psychiatry* **137**, 274–8 (1980).
23. Dickoff, H. and Lakin, M. Patients' views of group psychotherapy: retrospection and interpretations. *International Journal of Group Psychotherapy* **13**, 61–73 (1963).
24. Macaskill, N. D. Therapeutic factors in group therapy with borderline patients. *International Journal of Group Psychotherapy* **32**, 61–73 (1982).
25. Marcovitz, R. J. and Smith, J. E. Patients' perceptions of curative factors in short-term group psychotherapy. *International Journal of Group Psychotherapy* **33**, 21–39 (1983).
26. Schaffer, J. B. and Dreyer, S. F. Staff and in-patient perceptions of change mechanisms in group psychotherapy. *American Journal of Psychiatry* **139**, 127–8 (1982).
27. Berzon, B., Pious, C., and Farson, R. The therapeutic event in group

psychotherapy: a study of subjective reports by group members. *Journal of Individual Psychology* **19**, 204–12 (1963).
28. Sherry, P. and Hurley, J. Curative factors in psychotherapeutic and growth groups. *Journal of Clinical Psychology* **32**, 835–7 (1976).
29. Butler, T. and Fuhriman, A. Patient perspective on the curative process. A comparison of day treatment and out-patient psychotherapy groups. *Small Group Behaviour* **11**, 371–88 (1980).
30. Butler, T. and Fuhriman, A. Level of functioning and length of time in treatment variables influencing patients' therapeutic experience in group psychotherapy. *International Journal of Group Psychotherapy* **33**, 489–504 (1983).
31. Bloch, S. Assessment of patients for psychotherapy. *British Journal of Psychiatry* **135**, 193–208 (1979).
32. Rohrbaugh, M. and Bartels, B. D. Participants' perceptions of 'curative factors' in therapy and growth groups. *Small Group Behaviour* **6**, 430–56 (1975).

10 Conclusion

In this concluding chapter we examine critically the 'state of the art' with respect to therapeutic factors in group therapy. Arising out of our review are four main questions: (1) Why has relatively little attention been paid to the study of the subject? (2) In the light of the work that has been done, what have we learned about therapeutic factors? (3) How can research be improved in the future? and (4) How important is the subject to the field of group therapy? In tackling these questions we hope to achieve a valid appraisal of all the material dealt with in the preceding chapters.

Relative neglect of therapeutic factors

We have emphasized repeatedly the watershed contribution in 1955 by Corsini and Rosenberg.[1] In concluding their paper they expressed the hope that their classification might facilitate better communication between therapists and provide a framework for research into therapeutic factors. Have their hopes been fulfilled? In terms of the volume of research done, the answer must be, disappointingly, in the negative. Although we have identified a reasonable corpus of work in this volume, we would have expected more comprehensive research. Considering the importance of the topic, the number of systematic investigations in particular is discouraging. Our impression is supported by several workers in the field.[2,3,4,5] How can we explain this picture?

Several factors have probably contributed. Firstly, and fundamentally, the practising group therapist has tended to assign a low priority to research. His preoccupations with day-to-day clinical functions have crowded out the interest he may harbour in research. What interest he has cultivated has been almost invariably in the sphere of theory.[6]

This brings us to the second factor. Most clinicians need to operate within a theoretical framework. They require a conceptual model to guide their decisions. And this is indeed fair enough. Without a model a therapist would be anchorless, his group buffeted by the *ad hoc* status of his every clinical judgement. Therapist and group members would soon be blown off course, with treatment becoming directionless and baffling. But adherence to theory has a price. Therapeutic factors, as we have seen, represent the common ground between the conventional schools of group therapy but have been relegated to a secondary position. The pattern is comparable to the lesser weight given by psychotherapists generally to the concept of non-specific factors (a misnomer if ever there was one—more aptly termed 'common basic factors'). Jerome Frank, the central figure in studying this concept, has aptly remarked: '. . . little glory derives from showing that the particular method which one has mastered with so much effort [in the context of our discussion, a specific theoretical approach] may be indistinguishable from other methods in its effects'.[7] Here, he is referring to the well-known comparability of the effect achieved by different forms and schools of therapy. The group therapist, like all psychotherapists, has not been immune from zealously protecting his chosen methods, a position which precludes curiosity about other forms of group therapy, no matter how different they might appear on first inspection. They all have a finite number of basic therapeutic factors in common.

By contrast, the 'social scientist' (one more concerned with the study of group processes rather than of therapy itself) has exhibited a ready commitment to the study of these factors. Since he is not a practising therapist, he is spared the professional identity problems alluded to above. On the other hand he is perhaps less qualified to identify clinically relevant questions to tackle in research. His predilection for tightly controlled, methodologically rigorous experiment in which a hypothesis is tested and specific conditions manipulated, frequently leads to a well-executed study but one with little or no appeal to his therapist colleagues.[4] A paucity of meaningful dialogue between the social scientist and the therapist is the unfortunate sequel, one exemplified in the preceding chapters by the different sets of journals in which the two groups tend to publish their work. The social scientist opts for a forum which favours the experimental mode of enquiry, the therapist for a clinically orientated publication. However, some journals do attempt to straddle the divide. A perusal of the *International Journal of Group Psychotherapy*, for example, will soon reveal that links do exist between social science and clinical treatment. Our point is that these links are fragile, and in need of substantial reinforcement.

The social scientist's preference for the strictly scientific posture, at the possible expense of clinical relevance, is not altogether surprising and brings us to another factor likely to explain the relatively undeveloped research output on therapeutic factors. The direct study of a therapy group is fraught with complexity. Our review has revealed this repeatedly. The phenomena involved do not lend themselves easily to precise specification and measurement; controlled conditions are difficult to achieve; the manipulation of variables is not straightforward; and ethical difficulties abound because of the problems in mounting experiments which will not jeopardize the interests of patients. How much easier therefore to conduct an analogue study in which these hurdles may be avoided or surmounted more readily. The demanding quality of research on clinical groups is obviously not restricted to therapeutic factors. Group therapy as a whole has been the victim. No wonder that an astute observer of research into psychotherapy like M. B. Parloff has concluded: '. . . the entire field of group psychotherapy may assume the unhappy nature of being the Peter Pan of psychotherapies . . .' This quotation is extracted from a paper in which Parloff expressed his long-standing pessimism about the limited progress that had been achieved.[8]

Although a decade and a half later the picture has not altered radically, there is room for guarded optimism regarding the study of therapeutic factors and we felt the work on this subject justified a comprehensive review. The resultant volume, we hope, testifies to this progress. Even if not as extensive as we would have wished, a body of interrelated clinical lore, theory, and systematic research *has* materialized; a body of knowledge which contains useful information for the practitioner and serves as a basis for continuing research. This brings us to the second question we posed at the outset of the chapter.

What have we learned about therapeutic factors?

This section constitutes a summary of the knowledge that has accrued concerning therapeutic factors as a whole (see Chapters 1 and 9) and individually (see Chapters 2–8). Our aim is to assemble in one place the chief findings and give the reader an overall impression of the 'state of the art'. We comment on the quality of this work in a later section.

Definitions

There appears to be consensus that a *therapeutic factor* is an element of the group process which exerts a beneficial effect on group members. But the concept remained blurred until recent years by failure to distinguish between a therapeutic factor, as defined above, and two closely related phenomena—a condition for change and a technique.

A *condition for change* is necessary for therapeutic factors to operate but does not have intrinsic therapeutic effects. A group, for example, needs to enjoy a shared sense of motivation for therapeutic factors to come into play but its members will not improve as a direct consequence of this quality alone.

A *technique* similarly does not exert therapeutic effects (except occasionally as a spin-off); it is merely a device available to the therapist to promote the operation of therapeutic factors. Thus, the technique of 'doubling' may enable an emotionally blocked patient to overcome his inhibition and thus go on to benefit from the therapeutic factor of catharsis (see Chapter 6).

Classification of therapeutic factors

Definition and taxonomy move in tandem. Ideally, the elements of a classification should be mutually exclusive and jointly exhaustive. As we have seen in Chapter 1, various classificatory efforts over more than twenty-five years have made substantial progress in trying to attain this ideal and considerable agreement has been achieved about the basic factors in group therapy. It is also generally understood that their relative importance in a particular group is a function of the group's goals, size, composition, duration, stage of development, and so forth. Although the emphasis has varied and terminology has been inconsistent, a general pattern has evolved. The number of factors has ranged between nine and twelve. They have covered three spheres: emotional, cognitive, and actional (behavioural). Here then we list and briefly define those factors about which there is substantial agreement (alternative terms in parentheses):

1. *Acceptance*—the patient feels a sense of belonging and being valued (cohesiveness).
2. *Universality*—the patient discovers that he is not unique with his problems (universalization).
3. *Altruism*—the patient learns with satisfaction that he can be helpful to others in the group.
4. *Instillation of hope*—the patient gains a sense of optimism about his potential to benefit from treatment.
5. *Guidance*—the patient receives useful information in the form of advice, suggestions, explanation, and instruction.
6. *Vicarious learning*—the patient benefits by observing the therapeutic experience of fellow group members (spectator learning, identification).
7. *Self-understanding*—the patient learns something important about himself, usually through feedback or interpretation (insight, intellectualization).
8. *Learning from interpersonal action*—the patient learns from his attempts to relate constructively and adaptively within the group (interpersonal learning, interaction).
9. *Self-disclosure*—the patient reveals highly personal information to the group and thus 'gets it off his chest'.
10. *Catharsis*—the patient releases intense feelings which brings him a sense of relief (ventilation).

The relative value of therapeutic factors

Arising out of their classification has been the development of various methods to ascertain which therapeutic factor group members, and to a much lesser extent, group leaders, find helpful or unhelpful. Yalom's direct questionnaire enquiry and the 'most important event' questionnaire are the two most favoured approaches (see Chapter 9). The inconsistency of the findings is undoubtedly due to differences in the populations studied, the different instruments employed, the timing of their administration, the forms of group therapy given, the different theoretical schools favoured by the therapists involved, and finally, in the way patients actually perceive the therapy.

However, a careful sorting of the data produces at least the fragments of a pattern. In terms of the comparative effectiveness of therapeutic factors, some form of insight appears to be linked to improvement; acceptance and self-disclosure are also relevant, though to a lesser degree. The weakest correlations with outcome are vicarious learning and guidance. Irrespective of outcome, the factors perceived by patients as most and least helpful cover a wide range. For example, if we consider *out-patient groups* (whether relatively short- or long-term), LIA, insight, and self-disclosure are emphasized as helpful, whereas guidance and vicarious learning are regarded as unhelpful. Altruism, and to a lesser degree acceptance and insight, are the helpful factors for members of *in-patient groups*; guidance and vicarious learning are seen as least helpful.

Applying another perspective, we find in relatively *short-term groups* (whether in-patient or out-patient), universality, acceptance, and to a lesser extent, altruism and self-disclosure, are regarded as the most helpful, with guidance and vicarious learning remaining as the least helpful pair. In relatively *long-term groups*, insight, LIA and self-disclosure are stressed positively, and guidance, vicarious learning, and universality negatively.

If we now consider the findings overall (admittedly this is a crude exercise) guidance and vicarious learning emerge repeatedly as unhelpful components in all types of group treatment. In relatively long-term out-patient groups, LIA and self disclosure are clearly important to group members; in relatively short-term in-patient groups, no particular factors predominate.

Theoretical models Innovatory theoretical models which incorporate a set of therapeutic factors or an equivalent thereof, have been devised. In Papanek's model, the therapist influences the group to form a culture based on three humanistic values: egalitarianism, honesty, and altruism (see p. 213). Kelman sees the group as a social influence with its therapist the primary agent of influence; it proceeds along the steps of compliance, identification, and internalization (the last is a blend of insight and interaction) (see p. 214); finally in Maxmen's view, the group (in-patient, short-term) is an educational forum in which patients are taught to think in a clinical way about their problems (see p. 219).

Therapeutic factors individually

Having dealt with therapeutic factors overall, we can now summarize what has been learned about each of the ten factors individually.

Insight (self-understanding) Although insight is essential to most forms of group therapy, its intricacy has made its study difficult. No consensus has emerged about its definition. Consequently, the term covers several forms of learning, including the understanding of dreams, the recognition of resistance, greater self-knowledge, and the appreciation of the origin of symptoms. None the less, two main categories of insight have been teased out: the patient's understanding of his own feelings, thoughts, and fantasies (intrapersonal or intrapsychic); and understanding of his relationships with others (interpersonal). These two forms are closely bound up with the psychoanalytic and interactional schools of group therapy respectively. The humanist-existential school has favoured yet another view of insight—as a process of self-discovery leading to authenticity.

These theoretical differences and the general complexity of the subject have contributed to the lack of systematic research. In the few studies in which there has been an effort to manipulate insight as an experimental variable, the results are inconsistent. This is no doubt due to the considerable differences in the clinical samples selected (ranging from volunteers with speech anxiety to chronic schizophrenic inpatients) and in the experimental designs deployed (for instance, comparing rational-emotive therapy with systematic desensitization; comparing two treatment conditions, one stressing insight and the other interaction; and comparing insight-orientated therapy with assertiveness training). Considering these differences, it is no great surprise that insight has been found to exert either equal, greater, or lesser effects compared to other treatment modalities. The effect of combining insight with another therapeutic ingredient, such as interaction, emerges as a more consistent trend and suggests that learning of whatever form may be more efficacious when it occurs in conjunction with certain other group processes.

Another finding of note, arising from what is probably the best study in this context (see p. 42), is the relevance of insight for a specific sub-group even in a sample as ostensibly homogeneous as young volunteers with speech anxiety. In the present state of knowledge, it seems that insight is a genuine therapeutic factor in group therapy but only for certain categories of patient. This is neatly reinforced by the results of a study in which psychologically minded group members improved more than their less psychologically minded colleagues, when receiving insight-orientated treatment. This difference was not observed in non-insight-orientated therapy groups.

The value of *feedback*—particularly relevant in the acquisition of interpersonal insight—has been usefully investigated. One research team is notable for its continuing effort to test how feedback can be best provided (see p. 53). Discriminating between positive and negative feedback on the one hand, and between behavioural, emotional, and mixed behavioural-emotional on the other hand, it is found, at least in volunteer students participating in brief sensitivity-training groups, that positive emotional feedback has most impact. This shifts to negative emotional when the feedback is given anonymously. The team's findings on the optimal sequence for offering feedback—negative or positive first—are contradictory.

Most studies of the role of videotape in feedback are descriptive but in one investigation greater adaptive behaviour was seen in patients who were systematically given such feedback, following each therapy session compared to controls (see p. 62). One useful review (see p. 61) of video feedback proffers firm hypothesis concerning its relevance, source, and acceptability, but there has been precious little effort to test any of them.

Learning from interpersonal action (interaction) Interaction between group members, including the therapist, is a basic condition for change; learning from such interaction is often regarded as an important therapeutic factor. Theoretical contributions on the latter are best appreciated in terms of the predominant relationship with which learning is linked. Two chief relationships can be distinguished: patient to therapist and patient to patient. A third, patient to group, has been examined in the context of forces that hamper the group's therapeutic task. The patient to therapist form is intimately bound up with psychoanalytic theory, and amounts to the group member developing a transference tie with his therapist and acquiring certain insights as a consequence of this involvement. Modifications of the classical transference pattern that obtains in individual therapy have been advanced. It may be diluted because of the simultaneous transferential links between each patient and the therapist and the occurrence of transference between patients. Also, the nature of transference may change as the group develops.

In the patient to patient model, variously labelled as dynamic-interactional, interpersonalist, and experiential, the group is viewed as a social microcosm which enables the member to experiment with new ways of relating in a group, using self-observation and feedback. His efforts are monitored for appropriateness and effectiveness. This learning from interpersonal action is then transferred to everyday life.

Dissatisfaction in recent years with what are considered limited and incomplete models of interaction has led to the adoption by some notable theorists of general systems theory (GST). The argument is made that GST enables patient to patient as well as patient to therapist frameworks to be integrated on a 'higher level of theoretical organization'. This is because the therapist attaches equal importance to a variety of systems—the group, the individual members, and their personality subsystems—and recognizes that a change at any one point in the overall system axiomatically leads to changes elsewhere in the system. Furthermore, because the therapy system has permeable boundaries, the reciprocal effects of the patient's experience in treatment and such factors as his marriage, family, and work are also closely noted and dealt with.

In contrast with the theoretical work, systematic research, both in amount and quality, has been disappointing. Investigators have opted to focus on interaction *per se* rather than on the learning that results therefrom, probably because the former is much more amenable to research methods. The foci of study have been the classification of interpersonal behaviours, the therapist's influence on patterns of interaction, the relationship between interaction and certain group variables, and the correlation between interaction and outcome.

The sporadic attempts to measure and classify forms of relating that take place in therapy groups have yielded useful information. Important dimensions appear to be dominance, submissiveness, disorganization, support, and sensitivity, although the work thus far has had little direct bearing on interpersonal learning.

The links between interaction and personality factors emerge as complex, and tentative. One highly specific factor, the capacity for mutual dependence (i.e. the ability to handle both dependence and independence appropriately) is associated with greater interaction among group therapy patients. Risk-taking is similarly associated, though influenced by sex and the group's level of structure. Apart from structure, the size of the group seems to be relevant, with more interaction reported after the addition of one or two extra members. Stable membership emerges as another correlate of interaction. The phase of group development is also directly associated, older groups being more interactive than newly-formed ones.

The role of the therapist in influencing the level and direction of inter-patient interaction has attracted the attention of several investigators. The findings are not altogether consistent. Redirection—the therapist responding to a patient's comment or question directed towards himself by involving another patient—is associated with more interaction than other responses, such as silence or direct response. But this effect was not noted among a sample of chronic in-patients, presumably because they were too impaired to dispense with the therapist's explicit, guiding hand. Both the quality and the intensity of the leader's responses are also important. Critical responses, for instance, lead to a reduction in positive forms of interaction between members. But, the relatively gentle expression of critical comments by the group leader promotes inter-member interaction overall. The least that can be said about these studies is that the therapist acts as a model for a particular interactional pattern within his group.

Finally, a brief comment on the links between interaction and outcome, a topic much neglected by the systematic researcher. In the only study to yield meaningful data and then on a non-clinical sample, behavioural change was correlated with interaction, but of a particular kind—that which occurs between members and is emotionally involving. This change immediately followed a concentrated group experience and the effects had waned eight months later (see p. 93).

Cohesiveness Although cohesiveness has been commonly regarded as a fundamental ingredient of the group therapeutic process, the vagueness of the concept has tended to hinder its proper study. In particular, insufficient attention has been given to the difference between group cohesiveness—the group's *esprit de corps*—and individual members' feelings of belonging and being accepted. The former is best conceptualized as a condition for change, since it probably enables various therapeutic factors to operate; acceptance, by contrast, has the features of a therapeutic factor and is best regarded as such. Even these distinctions are not enough since it appears as if both condition for change and therapeutic factor are multidimensional. Thus, cohesiveness embodies several aspects, including attraction to peers, attraction to the leader, and agreement with the group's goals.

Theoretically, cohesiveness has been approached in terms of its likely determinants or antecedents and its consequences or effects. Among the determinants, note has been made of three interrelated factors: (a) the association between the attractiveness of the group to its members and their expectation of favourable outcomes; (b) the group's 'incentive properties', such as its prestige and objectives; and (c) the influence of the individual's 'motive base', i.e. his need for security, recognition, or other value. Consequences of cohesiveness include maintenance of membership, the group's power to influence its members, increased participation, and an enhanced sense of security. The distinction between determinants and consequences however needs to be qualified. They are better viewed as components of a circular process inasmuch as a consequence can readily become a determinant.

Similar theoretical notions have been applied to the clinical context. Thus, it has been noted that in a therapy group cohesiveness may be promoted by, *inter alia*, members' liking for one another, the appeal of its activities, and its prestige. The therapeutic effects are highly salient: the patient is influenced by the group if he is attracted to it, and his experience of shared power and responsibility is associated with an elevated sense of personal competence.

There is a fair amount of systematic research on group cohesiveness. Studies have included the relationship between cohesiveness and outcome, the relationship between cohesiveness and various therapeutic factors, the therapist's role in promoting cohesiveness, and the link between cohesiveness and compatibility. To our knowledge, there has been no research on acceptance.

Inconsistent findings characterize the cohesiveness/outcome association, and appear to be influenced by the type of measurement used. For instance improvement assessed through self-report bears a stronger tie to cohesiveness than when using more objective measures. But in most studies the pattern still emerges of a positive correlation. In the only study yielding a negative association, the unique features of the sample—involuntarily treated sex-offenders—militate against the result being generally applicable.

Several studies point to a consistently positive relationship between cohesiveness and self-disclosure (see below); cohesiveness and interaction are also linked, but less strongly. A single study revealed that a highly cohesive group was able to withstand confrontation and challenge more effectively than a group low in cohesiveness (see p. 133).

Empirical work demonstrates the central role of the therapist in the promotion of cohesiveness. This can be achieved by various means. One such strategy is the prompting and reinforcing by the leader of statements made by patients which reflect cohesiveness. Also, the leader or co-leaders should adopt a caring style of leadership. Another factor concerns organization of the group: cohesiveness is associated with extended marathon sessions, with small rather than large groups, and with mixed-sex rather than single-sex composition.

Finally, some attention has been paid to the association between cohesiveness and compatibility, a link which has obvious implications for patient selection and group composition. All the work on this topic is based on the theoretical ideas of Schutz and incorporates his method of measuring compatability (see p. 117). The resultant picture is confusing. Although a positive correlation between cohesiveness and compatibility is commonly found, this is contradicted in one major study and influenced by the degree of compatibility in another. Compatibility probably does exert an effect on cohesiveness but compatibility is unlikely to be a unitary factor and does not appear to be stable over time.

Self-disclosure Probably because it is directly observable, self-disclosure has attracted a considerable volume of research, chiefly on analogue groups. The development of the Jourard scale, a measure of the inclination to divulge personal information, has provided the means for much of this systematic research though attempts to validate the scale have proved disappointing. Theoretical discussion has, by contrast, been slender. Jourard's contribution is paramount in this regard (see p. 129). His theoretical stance is readily encapsulated in his quotation: 'Make thyself known, and thou shalt then know thyself'. In other words, self-disclosure facilitates heightened self-awareness and this in turn paves the way for the achievement of authentic being. Conversely, the person who conceals his true self from others is alienated from himself.

Systematic studies cover the following areas: the association between self-disclosure and group cohesiveness; the group leader's role in influencing self-disclosure; the links between self-disclosure and the need for social approval, popularity, and reciprocity; and the relationship between self-disclosure and outcome. What do these studies show? Self-disclosure and cohesiveness are closely related, at least in laboratory groups, with the former seeming to be both an effect and a cause of interpersonal attraction. Here is an obvious example of the interdependence of a therapeutic factor (self-disclosure) and a condition for change (cohesiveness). The results of the several studies examining the influence of group leadership on group members' self-disclosure are inconsistent, probably because of differences in sample and methodology. Notwithstanding, it would appear that the leader—most studies are analogue in type—has the wherewithal to affect the pattern of self-disclosure in his group, particularly by setting an explicit norm that encourages members to reveal personal information. The leader's actual modelling of self-disclosure was found to be influential on group members in one study but not in two others. The question of whether therapist self-disclosure is advantageous is highly complex and can, as Dies suggests, only be usefully examined when broken down into specific parts—when, where, why, to whom (see p. 146).

The relationship between self-disclosure and the need for social approval is curvilinear, with maximum self-disclosure in patients with an intermediate score on social desirability; those with a great need for social approval probably avoid revealing themselves because it is regarded as a threat to their acceptance by their peers. A related finding is the association between the liking of group members for each other and the extent they perceive each other as self-revealing. A member's self-disclosure appears to promote his popularity, particularly in the initial phase of a group.

Reciprocity is a relevant facet in self-disclosure. Two analogue studies demonstrated that group members reveal intimate details about themselves if their fellows act similarly. These results can be explained in terms of theories on social interaction: the receipt of a self-disclosure is a social reward: greater rewards are associated with greater social attraction; therefore, a person who provides rewards will be liked and will tend to extend more social rewards to those whom he likes. This process is linked to the phenomenon of reciprocity, with mutual self-disclosure and mutual liking developing between pairs of group members. Based on this work, it may be hypothesized that a 'large inter-member discrepancy in self-disclosure' is disadvantageous to a group and that this is best dealt with at the point of patient selection, by avoiding any major disparities in the tendency to be self-revealing.

Finally, the question of the association between self-disclosure and outcome has only been studied by three research groups and the results are contradictory. For instance, a positive correlation was found among psychiatric in-patients, and a negative one among juvenile delinquents and chronic schizophrenics. Among volunteer students participating in encounter groups, self-disclosure with concomitant insight is reported more commonly by those with favourable outcomes compared to those with neutral or negative outcomes. Self-disclosure *per se*, apparently, is not the crucial factor. What seems important is how it is applied by its protagonist for cognitive understanding. Another relevant factor would seem to be the social appropriateness of self-disclosure. If made ineptly, this may well evoke critical feedback and prove counterproductive. The limited work on the self-disclosure/outcome link points again to the need to break down broad questions into their component parts. In this case the pertinent and difficult questions are: what sort of patient with what sort of problem benefits from what form of self-disclosure, to whom, and in what form of group therapy?

Catharsis The elusiveness of a unitary definition of catharsis has no doubt hampered the study of this factor, and it remains relatively under-researched. Confusion, between catharsis and self-disclosure for instance, has obscured the inherent nature of catharsis, namely, the release of strong emotions which brings relief. Learning *how* to express feelings, similarly, is best distinguished from catharsis. Clinicians appear to agree that the ventilation of feelings on its own is limited in its effects, and needs to be complemented by subsequent cognitive appraisal—what does this grief, sadness, anger, envy, and the like, signify? This notion is supported by the findings of the Stanford encounter group study, which show not only that catharsis does not contribute to improvement but also that the ventilation of aggressive feelings is associated with a poor outcome. The potential negative effect of catharsis is apparently important, and in need of focused investigation.

The paucity of systematic research is striking. The available studies indicate that catharsis has a role in influencing subsequent interaction within the group, that the format of the group can facilitate the expression of negative feelings, and that the therapist is in a position to manipulate catharsis by group members directed towards himself but without influencing outcome. The last study shows convincingly that catharsis can be systematically investigated to provide potential guidelines for the clinician.

Guidance This factor is not generally considered important but there has been little attempt to test this assumption despite the widespread use of didactic methods by self-help groups. The chief theoretical contribution is by Maxmen (see p. 172). His 'educative' model, devised for short-term in-patient group therapy, is exemplary for its clarity, specificity, and rational links with his own empirical work. Barely any systematic research has been done on guidance. The solitary study of the effect of various forms of advice suggests that the concept of guidance needs detailed elaboration. Guidance was found to be advantageous but the clinical sample, involuntarily detained sex-offenders, was a very special one.

An impressive volume of work has been devoted to pre-therapy training, a phenomenon closely related to guidance, in which patients are prepared for group treatment in one of several ways, including watching a film, listening to a tape, or receiving a set of instructions. A consistent finding emerges: preparation, in both analogue and clinical studies, enhances such aspects of the group process as interaction, a personal rather than impersonal focus, feedback, faith in therapy, and patient satisfaction. Effects on outcome, untested for the most part, are inconsistent.

Universality, altruism, vicarious learning, and instillation of hope- Very little can be said about this quartet of factors since the attention paid to them has been so scanty. This neglect is probably because they are subtle and covert, rarely made explicit, and therefore confined to the 'small print' in the chronicle of the group. *Universality* has gained more recognition recently in the context of the self-help movement. Theoretically, it appears that the self-help group is organized around the goal of maximizing the commonality of experience, and this in turn paves the way for a reduction in stigma. A group member's perception of his own uniqueness and oddity is dispelled by his participation in a group composed of people similar to himself. *Altruism* has, like universality, achieved more prominence as a result of the study of self-help groups. It is categorized in an authoritative review (see p. 193) as one of the seven shared properties that typify such groups, and conceptualized as the helper obtaining satisfaction from his altruistic act, and through this experience becoming less self-absorbed and more sensitive to others.

One would have anticipated that *vicarious learning* in the context of group therapy would be an attractive subject for study since the co-participation of several peers obviously provides a splendid opportunity for a patient to profit from the observation of their therapeutic experience. This is not the case. The only contributions have been a review of the process of identification in group treatment—a key dimension of vicarious learning—and a systematic study of the effects of identification with fellow-patients. The latter study, an investigation of limited scope, suggests that peer identification is linked to improvement. Vicarious learning is clearly in need of more theoretical and empirical examination.

The impressive work done on *hope* as a non-specific placebo factor in psychotherapy generally has not been applied to its role in group therapy. Thus, how the arousal of hope operates therapeutically in the group remains obscure. By implication, clinicians assume that anticipation of benefit is advantageous, and extrapolation from the work on pre-therapy training suggests that this may be so.

How can the study of therapeutic factors be improved?

At many points throughout the preceding chapters we have commented critically on the flaws in the study of therapeutic factors. Rather than catalogue those criticisms here—an exercise bound to demoralize and discourage the reader, and ourselves!—we prefer to outline ways in which future progress might be enhanced. These can be conveniently dealt with under three headings: definition of concepts, theory, and research methodology.

Definition of concepts

A fundamental requisite of any scientific endeavour is the clear identification and accurate definition of the phenomena under scrutiny. More assiduity is required at this basic level. Although the concept of what is a therapeutic factor has achieved a measure of clarity recently, the picture remains blurred in several areas. One is the question of nomenclature. Thus we still find a duplication of terms, therapeutic factor, change mechanism, and curative factor all for the same concept.

The differentiation of therapeutic factors from conditions for change and techniques must be constantly borne in mind since it is all too easy to neglect the distinctions between them and thus to lose sight of the intrinsic properties of a therapeutic factor *per se*. An obvious illustration is the perpetuation of group cohesiveness as a therapeutic factor rather than as a condition for change and the resultant obfuscation of acceptance, the genuine factor within it (see Chapter 4).

Continuing attention must be paid to the development of a comprehensive and mutually exclusive set of factors. We have laboured this point repeatedly in earlier chapters for the simple reason that imprecise delimitation of factors, resulting in overlap or admixture of therapeutic elements, leads to equally imprecise research findings. The example given in Chapter 5 of the lumping together of self-disclosure and catharsis reveals the handicaps imposed on the investigator when factors are not handled as discrete items. Thus, virtually all studies which involve catharsis are characterized by the same defect: the difficulty of establishing the exact nature of the process to which reference is made.

This problem is well illustrated on inspection of the most popular therapeutic factor questionnaire deployed in research, the one by Yalom. If we stick to catharsis, we note how its five constituent items cover no less than three different dimensions: the disclosure of personal information; the process of learning *how* to express feelings; and the here-and-now expression of feelings towards peers or therapist. To arrive at a clear definition of catharsis using this variegated assortment of items is made all the more difficult (see p. 161). (We will return to the important topic of the measurement of therapeutic factors a little later.)

In summary then, greater precision in definition and taxonomy is a high priority. Researchers continue to apply terms and definitions uncritically, often because this makes for an easier life. We recommend that they tackle instead the task of improving conceptual clarity, so that we arrive at a consensus on specific therapeutic factors, that is well grounded and has a substantial degree of validity. In this pursuit, the astute clinical observer, the systematic investigator, and the theorist have equally important roles to play. The last has a crucial role too, in incorporating well-defined therapeutic factors in his theorizing about how groups work, a topic to which we now turn.

How to advance theory about therapeutic factors

The need to formulate theoretical models of group therapy is ever present. Here we must distinguish between two approaches to theory. In the first, scant regard, if any, is given to the role of therapeutic factors. In the second, these factors are stressed above all else. Both have a place in the attempt to understand the group process. Consider as an example of the first approach the contribution of Bion.[9] His differentiation of the work-group and basic-assumption group, and the elaboration of various forms of the latter, shed light on potentially disruptive features of group therapy (see Chapter 3). We learn little about what makes groups therapeutic but we are provoked to ponder about what gets in the way. The second approach is, however, more relevant to our topic. Here, a theory is formulated which recognizes the role of therapeutic factors and strives to explain the underlying basis of their operations.

Although useful contributions have been made in this context many more are needed. The educative model devised by Maxmen (see p. 219) illustrates what is required. We have already expressed our admiration for his contribution of a theoretical model of group therapy specifically designed for in-patients who remain as group members for only days or weeks. In so doing, Maxmen has demonstrated convincingly what can be accomplished. Firstly, eliminate the uniformity myth.[10] There is no such thing as 'group therapy'. Instead, there are specific therapeutic methods applied in the context of a group in order to reach the specified goals of a particular sample of patients. Obviously, relatively ill psychiatric patients, resident in a hospital ward for a limited period, and who wish to return to the community, require a model of group treatment which takes all these features into consideration.

Secondly, observe carefully which aspects of treatment such patients appear to profit from; seek out their views more systematically if necessary. Then, having identified objectives that are realistically attainable, and having appraised the feedback of the 'consumer', devise an appropriate model of group therapy which incorporates a specific set of therapeutic factors.[11]

Obvious in this sequence is that the development of the model is closely bound up with clinical reality. Nothing esoteric or abstract here. Clinical observation begets theory; theory is translatable into clinical action; and clinical experience subsequently illuminates aspects of theory which need to be modified. Another desideratum concerns the testability of the theory or dimensions of it. The closer the links between theory and clinical practice, the more likely it is that testable hypotheses can be erected. A theory which is beyond the bounds of experimentation may be of the utmost fascination but is of limited value in elucidating the nature of the group process. Indeed, we may confidently assert that the utility of a theory is a function of its capacity to point to new pathways of research, either through subsequent, more refined theoretical advances or through the production of new hypotheses for testing.

In using Maxmen's work to illustrate these points about theoretical developments, we are focusing on a model of group treatment involving a constellation of therapeutic factors. Also necessary is the formulation of theory and hypotheses about individual factors to enable a better understanding of their specific contribution in treatment. What the subject needs is a concerted theorizing effort which draws on notions and empirical findings from a number of interrelated fields. We can see the potential for this line of work when regarding Robinson's comments on destigmatization in self-help groups (see p. 190). By examining the concept of stigma in a type of group which stresses the commonality of experience, greater understanding of the mechanisms underlying universality is bound to emerge.

Progress will be thwarted however by the lack of specification of terms. Thus, in advancing theories about individual therapeutic factors, a point we made earlier in this section applies: precision in the definition of these factors and in their classification is critically relevant. Preciseness of definition and testability of theory, we have now noted, are essential steps to solid systematic investigation.

We conclude this section on how research may be improved by looking at what else is required of the empirical researcher in overcoming deficiencies that have typified the study of therapeutic factors in the past.

How to improve empirical research of therapeutic factors

The areas of research that seem to us to warrant particular attention are: specification of experimental variables, replication of studies, a cumulative approach, and the measurement of process. Of course, this is not to negate the general need for better measures of outcome, sufficient sample size, controlled conditions, and the like. But these aspects have been well covered elsewhere and need not be repeated here.[12]

Specification of research variables This has been noticeably lacking in the work on therapeutic factors. It is common to find accounts containing little description of the sample, the group leader, or the type of group treatment used. In the case of the sample, we need the fullest information about such factors as age, sex, occupation, education, socio-economic status, diagnosis, severity of illness, previous therapy and response thereto, concurrent therapies, whether in-, day- or out-patient, and motivation. Similarly in analogue studies, a complete account of the sample is required. A comprehensive specification of qualities of the therapist or leader is equally important, including his school of therapy, level of experience, level of training, and values held. The uniformity myth[10] is especially applicable to the poor description of the type of group treatment used in a particular study. Often, we are only told that the group met at such and such a frequency and patients participated in an average X sessions. Apart from frequency and duration of sessions, we need information about many other aspects. How many therapists were involved? What was the average size of the group? How was it composed? Were patients prepared for the group experience in any way? Was any form of homework assigned? What was the theoretical approach used? What were the goals of the group? What role did the therapist play?

Only with such detailed specification can we properly evaluate research findings, particularly if any matching procedure is employed. Specifically, three advantages result. If we know under what conditions any particular research findings apply, and can possibly through extrapolation judge under what other conditions the same findings would also obtain; other researchers can replicate a specific study; and comparative studies can be made, with variations in sample, type of leadership, or type of treatment.

Replication Replication, either exactly or with some modification of experimental design or of specific variables, is conspicuously absent in the literature on therapeutic factors (the work on pre-therapy training is an admirable exception—see Chapter 7). Exact replication of a study to yield similar data strengthens confidence in the findings. Conversely, inconsistent or contradictory findings may reveal flaws or previously overlooked variations in research design, sample, methodology, etc.

The studies on patients' perceptions of the relative helpfulness of therapeutic factors, described in Chapter 9, illustrate, paradoxically, both the advantage and disadvantage of replication. The obvious potential advantage lies in the knowledge gained about what various patient samples find useful in their group therapy experience; the disadvantage is the confused pattern of findings that emerges. The latter, however, is directly ascribable to the substantial variations in, *inter alia*, the questionnaires used, the timing of their administration, forms of group therapy, and the handling of the data. In other words these studies resemble each other, but the authors do not attempt genuine replication or even replication with limited, specifiable modification.

A cumulative approach The lack of replication or 'approximate' replication in therapeutic factor research is matched by its non-cumulative nature. During nearly three decades of systematic work, not only have few studies been replicated but also the methods and findings of previous work have been insufficiently considered when devising new experimental studies. As a result, studies covering diverse aspects of individual therapeutic factors relate poorly to one another and fail to provide a distinct body of knowledge. Certainly, programmed research is a rare jewel. This need not be so, as is demonstrated by the series of studies on feedback by Jacobs and his colleagues, which we discussed in Chapter 2. The field is in pressing need of this type of approach.

If researchers were governed by the principle that knowledge accrues and gains effect when a research question is tackled in a coherent, step-by-step fashion, much of their effort would not be so squandered as has been commonly the case hitherto. The odd investigation popping up out of nowhere or only with the most tenuous of links with previous research is bound to meet the unfortunate fate that its methods and results are not absorbed into the mainstream of thinking on the topic but left to bob along to little effect.

Investigators are not always so fortunate as to operate within a stable, continuing colleagueship which affords an opportunity to probe a particular set of issues systematically, especially by devising the next experiment as a rational sequel to its predecessor/s. None the less, any person eager to work in the field would maximize the value of his contribution if he were intimately aware of the extant literature and saw his task as building on that basis of knowledge currently available. This does not preclude those rare occurrences of genuine new insight or a paradigmatic breakthrough.

Measurement These comments on non-cumulativeness are linked to one final recommendation for how systematic investigations may enjoy an improvement in quality—the need for instruments adequate to the task of measuring, validly and reliably, therapeutic factors and associated process variables. Not only have few process measures been devised, but those that have are frequently of dubious validity. We have noted, for example, how the Jourard scale (see Chapter 5), an instrument purportedly measuring self-disclosure, may merely reflect a respondent's stated tendency to reveal himself, not his actual self-disclosing behaviour. However, the novelty of the Jourard scale did not deter a whole host of research workers from snapping it up eagerly. The snag was that their critical faculties were outpaced by their zeal. By the time the scale's validity had been impugned, a plethora of studies incorporating it had been performed. They are all suspect as a result. The Jourard saga teaches us some obvious lessons, besides revealing how hungry the research community is for measures of process. To avoid a similar error, we must rectify the inadequacies of existing measures and create new measures—all to be subjected to the usual tests to establish validity and reliability.

Fuhriman and his colleagues[13] demonstrate the value of tackling these tasks. Starting with the observations that Yalom's therapeutic factor questionnaire has been the most widely used in research, and that four of the factors in it have been assigned high priority by a number of clinical samples—cohesiveness, catharsis, interpersonal learning, and insight—Fuhriman *et al.* opted to refine this section of the questionnaire by achieving a clear definition and separation of the four constructs involved. As a first step, the literature was examined for the clearest possible definitions of the constructs. Then, the items in Yalom's questionnaire covering the four factors were 'refined, made more clear, or eliminated'. Omitted items were replaced by more suitable ones. Finally, a pilot study was done to check whether the four modified scales would, like their predecessors, be relatively valued above other factors in the original Yalom questionnaire. This was found to be the case.

A factor analysis was then carried out on the responses from 161 members of a variety of groups, who had completed the refined scale covering the factors of cohesiveness, interpersonal learning, catharsis and insight. Cohesiveness, insight, and catharsis emerged as separate entities and also showed 'moderately high internal consistency'. By contrast, the items on the interpersonal learning scale did not load together, leading the researchers to suggest that the construct it purports to reflect is not a separable therapeutic factor but rather an underlying process whereby all forms of learning in groups occurs.

Even without entering further into the technical detail of this work, we can note the ample scope there is to improve the psychometric qualities of Yalom's questionnaire and its derivatives. We can also join Fuhriman and his associates in their expression of hope that '. . . future research will provide behavioural instruments capable of measuring the curative [therapeutic] factors . . . and relate their evidences to outcome'.

How important are therapeutic factors anyway?

Bearing in mind the desiderata for research, both theoretical and empirical, outlined in the previous section, and the rather slow pace of progress in the fields, the sceptic may be tempted to surmise along these lines:

> Why do not group therapists simply get on with the job of helping their clientele by relying on clinical lore? After all, this consensual body of information, derived from careful and astute observation, has served the therapist well for decades. Systematic research on the other hand has added comparatively little to clinical acumen and there are no grounds to anticipate that future research will do any better. Moreover, research will inevitably continue to fail to do justice to the intricacy of the group process and to the complexity of the people who participate in it.

We consider this view a reflection of cynicism and nihilism rather than genuine scepticism. The group therapist can ill afford to be complacent. His record of achievement hitherto is rather modest. Reviews of the literature on outcome testify to that.[14] In one notable study, not only were the results of treatment poor but the patients were also dissatisfied, even resentful, about what they regarded as a bewildering, unhelpful process.[15]

Merely to perpetuate old models of group therapy because the theories behind them are appealing is not the way to achieve advances in the field. Neither is the adoption of one of the many new models which compete with one another for the therapist's attention. They are usually characterized by a superficiality of conception and a lack of durability. In any event, what purports to be innovative is mostly an existing notion clad in bright new clothing, which soon wears thin!

In our view, the most desirable course of action to be taken by those working in the field of group therapy, whether as clinician or researcher, emerges clearly from what has been covered in the preceding chapters. Firstly, it is to harness the knowledge that has accrued to routine clinical practice. Although most of the research is incomplete, intelligent, informed, and judicious application of the available research findings, in the light of relevant, established clinical lore and pragmatic models, is more likely to lead to advances than exclusive reliance on any one source of knowledge. The terms 'intelligent', 'informed', and 'judicious' are chosen intentionally—the therapist must use his critical faculties to the utmost in considering a number of variables at the same time, such as the goals of the group he is leading, its duration, and the particular needs of his patients. In order to do this effectively he must be acquainted with the findings of systematic research. But he must also be cautious and not seduced by every new contribution he stumbles upon.

Secondly, theorists and systematic researchers must persevere. Although slow and often erratic, there has been progress. The theorist should heed Maxmen's advice, namely, that pragmatic considerations should dictate new conceptual models.[16] In the end, patients must 'survive our theories' and groups should help their members. Furthermore, exotic theories which are immune to testing, may titillate and even stimulate, but will not contribute substantially or enduringly to clinical practice.

The systematic researcher must take care not to replicate the defects of previous research. Assuming these defects can be minimized, many aspects of therapeutic factors deserve attention in the future. Some have been examined previously but require replication while others await the investigator's first efforts. What is the relationship between therapeutic factors and group differences? (e.g. long versus short-term, in-patient versus out-patient, homogeneous versus heterogeneous). Are therapeutic factors related to individual differences? (e.g. diagnosis, psychological-mindedness, intelligence). What is the association between particular therapeutic factors and outcome? Here we urgently need research that would point to those factors that can be manipulated to enhance the effectiveness of group therapy. Is there an association between therapeutic factors and group development; i.e. are some factors more relevant than others at particular phases of the group? What is the relationship between various therapeutic factors, conditions for change, and techniques? How can therapeutic factors best be measured?

In facing up to the daunting task of conducting research of good quality on these and related questions, the investigator can be emboldened to proceed by the words of J. D. Frank, a doyen of psychotherapy research. In assessing a quarter-century of group psychotherapy research some years ago, he expressed his belief that such activity could contribute to clinical practice.[17] His belief had 'managed to survive . . . [even] in the absence of very much nourishment'. Perhaps it would be well to end on such an optimistic note, by expressing the hope that group therapy will continue not only to be nourished but that the amount and quality of that nourishment will steadily improve.

References

1. Corsini, R. and Rosenberg, B. Mechanisms of group therapy: processes and dynamics. *Journal of Abnormal and Social Psychology* **51**, 406–11 (1955).
2. Yalom, I. D. *The theory and practice of group psychotherapy*. Basic Books, New York (1975).
3. Lieberman, M. A., Yalom, I. D., and Miles, M. B. *Encounter groups: first facts*. Basic Books, New York (1973).
4. Parloff, M. Group dynamics and group psychotherapy: the state of the union. *International Journal of Group Psychotherapy* **13**, 393–8 (1963).
5. Hill, W. F. Further considerations of therapeutic mechanisms in group therapy. *Small Group Behaviour* **6**, 421–9 (1975).

6. Coché, E. and Dies, R. R. Integrating research findings into the practice of group psychotherapy. *Psychotherapy: Theory, Research and Practice* **18**, 410–16 (1981).
7. Frank, J. D. Therapeutic factors in psychotherapy. *American Journal of Psychotherapy* **25**, 350–61 (1971).
8. Parloff, M. B. A view from the bridge: group process and outcome. *International Journal of Group Psychotherapy* **17**, 236–42 (1967).
9. Bion, W. R. *Experiences in groups*. Tavistock, London (1959).
10. Kiesler, D. J. Some myths of psychotherapy research and the search for a paradigm. *Psychological Bulletin* **65**, 110–36 (1966).
11. We cannot afford to be dogmatic in this regard in view of the authoritative view expressed by M. A. Lieberman. (See: Comparative analyses of change mechanisms in groups. In: *Advances in group psychotherapy. Integrating research and practice* (eds. R. R. Dies and K. R. MacKenzie). International Universities Press, New York, 1983.) He argues:

    'Therapeutic change does not appear to be maximized by the idiosyncratic match between an individual's specific group experience and particular events. Rather, it appears that the sheer number of different kinds of experiences or events a person encounters in a change-induction group will, on the average, lead to an increased likelihood of change.' (p. 207)

    We would accept some of the force of Lieberman's argument but feel that it tends to ignore the clinical reality of dealing with a wide variety of therapy groups.
12. See, e.g.: Garfield, S. L. and Bergin, A. E. (eds.) *Handbook of psychotherapy and behaviour change*. Wiley, New York (1978), and *Psychotherapy research. Methodological and efficacy issues*. American Psychiatric Association, Washington D.C. (1982).
13. Fuhriman, A., Drescher, S., Hanson, E. *et al.* (Unpublished MS) University of Utah (1983).
14. Parloff, M. B. and Dies, R. R. Group psychotherapy outcome research. *International Journal of Group Psychotherapy* **27**, 281–319 (1977).
15. Malan, D. H., Balfour, F. H., Hood, V. G., *et al.* Group psychotherapy. A long-term follow-up study. *Archives of General Psychiatry* **33**, 1303–15 (1976).
16. *Psychiatric News*, 19 March 1982, p. 33.
17. Frank, J. D. Group psychotherapy research 25 years later. *International Journal of Group Psychotherapy* **25**, 159–62 (1975).

Appendix

Superior figures refer to lists of references for each chapter.

Chapter 2: Insight (self-understanding)

Author	**Sample**
Abramowitz and Abramowitz (1974)[31]	12 female and 14 male volunteer students, average age 21
Abramowitz and Jackson (1974)[32]	15 male and 13 female volunteer students, average age 21

Method	Findings
Students randomly assigned to one of four groups led by the same experienced therapist. Groups—two 'insight orientated' and two 'non insight-orientated' met for 10 sessions. Independent judges assessed transcripts to validate this distinction. Psychological-mindedness measured pre- and post-therapy using an 'Insight' test. Outcome measured by battery of scales combined into global 'direction of change' index.	1. In the insight groups a greater number of the more psychologically minded members improved than the less psychologically minded. 2. No such differences observed in the non insight groups.
Students randomly assigned to one of four groups led by the same therapist: (a) therapist makes there-and-then interpretations about links between present behaviour and past history; (b) therapist makes here-and-now interpretations—on intra-group behaviour; (c) combined there-and-then/here-and-now interpretations; (d) attention-placebo—therapist makes no interpretations at all. Groups met for 10 sessions. Independent judges validated distinctions between groups. Outcome assessed by battery of self-	No significant interactions found between type of therapeutic condition and outcome although trend for combined here-and-now/there-and-then group to be superior to other groups.

Bailey (1970)[49]	24 female prisoners
Coons (1957)[26]	66 in-patients, mostly schizophrenic
Danet (1969)[50]	Two groups of seven students with neurosis or personality disorders

report measures, including anxiety, self-esteem, shame, and guilt.	
Subjects randomly allocated to three groups—regular group therapy, a self-confrontation group using audio feedback, and a control group. Thirty group sessions over six weeks. Alternate sessions of the two treatment groups taped. Self-confrontation group spent alternate sessions listening to audio playback of previous session. Segments from tapes analysed for level of participation. A self-ideal Q-sort pre- and post-therapy.	1. Q-sort measure showed no differences in the three groups. 2. The level of participation was greater in the group receiving audio-playback.
Patients randomly assigned to one of three treatment conditions: (a) interaction—basically supportive therapy, with the emphasis on generating a warm, accepting, and permissive environment; (b) insight—patients encouraged to examine personal problems, their origins and solutions; and (c) control—no planned group therapy, but patients subject to 'usual hospital routines'. Patients received between eight and 90 hours of group therapy. Groups similar in terms of economic status, diagnosis, education, intelligence, age, duration of illness. Assessment pre- and post-group therapy using Rorschach and Wechsler-Bellevue adult intelligence scale.	Interaction group showed significantly greater improvement 'in adjustment' than did insight and control groups, on both forms of assessment.
Each group run by same pair of therapists. Both groups videotaped. Experimental group received 10 minutes videotape playback from previous meeting at beginning of sessions 2–10. Control group received no such feedback. Patients and therapists were interviewed, and completed non-standardized questionnaires.	1. Presence of camera influenced the course of meetings; minority found it inhibiting. 2. Videotape feedback affected group interaction, increasing cohesiveness.

Jacobs, Jacobs, Gatz, *et al.* (1973) [36]	46 students
Jacobs, Jacobs, Feldman *et al.* (1973)[40]	48 students
Jacobs, Jacobs, Cavior, *et al.* (1974)[42]	48 students
Lieberman, Yalom, and Miles (1973)[16]	See appendix for Chapter 9

Subjects participated in one of six groups lasting eight hours. Each student selected two statements from a list prepared by the researchers to give as feedback to half of his co-members, after one group exercise; procedure repeated following a second exercise. Three experimental conditions were compared (containing two groups each): (a) positive feedback given first; followed by negative feedback; (b) negative feedback given first, followed by positive feedback; (c) positive and negative feedback given together on each occasion. Subjects rated feedback for credibility and desirability.	1. Positive feedback more credible and desirable than negative feedback, overall. 2. Feedback rated as more credible and desirable when negative form given first, and positive form second. Subjects receiving positive and negative feedback on both occasions valued the group experience least.
Subjects participated in one of six groups lasting six hours. Each subject selected two statements from a list of 14 prepared by the researchers to give as feedback to each of the other group members. Subjects then rated feedback statements for accuracy, desirability, and impact. Feedback classified along two dimensions: (a) behavioural (identifying an aspect of behaviour), emotional (emotional reaction of the subject giving the feedback), and mixed; and (b) positive or negative.	1. Positive feedback more credible than negative feedback. 2. Positive-emotional feedback the most credible and negative-emotional feedback the least credible. 3. Positive-behavioural feedback enhanced by the addition of positive-emotional feedback.
As in Jacobs *et al.*[40] but the feedback given anonymously.	1. Positive feedback more credible than negative feedback. 2. Negative-emotional feedback the most credible of the negative feedback conditions and positive-emotional feedback the least credible of the positive feedback conditions. 3. Subjects who received behavioural-feedback only (positive or negative) reported most gain from group experience.

Lomont, Gilner, Spector, and Skinner (1969)[30]	12 in-patients, average IQ 94
Meichenbaum, Gilmore, and Fedoravicius (1971)[23]	53 volunteers, mostly young students, with speech anxiety
Roback (1972)[29]	24 male in-patients hospitalized for an average of 10 years. 20 diagnosed as schizophrenic. Average age 36
Robinson and Jacobs (1970)[48]	40 adult in-patients, 'relatively verbal and in good contact', aged between 20 and 49, hospitalized for less than 18 months

Two groups matched on IQ, MMPI and other measures met daily for six weeks. One group emphasized insight (the understanding of past and present behaviour) and the other was run as an assertiveness training group. Change assessed using MMPI and Leary interpersonal checklist administered pre- and post-group.	Assertiveness group showed greater reduction on MMPI clinical scales.
Subjects randomly assigned to one of four treatment conditions: (a) insight (derived from Ellis's rational-emotive therapy); (b) desensitization; (c) both combined; and (d) placebo group as control for non-specific factors. Groups met for eight, weekly sessions. Assessment at termination and at three month follow-up, including self-report and a test speech rated by trained judges.	1. Insight and desensitization groups achieved greatest, and about equal, improvement on all measures, at termination and at follow-up. 2. Subjects divided into two groups: speech anxiety only and speech anxiety as part of diffuse social anxiety. Subjects with speech anxiety only benefited significantly more from desensitization and significantly less from insight and combined treatment compared to subjects with diffuse social anxiety.
Patients randomly assigned to one of four groups: (a) therapist emphasized insight and interaction; (b) therapist emphasized interaction but not insight; (c) therapist emphasized insight but not interaction; and (d) control group—watched films. Hourly sessions three times a week for 10 weeks. Sessions tape recorded, segments transcribed and rated for levels of insight and interaction shown by patients. Several outcome measures, including MMPI, symptom checklist, WAIS, days out of hospital.	1. Satisfactory reliability obtained for ratings, and treatment conditions met. 2. A trend for the insight-interaction group to show more consistent indications of improvement than the other three groups.
Six groups met on six occasions over two weeks. All meetings videotaped. Three experimental groups had a one-hour video feedback led by therapist immediately following each therapy session; control groups had similar session without video feedback.	1. Judges' ratings of adaptive behaviour three times greater in experimental group than in control. 2. No significant differences between groups on self-ratings of adaptive behaviour.

Author	**Subjects**
Schaible and Jacobs (1975)[39]	60 female students

Chapter 3: Learning from Interpersonal Action

Flowers (1978)[35]	Nine student volunteers, six women, three men, in laboratory group for 15 weekly sessions, 'to discuss their personal problems'
Flowers, Booraem, Brown, *et al.* (1974)[34]	Four male and two female 'severely disturbed' out-patients in supportive, weekly group therapy

Method	Findings
Feedback sessions were audiotaped and rated by two naïve judges for level of feedback given by therapists. Four other naïve judges rated adaptive behaviour of patients on the first and fifth videotape. Patients also rated themselves on this dimension.	
Same as for Jacobs, Jacobs, Gatz, and Schaible (1973) except that group session was half the length; subjects gave feedback to only one designated co-member. Treatment conditions included: no feedback after first exercise, then positive feedback after second exercise; no feedback after first exercise, then negative feedback after second exercise; and positive and negative feedback given together on each occasion.	1. Positive feedback more credible and desirable than negative feedback, overall. 2. Feedback rated as more credible and desirable when positive form given first and negative form second.
Method same as for Flowers *et al.* (1974) with regard to use of tokens (see below) but experimental design is AB_1AB_2A. In phase A, therapists instructed to deliver mostly positive statements to group members. In phase B_1, therapists instructed to deliver mostly negative statements, but of low intensity (criteria for this not defined). In phase B_2, therapists instructed to deliver mostly negative statements, but of medium intensity (again not defined). After each group session, subjects completed questionnaire covering satisfaction with session and level of trust.	1. Design validated by token count of therapists' statements; level of intensity assessed by independent raters rating audiotapes of B_1 and B_2 sessions. 2. Level of interaction between members significantly increased during B sessions but no significant difference between B_1 and B_2 sessions. 3. B_2 sessions associated with decrease in members' satisfaction with group and their self-report level of trust. 4. B_1 sessions associated with slight increase in satisfaction, and significant increase in trust.
Patients met twice a week over 12 weeks. In phase A—first 12 sessions—patients and therapists distributed tokens to one another to reflect their	1. Token use found to reflect accurately the proportion of positive and negative statements given (through independent ratings of

Grosz and Wright (1967)[39]	Male in-patients attended for an average 5.5 sessions of a weekly, open group. Average 5 patients per session.
Grosz, Stern, and Wright (1965)[36]	Male in-patients participating in one of five weekly, open groups. 146 patients involved during period of study, which covered 74 sessions. Attendance varied from between four and six

feelings: red, when making a negative statement, and blue, when making a positive statement. In phase B—next six sessions—tokens not used, to serve as control condition. In phase C—final six sessions—tokens again used. In last nine weeks, independent observers rated frequency of therapist–patient and patient–patient interactions.

segments of audiotaped sessions).

2. Number of patient–patient interactions significantly higher when tokens in use than when they were not.
3. Number of therapist–patient interactions significantly lower when tokens in use.
4. Use of tokens seems to be associated with increase in proportion of negative, feedback statements made by the therapist.

Three therapists ran group sessions in turn; non-directive, encouraging patient–patient interaction. Observer/co-therapist kept record of all verbal interactions between patients and between patients and therapist. Frequencies of verbal interactions (uninterrupted segments of speech) computed for each group member.

1. Patient–patient verbal interactions increased steadily over first 16 sessions, despite changes in group's composition, and changes in therapists.
2. During sessions 16–26, interactions stayed at high level although fluctuating greatly.
3. Therapist–patient interactions—no significant differences between therapists in their interacting behaviour.
4. Steady group composition from one session to another associated with increase in patient interactions; change in membership associated with increase or with decrease in such interactions.

Each group run by different therapist, but all aimed to promote interaction. Observer/co-therapist kept record of all verbal interactions between patients and between patients and therapist. Frequencies of verbal interactions (uninterrupted segments of speech) computed for each group member. Correction included to eliminate the effect of unequal distribution among therapists of different-sized groups.

1. The group led by most experienced therapist had highest number of patient–patient interactions.
2. No consistent relationship between therapist–patient interactions and patient–patient interactions.
3. Patient–patient interactions increased with greater group size but this was inconsistent over groups; only consistent when data from all five groups pooled.
4. Group size not related to number of patient–therapist interactions.

Heckel, Froelich, and Salzberg (1962)[31]	Seven acutely ill psychiatric in-patients
Kaye (1973)[40]	Two T-groups (14 and 13 members) chosen at random from academically unsuccessful students. 'Comparison groups': 10 'ballotted' out of participation, 13 who had declined the invitation, and 30 academically successful students.
Land (1964)[33]	Experiment I—two experimental groups; each with ten in-patients, *long-term* residents in closed ward. Plus control group. Experiment II—two experimental groups; each with ten acutely ill patients in maximum security ward. Plus control group. (None of the above groups were matched.)
Lee (1976)[29]	48 male, 48 female subjects chosen from 250 students on the basis of extreme scores on a risk-taking inventory

Six group sessions with one therapist who for sessions 1–3 referred therapist-directed comments to the group (redirection) and for sessions 4–6 did not. Therapist and patient statements coded from tape recordings; therapist's statements as redirection versus non-redirection and patients' statements as therapist-directed or interaction.	Interaction between patients directly related to proportion of redirection responses and inversely related to total number of comments by therapist.
Hill interaction matrix (HIM), Schutz's FIRO-B, and the Leary interpersonal checklist (ICL) were administered before and after a 10-day workshop, and eight months later. Controls completed FIRO-B and ICL at comparable times.	1. Short-term changes in perceived behaviour and in personal and interpersonal constructs (HIM, ICL) in experimental groups, but almost all changes reverted to pre-workshop scores after eight months. 2. No changes in FIRO-B for either experimental group or controls.
All patients, experimental and control, participated in four preliminary group sessions. Rated on Finney group therapy scale by two independent judges. Control groups then not seen until end of experimental period. Experimental patients had ten therapy sessions. In one experimental group, therapist talked actively and directly to individual patients; in the other experimental group, therapist was silent unless questioned directly, in which event he redirected the question to another patient. All sessions were taped to validate consistency of experimental conditions.	1. Interaction between patients increased when therapist was silent and redirecting in the acutely ill sample. 2. In the case of the chronic patients, it seemed to be necessary for the therapist to talk directly to patients to obtain their involvement. 3. None of the groups showed any major improvement on various measures of outcome.
Four types (high risk-taking males and females; low risk-taking males and females) further subdivided by allotting at random, members of each type to three groups of four. Each group experienced a simulated first session of group therapy consisting of three practice trials providing training in three prescribed behaviours: self-disclosure, feedback, and group	1. Structured groups were more effective in promoting prescribed behaviours than less structured groups, except in high risk-taking males. 2. Males and high risk-taking subjects displayed more prescribed behaviour than females and low risk-taking subjects.

Lorr (1966)[26]	45 groups totalling 194 patients with either neurosis, or psychosis in remission; 11 per cent female
McPherson and Walton (1970)[25]	Eight neurotic out-patients meeting weekly for 90-minute group therapy sessions
Ryan (1958)[28]	25 patients in two therapy groups

confrontation (all aspects of interaction in this context). Groups were high, moderate, or low in terms of structuredness. Sessions were taped and rated for prescribed behaviour. A scale of group cohesiveness was used.	
Four meetings of mature groups sampled by observers who rated interpersonal behaviour on a schedule of 75 items. Factor analysis to determine extent to which items could be grouped into previously hypothesized dimensions.	Interpersonal behaviour was classifiable into the following dimensions: 1. Dominance/attention seeking. 2. Hostility. 3. Leadership role. 4. Supportive role. 5. Succorance (help-seeking). 6. Submission. 7. Withdrawal. 8. Disorganized (psychotic). Second-order correlations yielded four categories: 1. Activity level. 2. Submissiveness/disorganized. 3. Supportive role. 4. Leadership role.
Group run along group-analytic lines. Seven experienced clinicians observed at least 25 meetings (one was the therapist). Each observer, using repertory grid technique, rated each patient for his intra-group behaviour. 16 bipolar constructs elicited from each rater. Seven individual grids combined and factors analyzed.	The three largest components, accounting for 70 per cent of total variance, were: 1. Assertive/dominant versus passive/submissive. 2. Emotionally sensitive versus emotionally insensitive (to others in group). 3. Hinders attainment of the group's goals versus aiding the same. These three components reflect 'very closely' content and size of dimensions used by each of the seven raters, i.e. substantial agreement on dimensions of interaction.
Groups studied for 16 weeks. A Rorschach-based scale designed to assess capacity for mutual dependence (comprising 'capacity for giving' and 'management of dependency' in	1. High capacity for mutual dependence correlated with involvement in the group. 2. Giving individuals were more involved in the group.

Salzberg (1962)[32]	19 psychiatric in-patients who met twice a week for ten weeks
Swarr and Ewing (1977)[41]	45 student–patients with long-standing interpersonal difficulties and low self-esteem, average age 22 years; 22 men, 23 women

relationships) of each member. This distinguished giving from non-giving; and dependence-flexible, dependence-acceptance, and dependence-denial individuals. Involvement in the group was measured by length of stay and therapist ratings.	3. Dependence-flexible individuals were more involved than dependence-acceptance and dependence-denial individuals.
Therapist used either silence, talking only when conversation lagged, redirecting (therapist brought one or more group patients into discussion), or directing (therapist spoke directly to a single patient only) in various combinations: silence-redirection; silence-direction; talking-redirection; and talking-direction. Observations made were: frequency of patient's responses to the four conditions; whether responses were interaction or non-interaction (dependent on whether patients spoke to one another); whether responses were environmental (about object or person outside group), personal (the patient talks about himself), or group (patient refers to another member).	1. No significant difference in total frequency of patients' responses between the four conditions. 2. Silence associated with significantly more interaction. 3. Redirecting associated with significantly more group-type responses i.e. patient refers to another member. 4. Talking-direction associated with greatest number of personal responses.
Ten small, out-patient groups meeting for two-hourly, weekly sessions. Patients served as own control by use of a waiting period of 11 weeks. They completed two self-report questionnaires—the group therapy evaluation form and the Illinois personal rating form—pre-group, at end of waiting period, after about three months of treatment, and at end of treatment, which lasted, on average, six months.	Positive changes occurred in some areas after three months of treatment, e.g. self-esteem, anxiety, self-confidence, motivation, activity. Variables not changing significantly at three months but doing so at the end of therapy, included interpersonal relating, trust, assertiveness, hostility. The latter changes possibly required group cohesiveness and trust, providing opportunity to experiment with new kinds of interaction and to experience success.

Chapter 4: Acceptance (Cohesiveness)

Author	**Sample**
Bugen (1977)[41]	Eight groups comprising 56 students on a counselling course
Costell and Koran (1972)[39]	11 weekly out-patient therapy groups studied for first 20 sessions. 41 men and 46 women, mostly 20–40 years old and middle socio-economic class.
Danet (1969)[22]	See appendix for Chapter 2.
Dies and Hess (1971)[32]	Six 'comparable' groups, each containing five ex-drug-addicts desiring psychotherapy
Edwards (1969)[43]	Six therapy groups (total of 32 students)

Method	Results
Four pairs of groups composed according to results of inclusion scale of FIRO-B: high; high-moderate; low-moderate; and low need for inclusion. Sensitivity-training groups for three hours a week for 15 weeks led by inexperienced leaders. Subjects also received didactic lectures on group therapy. One group of each pair received pre-group instruction stressing cohesiveness; the other a non-specific instruction. A 12-item cohesiveness questionnaire was administered at end of second, fifteenth, and twenty-eighth hour.	1. Specific pre-group instructions had little influence on the development of cohesiveness. 2. Cohesiveness developed to greatest extent in the two low-moderate inclusion groups, to an intermediate extent in the high-moderate groups, and least in the high and low inclusion groups. 3. Establishment of cohesiveness was complete by the mid-point in the group's development.
FIRO-B administered before treatment to measure compatibility between members. Group cohesiveness questionnaire completed after first and twelfth meetings by patients.	1. Cohesiveness remained almost unchanged over first 12 meetings. 2. Compatibility not significantly correlated with cohesiveness measured after first or twelfth meetings. 3. Compatibility unrelated to early drop-out.
Three groups run as 12 hour marathon, three as conventional group—one hour daily for 12 successive days. Three experienced therapists running one group of each kind. Tape recordings were made of hours 1, 4, 8, and 12 of each group. Cohesiveness was measured by patients and independent judges.	1. Cohesiveness increased linearly with time in both types of group. 2. On most measures, increase was greater in marathon groups.
The following measures were used: FIRO-B administered pre- and post-therapy to therapist and patients. Group opinion questionnaire was administered to provide outcome	1. FIRO-B compatibility among patients had little consequence for their improvement. 2. Kt was correlated with therapist ratings of improvement.

Hurst (1978)[28]	12 adolescent groups (six each from different cultural backgrounds) each of 6–10 adolescents
Kapp, Gleser, Brissenden, *et al.* (1964)[18]	47 members of 11 community discussion groups and 12 therapy groups. No indication of duration or frequency of group meetings

scores on personality improvement and ego involvement. Therapist ratings of improvement were made; a measure of 'compatibility with group' was obtained by pairing each patient with other members and obtaining means of FIRO-B scores. Total compatibility between patients and therapists (Kt) was similarly obtained.

3. Two individual FIRO-B scores were correlated with outcome—expressed control negatively and expressed affection positively.

Weekly meetings for 30 weeks led by two co-therapists. Four instruments were developed to measure: group cohesiveness; leadership style (self-expressiveness, caring, meaning-attribution, controlling); attitudes towards self; and attitudes towards others and external world. These were administered during the 30 weeks.

1. Caring positively correlated with cohesiveness.
2. Self-expressiveness correlated with cohesiveness to a lesser extent.
3. Caring was an essential element of a cohesive group but self-expressiveness facilitated cohesiveness only if caring was present.
4. The promotion of cohesiveness depended on both leaders of a pair exhibiting effective styles.
5. Increase in self-esteem positively correlated with cohesiveness.
6. Some correlation between caring and increase in self-esteem.
7. Differences between the two samples suggested that the effectiveness of leadership style was related to cultural background of patients.

A 'Group Opinion Questionnaire' completed by group members measuring self-perceived personality change, involvement in the group, and level of group cohesiveness, after they had spent substantial periods in group experience (up to 2 years).

1. Outcome, involvement, and cohesiveness were independent of age and education.
2. The three variables increased with duration of individual's group experience.
3. Involvement tended to a maximum at about 15 months.
4. Cohesiveness correlated with both involvement and outcome.
5. Therapy groups had higher change but lower involvement and cohesiveness scores than discussion groups.

Liberman (1970)[26]	Two matched, seven-member therapy groups
Ribner (1974)[34]	See appendix for Chapter 5.
Rich (1968)[25]	Two sets of laboratory groups comprised of normal individuals
Riley (1971)[40]	Three groups selected from 30 students

Two therapists with similar training and experience. Groups met weekly for nine months. In the experimental group, the therapist made comments designed specifically to prompt or reinforce expressions of cohesiveness. The therapist ran the control group intuitively. Ratings of interaction were made from tapes and by a non-participant observer using measures with high inter-rater reliability. Outcome measures—target complaints and symptom checklist.	1. Experimental group more cohesive. 2. Experimental group showed more rapid symptomatic improvement on both outcome measures and slightly better six-month outcome on symptom checklist. 3. Inferences drawn regarding optimum therapist behaviour: (a) Respond promptly to target behaviour. (b) Keep interventions simple. (c) Speak directly to patient. (d) Use reinforcement more than prompting. (e) Avoid excessive comment.
One set was selected to be highly cohesive, the other to be low in cohesiveness. Operational definitions of cohesiveness (attraction to task and to other members) and types of communication (persuasive and coercive). Extra member added to each group, instructed to express deviant opinion on group task. From audiotapes of group meetings, statements designed to change opinion of deviate were scored as persuasive or coercive.	1. Main hypothesis that communication to a deviate in a highly cohesive group would be more persuasive and less coercive than in a less cohesive group was not borne out. 2. Members of highly cohesive groups voiced disagreement with the deviate more often than members of less cohesive groups. 3. Members of less cohesive groups voiced agreement with deviate more often than members of highly cohesive groups.
FIRO-B compatibility was the basis for placement in group: two groups more compatible, one group less. Sensitivity-training group met three hours a week for 37 weeks. Focus on individual personality and personal development. Mid-year marathon session for each group. Following measures were used: Tennessee self-concept scale pre- and post-group experience; FIRO-B, and measures of cohesiveness before, during, and after group experience.	1. No correlation between compatibility and change in self-concept. 2. Positive correlation between compatibility and cohesiveness. 3. Level of interpersonal need as measured by FIRO-B changed with time.

Roether and Peters (1972)[21]	64 sex offenders in a mandatory group therapy programme, who had attended ten or more sessions
Smith (1970)[24]	Encounter groups; not further specified
Snortum and Myers (1971)[23]	A sensitivity-training group of 21 subjects, which met weekly for seven weeks
Weiss (1972)[20]	84 students: 56 group members; rest no-treatment controls
Yalom, Houts, Zimerberg, *et al.* (1967)[19]	Five new out-patient groups comprised of 40 patients with neurosis or personality disorder. Studied for one year of therapy

Four therapists rated the following in their groups: cohesiveness; expressed hostility to outside authority, outside others, and to peers in the group; whether the group was 'good' or 'bad'. Outcome measured as police arrests within one year of first assignment to therapy programme.	1. Therapists tended to rate cohesive groups as 'good'. 2. Patients attending more cohesive sessions were more often treatment failures. 3. Patients with successful outcome had more often attended sessions high in hostility (especially to outside others). 4. No evidence that hostility was more beneficially expressed in cohesive groups.
Member rating scale of group interaction comprised of nine variables (not further specified). Measure of development of cohesiveness also not specified.	Some support for the hypothesis that groups rated high in interaction develop a high level of cohesiveness.
Self-rating scales of closeness and hostility completed after earlier meeting.	Intimacy increased as a function of the frequency of interaction.
Six marathon groups of 12 hours duration. Personal orientation inventory (measure of self-actualization) and HIM-B (measure of interpersonal style) administered to experimental subjects pre- and post-treatment, and to controls at comparable times. Audiotapes of third, sixth, ninth, and twelfth hours rated on HIM-G (measure of therapeutic interaction). Two cohesiveness measures administered at end of each of the above hours.	1. No appreciable therapeutic gain for most members. 2. Linear development of cohesiveness in all six groups. 3. Two measures of cohesiveness intercorrelated. 4. Questionnaire measure of cohesiveness a moderate predictor of outcome. 5. Cohesiveness not correlated with ratings of therapeutic process.
Groups met weekly for 90 minutes led by novice co-therapist pairs, under supervision, and with interactional orientation. Following measures used: (a) pre-therapy—FIRO-B, Jourard self-disclosure questionnaire, psychological-mindedness test from California personality inventory; (b) during therapy—at sixth and twelfth	1. 20 patients dropped out, 11 before the twelfth meeting. Dropouts expressed dissatisfaction with the group. No patient dropped out between twentieth session and final assessment. 2. Numbers too small to demonstrate clear outcome differences between 'dropouts' and 'completers'.

Author	Sample
Yalom and Rand (1966)[37]	Five out-patient therapy groups (total of 40 patients) with similar composition, met weekly
Chapter 5: Self-disclosure	
Anchor, Vojtisek and Berger (1972)[36]	24 acutely ill, psychiatric, male in-patients, with good pre-morbid personality
Bundza and Simonson (1973)[24]	16 male and 29 female psychology students

Method	Findings
meetings, patients filled in a cohesiveness questionnaire and ranked peers on popularity; (c) at end of one year—patients assessed on three dimensions of outcome by independent judges and patients' self-ratings on same scales.	3. Cohesiveness correlated significantly with self-ratings of improvement but not with interviewer ratings. 4. Group popularity correlated strongly with both self- and interviewer-ratings of improvement.
Groups were studied for first 12 sessions. FIRO-B administered initially to assess compatibility. Measures of cohesiveness—questionnaires, attendance, and rate of premature termination.	1. Groups with greater group compatibility were more cohesive. 2. Early terminators less compatible with other group members. 3. Patients who were incompatible with at least one group member were less satisfied with group. 4. Compatibility with the therapist was not important.
Patients randomly assigned to one of four groups. Marlowe–Crowne social desirability scale completed prior to group meeting. Forty-minute, leaderless, videotaped discussion, beginning with topic 'friendship'. Tapes rated for number of personal and impersonal statements according to Anchor's group interaction profile by four naïve raters.	Patients with moderate scores on social desirability scale expressed a greater percentage of personal statements than either high or low scorers.
Subjects given transcriptions of simulated sessions in which therapist responses were either non self-disclosing, warmly supportive or self-disclosing (i.e. supportive statements containing reference to therapist's own experience). Subjects rated willingness to self-disclose to therapist via self-disclosure questionnaire and adjective checklist. Subjects were then interviewed by the therapist using standard, open-ended questions.	1. Actual self-disclosure to the therapists correlated with 'willingness to self-disclose'. 2. Self-disclosing therapists appeared warmest and elicited greatest willingness to self-disclose.

Certner (1973)[28]	64 unmarried students, 32 male and 32 female
Dies (1973)[22]	24 of the members of 10 therapy groups at a university counselling centre
Dies and Cohen (1976)[25]	108 psychology students

Subjects divided into groups of four and instructed to get acquainted. After 10 minutes subjects rated liking for other participants. A note-passing technique for exchanging personal information was used. Ten sets of seven personal questions ranging from high to low intimacy were presented. Each student exchanged a note with his three fellow members, specifying the number of the question the recipient was to answer and providing an answer to the questions requested of him. Subjects rated again how much they liked each other.	1. Positive relationship between initial self-disclosure and liking for both males and females. 2. Effect of self-disclosure on final liking was highly significant. 3. Intimacy of self-disclosure was reciprocal. 4. No differences between females and males in self-disclosure or in liking.
Clients completed postal enquiry asking: 1. How group leader would respond, and how client would like group leader to respond on the items of the group therapist orientation scale,[21] which rates attitudes to therapist self-disclosure. 2. Evaluation of therapist based on a set of 20 bipolar adjectives. Factor analysis of responses gave two main factors (1 and 2). 3. Number of group sessions attended.	1. Therapists judged to be self-disclosing were seen as friendly, open, and helpful (factor 1) but were less likely to be judged as relaxed, strong, stable, and sensitive (factor 2) than their non-disclosing counterparts. 2. Clients who rated their therapist low on factor 1 tended to desire a more self-disclosing therapist. 3. Preference for a more self-disclosing therapist increased with the number of group sessions attended.
Subjects were categorized according to experience of group therapy and willingness to join a group. They completed a questionnaire in which, using a seven-point helpful-harmful scale, they evaluated 65 statements reflecting therapist self-disclosure in therapy or encounter groups. Statements ranged from innocuous to intimate, and subjects judged their appropriateness for groups of different duration (1, 8, and 15 sessions).	1. Experience and willingness did not affect the attitude expressed. 2. Therapist self-disclosure was regarded as more helpful in encounter groups than in therapy groups. 3. Therapist self-disclosure was seen as more helpful in later group sessions. This was a more gradual trend in therapy groups. 4. Harmful effects of therapist self-disclosure were regarded as more likely in therapy groups. 5. Expression by the therapist of negative 'here-and-now' feelings about the group was seen as

Drag (1969)[20]	Not specified
Johnson and Ridener (1974)[12]	23 volunteer students
Kahn and Rudestam (1971)[34]	10 graduate psychology students, previously acquainted, in encounter group
Kirshner (1976)[13]	Eight groups of eight subjects
Lieberman, Yalom, and Miles (1973)[38]	See appendix for Chapter 9.
Nilsson, Strassberg, and Bannon (1979)[23]	120 male and 120 female introductory psychology students, average age 21,

Method	Findings
	particularly harmful: and particularly helpful were 'there-and-then' experiences from outside the group. 6. Preference emerged for a leader confident of his leadership abilities and emotional stability and willing to share personal and professional goals and normal emotional experiences.
Little detail available. Experimenter either self-disclosed or non self-disclosed in a 2-, 4-, and 8-person group.	Main conclusion was that self-disclosure occurs most easily in smaller groups and where there is a model to follow.
One male and one female group heterogeneous for self-disclosure (Jourard scale), and one homogeneous female group (all average scores). Four 30-minute discussion groups held on 'Higher Education'. Videotapes of these coded using interpersonal action analysis. Cohesiveness measured by 20-item questionnaire at end of programme.	Self-disclosure correlated with cohesiveness but not with members' level of participation.
Group leader was a faculty member known to students. Group met three hours weekly for 10 weeks. Data collected after meetings 1, 6, and 10. Each subject completed two rank-orderings of all other subjects: (a) person liked best; (b) person who had disclosed most.	1. Significant correlation between liking and self-disclosure. 2. Some indication that self-disclosure was important at the beginning of the group but other factors were more responsible for liking as interpersonal relationships developed.
Eight one-hour sessions of encounter-type exercises led by tapes. Two conditions—high- and low self-disclosure. Groups rated on various measures of cohesiveness.	High self-disclosure groups more cohesive than low self-disclosure groups.
One of a series of videotapes of a simulated counselling session made by	1. Both intrapersonal and interpersonal self-disclosure by

	mostly naïve to psychotherapy experience
Pino and Cohen (1971)[17]	44 students
Query (1964, 1970)[10, 11]	43 nursing students
Ribner (1974)[18]	96 single, male under-graduates

actors was presented to subjects. 'Counsellors' exhibited: (i) no self-disclosure; or (ii) interpersonal disclosure; or (iii) intrapersonal disclosure, in otherwise similar scripts. Subjects completed a questionnaire related to counsellors' personal and professional characteristics.

counsellors were evaluated more favourably than non-disclosure.
2. Intrapersonal self-disclosure was viewed more favourably than interpersonal self-disclosure.
3. Subjects regarded themselves as more likely to disclose to disclosing counsellors than to non-disclosing counsellors.
4. No differences were noted between male and female counsellors and subjects.

Two leaders each had two T-groups. Each leader used a 'leader-guided' style with one group and a 'group-centred' style with the other. Members' self-disclosure was measured by self-reference content analysis.

Leader-guided style was more effective in promoting self-disclosure.

Subjects divided into three groups of high, medium, and low self-disclosure (Jourard scale). They met twice weekly for 12 weeks of group therapy. Leaders rated each student after each meeting on self-disclosure items adapted from Finney group psychotherapy scale. After their last meeting, the students: (a) rated individual members and the group as a whole on a nine-point scale of 'liking' (a measure of cohesiveness); and (b) completed self-disclosure questionnaire in terms of topics discussed.

High self-disclosure associated with high cohesiveness and positive attitude towards group.

48 subjects with high and 48 subjects with low self-disclosure (Jourard scale). 24 groups formed with four subjects each: eight groups of subjects with high self-disclosure; eight of subjects with low self-disclosure; and eight of two high and two low self-disclosure subjects. Groups met for one hour; session was taped and segments were rated for intimacy, frequency, and depth of self-disclosure. Half the

1. High inter-rater reliability of judges' ratings.
2. Contract encouraged frequency and depth but not intimacy of self-disclosure.
3. Contract encouraged group cohesiveness though mutual liking was lower than control.
4. Subjects high in self-disclosure showed greater cohesiveness and mutual liking than subjects low in

Scheiderer (1977)[19]	32 self-referred male clients of a university counselling centre. Average age 20; selected for moderate problem severity
Strassberg, Roback, Anchor, *et al.* (1975)[37]	18 male, long-stay, in-patient, schizophrenics, average age 36
Truax and Carkhuff (1965)[16]	40 psychiatric in-patients and 40 institutionalized juvenile delinquents in group therapy programmes
Weigel, Dinges, Dyer, *et al.* (1972)[35]	74 students requesting therapy. Divided into five sensitivity groups, two therapy groups, and two marathon groups
Weigel and Warnath (1968)[14]	20 graduate student volunteers

groups had an explicit contract which encouraged self-disclosure; the other half were merely instructed to get acquainted. Post-group ratings were made by members of how much they liked each other and the group.	self-disclosure.
Subjects were exposed to one of four conditions prior to the first clinical interview: (i) control (no instructions); (ii) specific detailed instructions stressing self-disclosure; (iii) modelling of self-disclosure via video of an interview plus commentary; (iv) instructions plus modelling. Audiotapes of clinical interview were rated for verbal content. Clients and therapists completed questionnaires about the interview.	1. Clients exposed to instructions and those exposed to modelling disclosed more personal material (both related and unrelated to problems) than controls. 2. This effect was stronger in the modelling condition; no èxtra effect from combined condition. 3. Both clients and therapists exposed to experimental conditions found their interviews more effective than those exposed to control condition.
Patients assigned to one of three groups which met for 30 sessions over 10 weeks. All sessions taped. Patients completed questionnaire to distinguish between those who perceived therapist as more caring or less caring. Patients' self-disclosure measured through tapes. Outcome assessed by self-reports, behavioural assessment, and WAIS.	1. Negative correlation between self-disclosure and outcome. 2. Patients who saw therapist as more caring made more self-disclosures.
Group therapy sessions audiotaped. Analysis of four-minute segments for patient and therapist transparency using the authors' 'depth of intrapersonal exploration' scale. Patient and therapist ratings of change were made.	1. Significant positive relationship between therapist transparency and patient self-disclosure. 2. High levels of self-disclosure (and self-exploration) significantly correlated with change—positively in psychiatric patients, negatively in delinquents.
Students ranked members of their groups on liking, mental health, and self-disclosure after several hours of therapy. They also ranked therapists.	1. Positive correlations between liking and mental health, and between liking and self-disclosure. 2. Negative correlation between perceived therapist self-disclosure and mental health.
15 students were assigned to one of two	1. No difference between groups on

Author	Sample
Weiner, Rosson and Cody (1974)[15]	9 patients in concurrent individual psychotherapy
Worthy, Gary, and Kahn (1969)[27]	48 female undergraduates

Chapter 6: Catharsis

Author	Sample
Haer (1968)[10]	12 patients; two therapy groups each three males and three females

Method	**Findings**
therapy groups; five to controls. 10 sessions. Pre-therapy measure of willingness to disclose was made using an adaptation of Jourard scale. One therapist self-disclosed, the other did not. Post-therapy measures were: Jourard rating of 'What I have told' in the group; and therapists and students completed questionnaires ranking each member on liking; their amount, depth, and change in self-disclosure; and their mental health.	willingness to disclose. 2. Disclosing therapist liked by group members more than non-disclosing therapist. 3. Non-disclosing therapist ranked higher on mental health than disclosing therapist.
Two experiments: 1. Two groups, A and B, formed according to measures of self-disclosure, including the Jourard scale. In group A, therapist self-disclosing for sessions 1–5 and not in 6–10. The reverse in group B. The last 30 minutes of group sessions videotaped and a 15-minute segment coded independently by three raters for self-disclosure. 2. Patients randomly assigned to two groups. In group A therapist self-disclosed, not so in group B. Videotape segments coded by one rater.	1. Jourard scale not predictive of affective self-disclosure. 2. Association between affective self-disclosure by therapists and by patients. 3. In experiment 2, no correlation between affective self-disclosure by patients and therapist.
Same as Certner (1973). See above.	1. Initially, self-disclosure was to those for whom there was greater liking. 2. Following mutual self-disclosure, a greater liking developed for those from whom intimate disclosures had been received. 3. Subjects exchanged more intimate information with those who disclosed similarly to them.
Tapes were made of 20 sessions of each group. Therapist encouraged	Frequency of aggressive responses significantly diminished after

Liberman (1970)[11]	Two matched, seven-member therapy groups
Lieberman, Yalom, and Miles (1975)[13]	See appendix for Chapter 9.
Myerhoff, Jacobs and Stoller (1970)[12]	17 psychiatric in-patients, two groups

Chapter 7: Guidance

Author	Sample
Bednar and Battersby (1976)[24]	Students: 24 male; 24 female

expression of feelings. Tapes coded for expressions of anger and aggressive responses. Frequency of aggressive responses in the 30 minutes preceding and 30 minutes following expressions of anger was tabulated.	expressions of anger.
Two therapists with similar training and experience. Groups met weekly for nine months. In the experimental group, the therapist made comments designed specifically to prompt or reinforce expressions of hostility towards him. In the control group, the therapist ran the group intuitively. Ratings of interaction and therapist-directed hostility were made from the tapes and by observers. Outcome measures—target complaints and symptom checklist.	1. Therapist prompting and reinforcing effectively promoted expressions of hostility directed to therapist. 2. Expressions of hostility to therapist were unrelated to symptomatic and personality change.
Marathon group met for three six-hour sessions over three days; the traditional group met for nine two-hour sessions over three weeks. Both were led by the same therapist. Patients completed adjective checklists after each two-hour period of treatment as a measure of emotionality.	1. Therapist acted consistently throughout experiment, as judged by non-participant observers. 2. Overall, degree of emotionality was similar in two groups. 3. There was a greater level of negative feelings experienced in the marathon group.

Method	**Findings**
Random assignment to eight different two-hour work-shops on interpersonal relations. Each group differed in initial written instructions and received either a general or a specific message about group process. Dependent variables were measures of: personal discomfort; attitudes towards group experience;	Specific, behavioural instructions were particularly associated with: (a) improved cohesiveness; (b) greater self-disclosure and feedback; (c) less 'conventional' social behaviour; (d) more favourable attitudes towards

D'Augelli and Chinski (1974)[23]	68 male, 70 female students; no prior experience of group therapy
Dick, Pawlick, and Woods (1982)[31]	105 patients referred for treatment in a psychotherapy unit. Experimental group of 33 females, 16 males; retrospective control group of 32 females, 25 males. Comparable in terms of age, diagnosis, length of previous treatment and past experience of therapy
Flowers (1979)[14]	32 male sex offenders compulsorily resident in prison hospital. Four groups of eight

group cohesiveness; and interpersonal behaviour.

group.
Personal discomfort did not vary significantly.

Assessment of interpersonal traits, such as empathic understanding, openness, and honesty yielded a measure of 'therapeutic talent' (TT). 12 'high TT' and 12 'low TT' groups formed. Two-hour leaderless session with taped instructions; three conditions;

1. Practice: detailed description of self-disclosure, talking about the here-and-now, feedback. Each subject practised each behaviour.
2. Cognitive: similar except no practice. Instead subjects verbally summarized instructions.
3. Control: 'attention-placebo' lecture on history of sensitivity training.

Two hour T-group, observed and audiotaped. Raters scored participants for personal discussion and feedback.

1. High TT subjects engaged in more personal discussion than low TT subjects. Overall use of feedback did not differ, but high TT subjects tended to use more personal feedback.
2. Groups exposed to experimental conditions had higher levels of personal discussion and feedback than control groups.
3. Against the authors' expectations, subjects in the cognitive condition engaged in more personal discussion and feedback than those in the practice condition.
4. Differences between the three conditions predominantly observed in high TT subjects.

All patients received daily therapy; one large group and three small groups for 12 weeks. Other activities included psychodrama, art therapy, physical activities. Experimental group received in addition a period of individual therapy as preparation for group work. Interviews with each patient in first and twelfth weeks of therapy, covering attitudes to self and satisfaction with life.

No significant differences between experimental and control either in the proportion of dropouts or in the parameters measured by the interview.

Therapists trained to give different forms of advice. Control therapists not so trained. Therapist behaviour in groups rated from audiotapes by independent raters for types of advice given: simple advice; offering alternatives; giving instructions; and advice about the group process itself. Each piece of advice was transcribed

1. Clients in trained therapists' groups showed greater improvement than clients in control therapists' groups.
2. Alternatives and instructions equally potent in promoting achievement of goals; more so than simple advice.
3. Group process advice not tested.

Hilkey, Wilhelm, and Horne (1982)[29]	90 male prison inmates, average age 28. Eight weekly group therapy sessions of 90 minutes each
Loranger (1973)[13]	25 problem drinkers sentenced to a treatment facility
Strupp and Bloxom (1973)[28]	122 patients referred for psychological counselling on the basis of low income and minimal motivation. Average age 29; average education 11 years. Approx. equal male and female, black and white. Wide range of psychological problems, but deemed 'suitable for psychotherapy'

into a goal. Patient's achievement of goal rated on a seven point scale by staff uninvolved with group.	
Partially matched groups of seven or eight subjects assigned to either experimental or control condition. Experimental subjects viewed a 30-minute videotape of group session in which therapist facilitated 'therapeutic behaviours'; then able to ask questions; and then guided to role-play client and therapist. Assessment pre- and post-treatment including state-trait anxiety scale, readiness for group counselling scale, and self-report scale on achievement of goals. Also therapist and peer ratings of outcome. Independent judges rated, with satisfactory reliability, interaction in groups, using Bale's interaction categories.	1. Pre-training associated with greater readiness for group experience. 2. No differences between experimental and control groups on quality of interaction, except for the first session. 3. Outcome—no significant difference using self-report, but experimental subjects more improved than controls, according to peer and therapist ratings. 4. No difference in attendance.
Patients allocated to three groups which ran for 13 weeks. One group received 'didactic educational therapy', the second 'group therapy and family orientation', and the third a combined treatment. Outcome assessed by the alcohol education instrument and the clinic evaluation instrument. Also by self- and therapist-ratings.	1. Knowledge of alcoholism increased in all groups. 2. Discrepancies between self- and therapist-ratings noted. 3. Education seemed to be most therapeutic tool (evidence for this not directly stated).
1. Balanced groups formed on the basis of age/sex/presenting problem etc. 2. Each group introduced to therapy by means of: (a) a role induction film; or (b) a role induction interview; or (c) a control film. 3. Four experienced therapists treated three groups each for 12 weeks, using eclectic techniques. 4. Battery of tests administered prior to group 1 and following groups 1, 3, 5, 7, 9, 11, and 12 by research	1. Matching of groups satisfactory. 2. Patient's satisfaction with therapy significantly better in groups with induction experience, especially film. 3. Role induction film associated with patients' ratings of improvement, but no consistent trends in therapists' ratings of improvement. 4. Symptom discomfort did not vary consistently between groups. 5. Attendance unusually good in all groups.

Whalen (1969)[25]	128 male student volunteers
Wogan, Getter, Amdur, *et al.* (1977)[30]	52 referrals with long-standing problems, from a university mental health clinic
Yalom, Houts, Newell, *et al.* (1967)[27]	60 patients with neurotic or personality disorders

personnel, including symptom discomfort and satisfaction with treatment. Patients and therapists unaware of experimental design.	
Groups of four, randomly assigned to one of four experimental conditions: two sets of groups viewed a film in which students modelled self-disclosing behaviour as a way of getting to know each other. All groups received taped instructions about the group, either detailed or minimal. Groups ran for 40 minutes, observed. Trained judges rated, *inter alia*, levels of personal discussion and feedback.	1. Good inter-rater reliability. 2. Groups receiving film and detailed instructions consistently resembled the filmed group more than other groups.
Nine out-patient groups: two control groups met without special instructions; three groups heard taped instructions stressing self-disclosure, feedback, and 'getting in touch with feelings'; two groups spent one hour in a structured group designed to facilitate disclosure of feelings; two groups met without leaders for one hour. Subjects completed target problem checklist before and throughout the study. First six sessions audiotaped and rated for interaction. Selected tape segments rated for personal/ impersonal, and group related/group unrelated content.	1. No clear differences between treatment conditions in early groups. 2. Small differences in improvement (problem checklist) when all meetings taken into account: tape condition showed greatest improvement; controls least. 3. Noticeable therapist effect confounding treatment conditions—active therapists associated with more successful groups.
Patients randomly assigned to one of three experimental or three control groups. Members of former had systematic talk on group therapy. Groups studied for first twelve, weekly meetings. Therapists blind to experiment. Measures of cohesiveness, faith in therapy, interaction, and attendance.	Three hypotheses were tested—that patients in experimental groups would: 1. Have greater faith in group therapy. 2. Have greater attraction (cohesiveness) to their groups. 3. Engage in more here-and-now discussion of relationships within the groups. Hypothesis 1 received some support, hypothesis 2 not supported, hypothesis 3 strongly supported.

Chapter 8: Vicarious Learning

Author	Subjects
Falloon, Lindley, McDonald, and Marks (1977); Falloon (1981)[18, 19]	76 psychiatric out-patients, neurotics and personality disorders, presenting with problems in social behaviour. 55 men, 21 women
Jeske (1973)[15]	20 patients, average age 38 years; 12 men, 8 women; with depression, other neurotic symptoms, marital and family problems

Chapter 9: Therapeutic Factors Overall

Author	Sample
Berzon, Pious, and Farson (1963)[27]	Two groups of 11 volunteer subjects. Mostly college graduates, married, aged 30–50. Inclusion criteria—functioning well in social roles, able to communicate subjective experiences

Method	Results
Patients randomly assigned to one of three conditions (but the first two conditions combined in subsequent analysis): modelling and role-playing (therapists modelled social interactions and then coached patients to do the same); modelling, role-playing, and homework assignments; and group discussion (activity limited to discussion of social difficulties and how to deal with them). Groups of between six and 10 patients met weekly for 10 weeks; led by pairs of co-therapists. Assessment on patients' target social problems, social adjustment, and self-report questionnaires of social anxiety, mood, and self-esteem at end of treatment, six months later, and an average 16 months later.	1. Patients in modelling groups showed greater improvement on virtually all measures of outcome at the end of treatment. 2. Effects endured at follow-up, both six months and average 16 months, although reduced in size. 3. Improvement associated with patients' attraction to the group and to its leaders.
Six weekly group sessions. MMPI administered pre- and post-group. Patients used concealed recorders to report occurrence of identification with other group members.	1. Patients who improved on MMPI recorded twice the number of identifications. 2. Most identifications related to problems articulated at intake assessment or in the course of therapy.

Method	Findings
Each group met weekly for 15 sessions. Following each session subjects completed 'most important event' questionnaire. Reports of important events assigned independently by three judges to one of nine therapeutic factors.	1. Satisfactory inter-rater reliability. 2. Most important two factors in both groups were (a) increased awareness of own emotional dynamics; and (b) recognizing similarity to others. 3. Next three most important factors

Bloch and Reibstein (1980)[29]	33 out-patients in one of six therapy groups; 18 men, 15 women, mostly with neurotic or personality disorders. Average age 27. 12 neophyte therapists, co-leading groups, trained to use an interactional model
Butler and Fuhriman (1980)[29]	28 day-patients, mean age 41, mostly female, majority single, 67 per cent diagnosed as psychosis, the rest as neurosis or personality disorder. Treated in day treament centre. 68 out-patients, mean age 35, 61 per cent female, mostly married, 84 per cent diagnosed as neurotic or personality disordered. Treated in out-

were
   (a) feeling positive regard, acceptance, sympathy for others;
   (b) seeing self as seen by others; and
   (c) expressing self congruently, articulately, or assertively in group.
4. Least important factors were
   (a) ventilating emotions, and
   (b) feeling warmth and closeness in the group.
5. Only a minority of 'events' involved therapists.

During the first six months of the groups, which met weekly, patients completed 'most important event' questionnaire at three-weekly intervals. Therapists completed the same questionnaire, at the same intervals, for each of their patients.

1. Satisfactory inter-rater reliability.
2. Patients' perspective—
   (a) most important factor was self-understanding, followed by self-disclosure, and interaction;
   (b) next three most important were acceptance, instillation of hope, and vicarious learning;
   (c) least important were altruism, catharsis, and guidance.
3. Therapists' perspective—
   (a) most important factor was self-understanding, followed by interaction, and self-disclosure;
   (b) apart from acceptance (10 per cent), six other factors accounted for a mere seven per cent of events.
4. Therapists tend to emphasize behavioural-type factors more than patients do.

Patients rated by their therapists on an operational scale for 'level of functioning'. Patients completed a variant of the 'How encounter groups work' questionnaire (used in the Stanford encounter group study), on one occasion only, during the course of treatment.

1. Groups differed markedly on level of functioning.
2. Day-patients valued cohesiveness as most important factor. Least valued were identification, guidance, and recapitulation of the primary family group. Other eight factors all bunched together.
3. Out-patients particularly valued

	patient therapy groups
Butler and Fuhriman (1983)[30]	91 out-patients, average age 33, majority female, mostly neurosis or personality disorder
Corder, Whiteside, and Haizlip (1981)[21]	16 adolescents, aged 13–17, from four therapy groups in different clinical settings
Dickoff and Lakin (1963)[23]	28 patients who had been in one of two psychotherapy groups for at least three sessions and an average of 11. 22 women, six men, mostly with neurotic or personality disorders (25 further patients refused consent for study)
Lieberman, Yalom, and Miles (1973)[19]	210 volunteer students

	self-understanding, universality, feedback, and catharsis. Least valued were recapitulation of the primary family group and identification. Greater and more subtle discrimination in evaluation compared to day-patients.
Patients rated as in Butler and Fuhriman (1980) on 'level of functioning'. Patients completed, on one occasion only during course of treatment, a version of Yalom's therapeutic factor questionnaire. Sample then divided at median on level of functioning, and perceptions of therapeutic factors compared. Sample also divided into three groups according to duration of group therapy (1–6 months, 7–24 months, 25+ months).	1. Higher functioning patients valued catharsis, self-understanding, feedback, and interaction significantly more than lower functioning patients. No significant differences in perceptions of other eight factors. 2. Patients treated for longer periods valued self-understanding, interaction, and cohesiveness more than those treated for shorter periods.
Groups met weekly for 9–12 months. All patients who had attended for at least six months completed Yalom's therapeutic factor questionnaire.	1. Items chosen as most helpful came from catharsis (two), interpersonal learning (two), existential, family re-enactment, cohesiveness, universality, and altruism. 2. Least helpful items came from insight (two), identification (two), catharsis, guidance, interpersonal learning, and existential. Difficult to assess data since only individual items were examined, not therapeutic factor categories.
Patients interviewed on several aspects of their group experience. Responses coded as: suppression (getting rid of worries); support (sharing problems); or tools for action (self-understanding). IQ scores on WAIS obtained.	1. Of the 28 patients, 16 emphasized support, eight suppression, and four tools for action. 2. Patients with higher scores on WAIS-vocabulary subscale emphasized tools for action.
17 encounter groups led by therapists of various theoretical schools. All met for a total of 30 hours. Subjects completed 'most important event'	1. 'High learners' rated insight, advice, cohesiveness, and recapitulation of family experience items significantly more often than unchanged

Marcovitz and Smith (1983)[25]	30 in-patients, mostly with depression or personality disorder
Maxmen (1973)[9]	100 consecutive in-patients, half with affective disorders and the rest including personality disorders, schizophrenia, and alcoholism. Severely disorganized patients excluded. Most aged 20–50; 58 women, 42 men
Schaffer and Dreyer (1982)[26]	100 in-patients and 30 staff in a crisis-orientated psychiatric unit

questionnaire on several occasions, and 'mechanisms of learning' questionnaire at end of group experience.	subjects. 2. Most important event questionnaire showed importance of cognitive mechanisms in high learners. 3. Catharsis relatively unimportant for outcome.
Patients participated in an average of eight group sessions, run along psychodynamic lines. Groups held four times weekly. Patients assessed on anxiety and depression measures at admission and discharge from psychiatric unit. Yalom's therapeutic factor questionnaire given immediately before discharge.	1. Catharsis, cohesiveness, and altruism ranked as most helpful. 2. Identification, family re-enactment, and guidance ranked as least helpful. 3. Intermediate were interpersonal learning, self-understanding, instillation of hope, and universality. 4. Patients improved significantly on two depression scales but no examination was made of the association between level of improvement and particular patterns of perception of helpful therapeutic factors. Anxiety measures not cited at all.
Patients participated in ward groups, average 9 sessions, with focus on here-and-now and free expression of feelings and problems. Modified Yalom's therapeutic factor questionnaire completed at unspecified time.	1. Patients ranked in order of importance hope, cohesiveness, altruism, and universality. 2. Least important were catharsis, insight, guidance, family re-enactment, and identification.
Patients on days one and eight of their hospitalization, and staff once only, chose two items most important to them from the questionnaire on 'How encounter groups work' (used in the Stanford encounter group study). Patients were in groups which met three times a day; average ten day hospitalization. Groups contained both patients and their relatives.	1. Patients' choices on days one and eight significantly correlated, suggesting stability of perception. 2. Correlations between patients and staff were small. 3. Patients rated self-responsibility and self-understanding as most helpful, followed by expression of feelings, advice, universality, and feedback. Least helpful were modelling, experimentation, self-revelation, and family re-enactment. 4. Staff perceived expression of

Sherry and Hurley (1976)[29]	17 volunteer subjects
Rohrbaugh and Bartels (1975)[32]	72 subjects participating in one of 13 therapy or human relations groups in various settings
Steinfeld and Mabli (1974)[20]	50 male prison inmates, participants in therapeutic community, rated by their therapists as having achieved successful outcome

	feelings, modelling, and experimentation as most important. All other factors rated very low.
Students participated in one of three groups. Ten sessions focusing on here-and-now interaction. Yalom's therapeutic factor questionnaire completed after final session.	1. Items ranked most important were interpersonal learning-input and catharsis. 2. Comparison of results with Yalom[15] showed high correlation, suggesting same factors important in short- and long-term groups.
Co-therapists of different theoretical persuasions ran various types of groups according to their normal practices. Yalom's therapeutic factor and cohesiveness questionnaires completed but not at standard time. Subjects rated by co-therapists as high or low learners. Construct validity of Q-sort tested by factor analysis.	1. Factor analysis yielded four factors: (a) Didactic versus experiential orientation to change. (b) Reliance on self versus reliance on others. (c) Giving versus receiving. (d) Acceptance of confrontation. 2. Group variables appeared more important than individual differences in subjects' evaluation of therapeutic factors, e.g. self-understanding emphasized more by therapy groups and relatedness (a mixture of cohesiveness and interaction) more by growth groups. 3. Of individual differences only educational level important—more educated group members valued relatedness and devalued existential awareness and guidance. 4. Age, sex, previous group experience, attraction to the group, verbal participation, and outcome were unrelated to therapeutic factors.
Subjects participated in 12–15 hours per week of group activities. Therapeutic model based on Glasser's reality therapy. 1–2 years later, before parole, subjects completed Yalom's therapeutic factor questionnaire.	1. Subjects rated in order of importance—insight, an existential factor, catharsis, interpersonal learning—input, interpersonal learning—output. 2. Least important were identification, universality, guidance, altruism, and family re-enactment. 3. Low correlation between ratings of

Yalom (1975)[15]	20 middle-class out-patients with neurotic or personality disorders, rated by their therapists as significantly improved

this sample and those of Yalom's sample (see below).

Mean duration of treatment 16 months, range 8–22 months. Improvement confirmed by self-ratings and assessment by independent judges. Patients completed Yalom's therapeutic factor questionnaire at termination.

1. Patients ranked in order of importance: interpersonal learning-input, catharsis, cohesiveness, and self-understanding.
2. Least important were identification, guidance, family re-enactment, and altruism.

Author Index

Note: Page numbers in *italics* refer to the appendix

Subject Index

Note: Page numbers in *italics* refer to the appendix.
LIA—Learning from interpersonal action